CITY ON A GRID

Endpapers: The 1811 Commissioners' Plan, the founding document of modern New York. Nearly nine feet long and defying easy print reproduction, the map appears here on the front and back endpapers, enclosing this book in a firm embrace, as the rigid linear grid plan itself did to Manhattan. *(New York City Municipal Archives)*

CITY ON A GRID

HOW 𝕹𝖊𝖜 𝖄𝖔𝖗𝖐 BECAME New York

Gerard Koeppel

DA CAPO PRESS
A MEMBER OF THE PERSEUS BOOKS GROUP

Designed by Jack Lenzo
Set in 11-point Goudy by The Perseus Books Group

Library of Congress Cataloging-in-Publication Data
Koeppel, Gerard T., 1957–
  City on a grid : how New York became New York / Gerard Koeppel.
     pages cm
  Includes bibliographical references and index.
  ISBN 978-0-306-82284-1 (hardcover : alkaline paper) — ISBN 978-0-306-82285-8 (e-book) 1. City planning—New York (State)—New York—History. 2. Streets—New York (State)—New York—History. 3. Grids (Crisscross patterns)—New York (State)—New York—History. 4. City and town life—New York (State)—New York—History. 5. Social change—New York (State)—New York—History. 6. Manhattan (New York, N.Y.)—History. 7. New York (N.Y.)—History. I. Title.

  HT168.N5K64 2015
  307.1'216097471—dc23

                        2015020980

Published by Da Capo Press
A Member of the Perseus Books Group
www.dacapopress.com

Da Capo Press books are available at special discounts for bulk purchases in the U.S. by corporations, institutions, and other organizations. For more information, please contact the Special Markets Department at the Perseus Books Group, 2300 Chestnut Street, Suite 200, Philadelphia, PA 19103, or call (800) 810-4145, ext. 5000, or e-mail special.markets@perseusbooks.com.

10 9 8 7 6 5 4 3 2 1

For Diane, Jackson, Harry, Kate, and Scrappy

CONTENTS

PREFATORY NOTE

THIS BOOK GOT its start after the attacks that brought down the World Trade Center towers in 2001. The original trade center was built in the 1960s over a wide area of its neighborhood, in particular the intersection of Greenwich and Dey Streets, where, at the northwest corner one January midday in 1810, a mother helped her child pump water from a public street well. The scene was painted in watercolor by a French émigrée, Anne-Marguerite Hyde de Neuville, a prolific artist of early America who then lived across the street. This casual—and my favorite—glimpse of Old New York showed modest wood and redbrick homes, dirt streets, bare trees, and a scattering of other New Yorkers—a lumberman, a housekeeper sweeping her sidewalk, two men talking, a few ladies walking, and other neighbors going about their business on what appeared to be a mild winter day. (Have a look online; the image, *Corner of Greenwich Street*, is easy to find.) Over a century and a half later, the intersection of Greenwich and Dey disappeared beneath the plaza of the first World Trade Center.

Then, in the rebuilding after 2001, a smaller trade center emerged and, with it, the long-lost segments of Greenwich and Dey streets, ironically just for foot traffic, much as they were used centuries earlier. This got me thinking that the street arrangement of now densely urban Manhattan is more plastic than I imagined. Streets and corners can come and go, and come back again.

Next, I thought what if it was not the World Trade Center but, say, the Empire State Building—not at an edge of the island but at the city's physical heart—that came down: a trauma to daily life in the very center of the city. (This was a depressing thought but no longer unimaginable—New York has joined the family of existentially traumatized world cities.) How would *that* rebuilding go? Should the rectilinear street grid conceived in the early 1800s to accommodate animal transportation be rebuilt as it was? Or should new or modified forms be introduced—radials, curvilinears, green spaces, water features—better suited to a mass-transporting, post-industrial, resource-conscious city?

How, I thought, could I be involved in a conversation about possible change—change prompted by malevolent intention, devastating accident, or enlightened choice—to the urban fabric of New York City? I'm not an architect, an engineer, an urban planner, a politician, or even an environmentalist who might claim direct input. I'm just an historian. (Historians are like people who yell fire in empty theaters: no one gets hurt, often no one hears, and sometimes the building burns down.) I could, as an historian of the city, examine its oldest and most essential piece of infrastructure—its famous rectilinear street grid—which shapes everything else about the city, and offer the findings to anyone interested.

What I found is that "the great grid" had a very humble, almost embarrassing, even unworthy, birth yet, like a common object fetishized over time, it resists attempts to change it. This history of two centuries and counting, I reckoned, may be of use when and if the time for change comes. It is easier to move forward after the grasping fingers of the past have been pried open, often revealing that the extraordinary is ordinary and not so difficult to change. In the meantime, what follows can also be taken as just another story in the epic of how New York became New York.

INTRODUCTION

There will come a time . . . when nothing will be of
more interest than authentic reminiscences of the past.

—Walt Whitman, *Brooklyn Daily Standard*, June 1861

But in analysing history do not be too profound, for
often the causes are quite superficial.

—Ralph Waldo Emerson, journal entry, November 1836

IF A PICTURE is worth eighty thousand words or so, one image cap-
tures what this book is about. And if every picture tells a story,
this image tells two. The photograph was taken during the winter
of 1882–83 from the roof of a millionaire brewer's new brownstone
mansion at the crest of Prospect Hill, on the east side of Fourth
Avenue between 93rd and 94th Streets. This was an evolving neighborhood of New York City, which then consisted of Manhattan only
(the boroughs came a little bit later). The avenue and streets on this
segment of the island had been laid in the 1850s, but development
had been stalled by the loud and dirty locomotives of the New York
and Harlem Railroad, running since the 1830s on surface tracks
through what was then and for decades after countryside. Only after
the tracks were sunk belowground and covered during the mid-1870s
did scattered squatter shacks, small factories, and aging farms give

way to merchant piles and developer dreams. The broad and freshly landscaped boulevard over the tracks would soon be renamed Park Avenue. And the hill's high prospects would soon transition from referencing the natural view to reflecting broader social expectation: Carnegie Hill, appropriating the name of the neighborhood's richest new millionaire.

The image that tells this book's stories, an albumen print by Bavarian-born Peter Baab, looks south from beer baron George Ehret's gabled roof at a city rising from the distance. On the right is the new avenue, airy and clean, visible for several blocks as it recedes into the sooty background; a scattered few of what will be solid walls of imposing apartment buildings front the avenue. Running across the middle ground is 92nd Street, intersecting the avenue as streets generally meet avenues on Manhattan: at a right angle. On the south side of the street, facing the camera, is a varied cast of structures representing the local past and future. From the corner stretches a new three-story brick row house with a half dozen entrance stoops greeting fresh sidewalk: a herald of comfortable multifamily living. Mid-block is the past: four modest but well-tended whitewashed wooden houses, each with a fenced yard and covered porch. The houses are relics: new construction in wood will be banned on Manhattan in a few years. Reaching high above the attic of the leftmost house is a side-yard tree, possibly the oldest thing in the image.

Only half of the house with the big tree is visible. The rest is obscured by a new neighbor across the street, with its back to the camera: the first of what promises to be a row of attached three-story brick apartment buildings. We know there will be more of them because this one has no windows on its western elevation, which will soon enough be mated with the eastern wall of the next new building very much like it.

And yet most of the space captured by the photographer is empty. The whole space from 92nd Street in the middle ground to 93rd Street just under the camera's view in the foreground, and from the avenue on the right to the new building at the left of the frame, is an expanse of open ground, as yet unimproved real estate. We know the void's days are numbered. Just as it will be filled from the north side of 92nd Street with brick buildings, much of the space along the avenue between 92nd and 93rd is ready to be filled with something even bigger: a large, deep rectangular pit has been excavated for the foundation of what will be a major Park Avenue address (now 1175 Park). Spied in the left foreground is the shadow of the first in a series of buildings that will fill any remaining space along 93rd Street.

At first glance, the image is no different from any that might have been captured of dozens of similar rectangular blocks in the city rapidly filling northward. Aside from the obvious visual juxtapositions of old and new, of empty and filled space, the chief value of the image for many observers is local and historic, or merely archival: information for a catalogue of urban development, land largely cleared of nature and prepared for permanent dense occupation. Seeking deeper meaning, some observers might focus on the redundant geometry, the thickening assemblage of rectangular shapes in different planes: the blocks of streets, the block-shaped new buildings, the rectangular building walls. The dominant new shape on the land will be replicated repeatedly in the air above it. In fact, the built forms are such a dominant theme that when this image has been occasionally reproduced over the generations, the lower half—the "empty" space—is usually cropped out. But this space too tells a story.

The main story of this book is the creation and long life of the iconic street grid of New York: the rectilinear plane of many parallel streets crossed at right angles by relatively few parallel avenues laid on the map of rural Manhattan two centuries ago that defined the urbanism of a rising city and nation. The grid was ordained in 1811 by a state commission, appointed in 1807, of three men—headstrong Founding Father Gouverneur Morris, longtime New York State

Surveyor General Simeon DeWitt, and major area landowner John Rutherfurd. Their grid, which started far south at the then suburban edge of the settled city in the 1810s, arrives before our eyes in the shot from Ehret's roof three-quarters of the century later.

The other story of this book is in the cropping of Baab's shot. In that empty space that reproductions usually edit out, the photographer—inadvertently, unwittingly—captured two faint but evident footpaths, formed in the dirt. One path runs from mid-block on 92nd Street through the center of the empty space toward the corner of 93rd Street and the avenue. The other path runs from the corner of 92nd and the avenue to mid-block on 93rd. The paths cross, not by design but by choice. No people were on the paths when the photographer took his shot, but in the compacted earth unknown New Yorkers had clearly marked a deep desire of living things: to reach their destination by the shortest possible route. Not by two lines around a right-angled corner, but by a direct path.

In that empty space and the urbanizing space framing it are the mystical and the magical: the organic, free, mystic movements through what remained of nature, and the autocratic, abstract, magical geometrics of the planned city. "Magical peoples, because of their rational spirit, arrive at geometric city formations," observed urban planner (and Nazi exile) Ludwig Hilberseimer in 1944, while "mystic peoples, in accordance with their principle of growth, arrive at organic city formulations." Geometric and organic formulations don't take precedence or priority over each other. They exist, thought Hilberseimer, as contemporary impulses, in different groups of people and within each person. Any city is made up of magic peasants and mystic nomads, willingly urbanized and willfully roaming. Manhattan, though, with more right angles than anywhere else in the world, is a profoundly magical place. It will be, for better or worse, until the rectilinear street grid is replaced, if it ever is.

In the 1800s, New York's grid, and the hundreds of thousands of rectangular lots, building forms, and interior spaces it inevitably produced, gave a sense of stability and rational purpose to a young city evolving into greatness. The pathways in the packed earth of verging Carnegie Hill are evidence of something more. As the emptiness is gradually filled with brick and masonry buildings, the paths will disappear, and the people who used them will experience loss. Though the shortest distance between two points is not around a right-angled corner, New Yorkers must navigate thousands. Perhaps this is what makes New Yorkers run, rushing from loss toward gain, around corners of street walls that protect private space from the public sphere.

The grid favors private interest over public convenience. The right angle values its interior space. Diagonal or nonlinear routes—dirt footpaths through an empty lot, curvilinear forms traversing natural topography—celebrate public space, the civic interest. A rectilinear-grid dweller moving from one point to another that is not on the same axis is obliged to go out of his or her way, to turn corners. Axial streets are urban moats guarding rectangular castles framing interior lives; these streets are pedestrian, common, subordinate. Diagonal or curving streets force private space into accommodations of shape; diagonals and curves make urban life a promenade, a public display, beautiful, grand, mysterious, mystic. This is not Manhattan.

It is often said that the street grid created by the commission of three respectable gentlemen represented the death of Old New York and the birth of the modern city—Old New York being the quaint, low-slung, but notoriously dirty and disorderly place of jumbled colonial and post-Revolutionary streets that sprouted from the southern tip of the island for nearly two centuries, modern New York being the rigid plain of rectangular blocks that brought order going forward. But death and loss are not the same thing. Something dead can't live again; something lost can be found. Someday, Manhattan may look different.

This book tells mostly of the creation and long life of the great grid, "the greatest grid" to some, who generally don't specify whether the superlative relates to quality or merely quantity. Weaving through this narrative of the great grid, like a New Yorker navigating Midtown at midday, is the lingering sense of loss: lost time, lost place, lost pathways in the packed earth, earth that's there beneath the asphalt, brick, concrete, steel, glass, and plastics, earth that of course will outlast all its human burdens.

FOR THE TIME being, New York is all about numbers and pretty much has been since the 1620s, when Dutch trappers and traders became market makers in exportable beaver pelts by the thousands. The numbers game called Wall Street opened for business here seventeen decades later. For nearly four centuries New York has been a commercial enterprise, with generations of gainers and losers. As Mark Twain (a numbers runner himself!) and others roughly put it, in Boston it's what you know, in Philadelphia who you are, and in New York how much you're worth. The New Yorker triumvirate appointed in 1807 to "unite regularity and order with the public convenience" announced a street plan four years later that converted Mannahatta—the Lenape "island of hills"—into a flattened landscape of numbers. If number crunchers dream of mythical cities, New York is what they look like.

Just inside their four-year deadline, the Commissioners* and their scrupulous chief surveyor mapped out 155 parallel streets crossing the island from river to river and intersecting at right angles with twelve parallel avenues running along the island's length, making for a ruthless, rigid, rectilinear grid of nearly two thousand largely identical blocks. The short, crooked streets of organic Old New York to the south had names of mostly topographical, geographical,

---

* To keep straight the various commissions that appear throughout the narrative, our 1807 Commissioners and their Commission will be capitalized (as they usually were in contemporary materials) and all others will not.

biographical, or cultural allusion, of Dutch, English, or local origin. Every one of the future city's scores of straight new streets and avenues beyond then aptly named North (now Houston) Street would be endowed with no more than an ordinal number and a cold Cartesian relationship to its linear kin.

The Commissioners placed their streets, from 1st to 155th, roughly two hundred feet apart and commanded that they all be made sixty feet wide, except fifteen that would be one hundred feet wide, at (mostly) regular intervals. The Commissioners' avenues, 1 through 12, were all to be one hundred feet wide, with mostly regular distances between them: after 1st and 2nd were placed six hundred fifty feet apart and 2nd and 3rd six hundred ten feet apart, it was nine hundred twenty feet between each avenue from 3rd to 6th, and eight hundred between all the avenues west of 6th. The only anomalies in the Commissioners' numerology were the abbreviated avenues A through D, which girdled the otherwise lanky island's short but ample eastern hip below 14th Street. Within a few generations, the bulk of Manhattan was covered in long straight lines of numbers. "Like the streets," observed city walker William Dean Howells, the avenues "are numbered, rather than named, from a want of imagination, or from a preference of mere convenience to the poetry and associations that cluster about a name, and can never cling to a number, or from a business impatience to be quickly done with the matter."

But Manhattan also remained a poetic place of names. Wall, Water, and William; Beaver, Bridge, Broad, and Broadway; Mott, Mercer, and Mulberry; Spruce, Cedar, and Pine: all remind us that New York was once and is still something more than just numbers. While numbered streets vastly outstrip named streets in total *mileage*, the nearly four hundred streets with names far *outnumber* the streets with numbers. Indeed, ever since the number and mileage of numbered streets and avenues peaked with the completion of the grid in the late 1800s, names have been gaining. From 1880 to 1890, in addition to 4th Avenue becoming Park, long uptown stretches of the numbered avenues to the west got proper and more marketable names: 8th became Central Park West; 9th, Columbus; 10th, Amsterdam; and 11th, West End. Riverside Drive had an immaculate conception, as did Madison and Lexington, added through the efforts of a real estate developer two decades after the plan was announced. Later, the geographic extensions of Avenues A and B emerged from the East River uptown as Sutton Place and York Avenue and East End Avenue. In recent decades, dispirited avenues and wide streets above Central Park have been reimagined as nominal boulevards: upper 6th Avenue, first named Lenox Avenue in 1887 for Scottish-born philanthropist Robert Lenox, was officially redesignated Malcolm X Boulevard a hundred years later; 7th Avenue has been named for Harlem congressman Adam Clayton Powell Jr. (1974), and 8th Avenue for Frederick Douglass (1977). The wide cross streets have been adorned with wishful boulevard status: West 106th Street for elegant Duke Ellington, who (like me) had lived there (1977); the four easternmost blocks of 116th for Luis Muñoz Marín, Puerto Rico's first governor (1982); 125th Street for Martin Luther King Jr. (1984); and 145th Street for early labor and civil rights leader A. Philip Randolph (2009). This is to name just a few of the major streets and avenues born with numbers and turned to boulevards with names; hundreds of other plazas, places, corners, and squares have been given official or honorary names where numbers or no designation appeared before. It seems we long for more than just numerical attachment to place. Like anxious parents wishing that toddlers would use their words, we want our places to have names like we do.*

---

* Accordingly, but mostly for narrative clarity, from here on in I'm going to use words rather than the Commissioners' figures for the numbered avenues, and retain figures for the numbered streets.

"IT'S FUN AND it's cathartic, it's, I dunno, it's entertaining to . . . look to the past," said recent New York mayor Michael Bloomberg, "but it doesn't do anything for the future." He was commenting in 2011 on blame for the nation's mortgage crisis: "We've just got to focus on how we move [on] . . . rather than why we got here and who did it." Sure, Bloomberg was speaking as a politician, but if the 108th mayor of New York genuinely believes that history is irrelevant, then he—who among other endeavors vainly sought to relieve the city's venerable and notorious street congestion that is a by-product of the grid—will have little interest in this book. This book explains, among other things, how the iconic street grid of Manhattan, proclaimed exactly two hundred years before Bloomberg's historical antipathy, helped make it such a congested place. At the same time, this book shows how the grid made New York, like the new American cities that copied it, an orderly place of energy and industry, a great and famous orderly place where history has been a step-cousin to commerce.

The Manhattan grid is loved, passionately, today mostly by people who need a city that is easy to comprehend, from tourists to transplants to spatially challenged natives. But the grid and the Commissioners and their surveyor who made it have appalled the sensitive and the cerebral from the get-go. The earliest of the outraged—Clement Clarke Moore, Edgar Allan Poe, Frederick Law Olmsted, and others with just two names—saw the grid plan become reality through the 1800s. "Our perpetual dead flat," mused Walt Whitman in 1849, "and streets cutting each other at right angles, are certainly the last things in the world consistent with beauty of situation." The gridded, unbeautiful city continued to distress through the generations. Henry James deplored his city's "primal topographic curse, her old inconceivably bourgeois scheme of composition and distribution, the uncorrected labor of minds with no imagination of the future and blind before the opportunity given them by their two magnificent water-fronts." James's gal pal Edith Wharton recoiled from "rectangular New York . . . this cramped horizontal gridiron of a town without towers, porticoes, fountains or perspectives, hide-bound in its deadly uniformity of mean ugliness." "We are all agreed—all of us, that is, who pay any attention to such things—," wrote Gilded Age architecture critic and *New York Times* editorial writer Montgomery Schuyler, "that the Commissioners . . . were public malefactors of high degree." Urban scholar Lewis Mumford spent a professional lifetime railing at New York's "civic folly," its "blank imbecility" and "long monotonous streets that terminated nowhere, filled by rows of monotonous houses." Mumford protégé Jane Jacobs lamented her city where "a street goes on and on into the distance . . . dribbling into endless amorphous repetitions of itself and finally petering into the utter anonymity of distances." Frank Lloyd Wright feared the "man-trap of gigantic dimensions" and its "deadly monotony." Igor Stravinsky gazed sadly from his last apartment at the "filing-cabinet architecture" of corporate Sixth Avenue. If he walked quickly, Jean-Paul Sartre felt at ease in postwar New York, but "if I stop, I get flustered and wonder, 'Why am I on this street rather than on one of the hundreds others like it?'" He found himself lost at the seemingly unambiguous intersection of Lexington and 52nd: "This spatial precision is not accompanied by any emotional exactitude."

Most recent urban scholars have been brutal critics. Cornell's John Reps: plagued by "mechanical dullness," topographical ignorance, too few avenues and too many congesting intersections, yet copied compulsively by new settlements rising across the spreading nation, New York's grid became "a disaster whose consequences have barely been mitigated by more modern city planners." Yale's Vincent Scully: with their "implacable gridiron" of puny public space, the 1807 Commissioners inaugurated the "American tendency toward private luxury and public squalor." Columbia's Peter Marcuse: a plane of real estate development instead of a textured urban form, Manhattan's grid is "one of the worst city plans of any major city in the developed countries of the world." Marcuse noted that *grid* is shorthand for *gridiron*, the medieval torture rack. And, of course, *gridlock*, the harsh neologism for urban and political impasse, was born in New York, during a 1980 transit strike that brought Manhattan street traffic to a standstill. "Even in 1811, the gridiron did not work well," says New York housing historian Richard Plunz. For one thing, "the solar orientation of the gridiron was reversed from the ideal. Had the long dimension of each block faced east-west, both front and rear facades of each house would have received sunlight each day." Instead, south facades got and get all the sun, north facades none. In addition, Plunz notes, as many others have, the lack of service alleys congested the overburdened streets. At its best, "the Manhattan grid was substandard."

Yet many smart people have embraced the grid. James Kent, the supreme scholar of law and politics in early New York, judged it brilliant. "The map and plan of the Commissioners," he wrote in 1836, "laid out the highways on the island upon so magnificent a scale, and with so bold a hand, and with such prophetic views, in respect to the future growth and extension of the city, that it will form an everlasting monument of the stability and wisdom of the measure." "The streets are at right angles to each other and the mind is liberated," gushed Le Corbusier a century later. "I insist on right-angled intersections." Mondrian found the geometric grail in his adopted grid city. Roland Barthes declared in 1959, "This is the purpose of New York's geometry: that each individual should be *poetically* the owner of the capital of the world." In the 2011 exhibit celebrating two hundred years of the "Greatest Grid," Uruguayan-born architect Rafael Vinoly said the grid of his adopted home "is the best manifestation of American pragmatism in the creation of urban form." Back in 1978, the Dutch architect (and non–New York transplant) Rem Koolhaas, echoing Kent, deliriously pronounced Manhattan's grid "the most courageous act of prediction in Western civilization."

This book doesn't judge. This book presents the story of the grid's creation by the primary men—three gentlemen Commissioners and their single-minded young surveyor—and the events in its lengthening life, and suggests you come to your own conclusion.

In the two hundred years of New York's grid, no one has written a book about it. In the same two centuries, dozens of books have been written about the other great and contemporaneous feat of anticipant design and engineering that enabled New York City's rise: the Erie Canal. Many of the same people were involved with both: brilliant but reckless Gouverneur Morris; preeminent if passionless surveyor Simeon DeWitt; and DeWitt's exacting but eventually deranged protégé John Randel Jr. The now long irrelevant canal remains the topic of endless books—recently one by me—while the most famous urban design of a living city, a design that defines daily life in this thriving city, has found not one biographer until now.

Why has the grid, which the New York essayist Phillip Lopate calls "a thing impossible to overpraise," never had a book—of praise or not—and why is now the time? Here is what I think. I think 9/11 shocked New York from young adolescence to the pimply insecurities of early adulthood, from a relatively young and untroubled existence, compared with the much longer lives and disordering traumas of other great world cities, to the first contemplation of its own mortality, from blithe self-assurance to the first pricks of introspection and wisdom. The vulnerability exposed by 9/11 has aroused a deeper examination of their city's past than New Yorkers have previously been willing to indulge.

I once wrote in a book review that "New York is a city that eats its history," where new readily replaces old that cities with deeper historical self-awareness would preserve or adapt. New York was founded as a commercial place and has remained so for centuries. "Unlike Rome, New York has never learned the art of growing old by playing on all its pasts," observed the French scholar of modern life Michel de Certeau. "Its present invents itself, from hour to hour, in the act of throwing away its previous accomplishments and challenging the future." De Certeau was writing in 1984, in a paean to

Manhattan's "wave of verticals" as he viewed them from the 110th floor of the World Trade Center, then "the most monumental figure of Western urban development."

But the towers are gone and, with Western-style urbanism now spread wide and high throughout the world, New York is unlikely again to be the supreme place of global monumentalism. For most of ten decades starting in 1870, the city was home to the world's tallest building, from the Equitable Life Building to 1 World Trade Center. The competition has moved elsewhere. Only six of New York's eleven onetime titleholders remain, yet the survivors suggest that the city is shifting from unadulterated, reckless, breakneck commerce to something more introspective and longer lasting. The Beaux-Arts icon Singer Building was demolished in 1968 at the tender age of sixty, the last former champion destroyed as a business decision. The city's now half-dozen ex-champs are all protected city or national landmarks. The Woolworth, Chrysler, and Empire State Buildings will never be the world's tallest again but they might eventually be the city's oldest, providing rare contemplation for many future generations of New Yorkers about how a city ages gracefully.*

Meanwhile, shipless river piers and abandoned freight railways are being transformed into inspired parks and public places. Baby strollers are pushing out brokers on Wall Street. ("There are some far-seeing people," it was observed way back in 1875, "who prophesy that when the present flood-tide which is carrying the population of New York further and further up town shall begin to ebb, its receding will bring the Battery again into favor as the dwelling of the wealthy and refined.") Traditional symbols of commercial energy—the Empire State Building, the fish market, the meat market—have

---

* Back in 1946, long before landmarking, Sartre caught glimmerings of a certain permanence and destiny: "I see in the distance the Empire State and Chrysler Buildings pointing vainly to the sky and it suddenly occurs to me that New York is on the point of acquiring a history and that it already has its ruins." Sartre, "New York, Colonial City," 133.

been transformed into places of tourism, dining, and domestication. The original World Trade Center itself was an anachronism, a misguided attempt by 1960s port officials to keep business downtown, lording over aging, sooty, limestone first-generation "skyscrapers" on cramped colonial streets, when business had already been drawn north to steel and glass obelisks along linear Midtown avenues.

New Yorkers—the amalgam of people born, living, or longing to be (back) here—now better see the city as a place in history, with a history that they want to know. Even the New-York Historical Society, formed in 1804 by some of the grid makers and on the verge of closing twenty years ago for lack of money and interest, has been reborn with must-see million-dollar exhibits; the Society's old-fashioned hyphen now seems a vigorous artery, not a vain anachronism. Just as Walt Whitman saw a future in history weeks after the outbreak of the Civil War, New Yorkers in body and spirit now look to the city's past for clues about its future.

Now, at last, is the time to tell the grid's story: the circumstances that led to it, how the Commissioners and their surveyor came up with their plan; how the life of the city has been utterly shaped by it. Whether one considers New York's grid "one of the worst city plans of any major city in the developed countries of the world" or "the most courageous act of prediction in Western civilization," here now is the story of how it came to be, who created it and why, who has tried to change it and how, and what might become of it.

CHAPTER 1

COME HITHER OLD GRID

They were like children, to whom repetition is more pleasing than variations or novelty.

—Jorge Luis Borges, 1971

THOUGH NEW YORKERS sometimes think urbanity began with them, grids are nothing new, nor are the arguments pro and con. On the plus side, grids use space efficiently, distribute property equitably, can be extended indefinitely, are simple to draw and build, and are easy to control militarily. On the negative side, grids ignore natural topography, impose conformity of building alignment and shape, neglect the travel efficiencies of radials and the beauty of radials and curvilinears, and are dull and ugly generally. Modern negatives of the dense, unbroken urban grid include congestion and environmental issues of limited light, air, green space, and natural drainage, and poor solar energy siting.

Few of these concerns were relevant in the oldest urban grid we know a bit about, at Mohenjo-daro, founded nearly 5,000 years ago and abandoned a thousand years later in what is now Pakistan. Possibly the most important among numerous Indus Valley cities, Mohenjo-daro when it flourished covered roughly 750 acres and was home to 40,000 people. After it was rediscovered less than a hundred years ago, the first excavations suggested to archaeologists that the city was laid on an extensive rectilinear grid, aligned north-south and east-west. More recently, scholars have confirmed only some straight, rectilinear streets, ranging in width from twenty to thirty feet, and many more irregular streets. Whether or not Mohenjo-daro was "the birthplace of the grid" is an ongoing debate for others. For our purposes, Mohenjo-daro means only that Manhattan had a precursor whose streets were shaped at least in part like its own as long as 5,000 years ago, an important city that flourished and was abandoned when its culture, for as yet unknown reasons, died.

Other cities in later civilizations certainly had rectilinear street grids, but the continuous record to us begins, as usual, in Greece. It is generally believed that the urban grid in what we call the Western world debuted at the ancient Greek city of Miletus circa 479 BC. First settled three millennia earlier as Aegean islands, Miletus in its heyday was a manufacturing and trading center on a peninsula, thanks to lowered sea levels and extensive silting of its deep bay. (That process has continued: for the past half millennium Miletus has been inland Turkish ruins.) Native son Hippodamus earned his town's place in the urban planning hall of fame by planning and assembling its center with a rectilinear street grid, a concept he did not invent but probably knew or heard of from previous, now lost examples. After giving Miletus its tight, regular grid, the reputed "father of urban planning" did the same for Piraeus, Rhodes, and other Greek cities.

Much of what we know about Hippodamus and his planning activities we know from Aristotle, who followed Hippodamus by a century. Aristotle agreed with Hippodamus that cities should be planned but, unlike Hippodamus, he believed that planning should incorporate more than just one form.

> The arrangement of private houses is considered to be more agreeable and generally more convenient, if the streets are regularly laid out after the modern fashion which Hippodamus

introduced, but for security in war the antiquated mode of building, which made it difficult for strangers to get out of a town and
for assailants to find their way in, is preferable. A city should
therefore adopt both plans of building: it is possible to arrange
houses irregularly, as husbandmen plant their vines in what
are called "clumps." The whole town should not be laid out in
straight lines, but only certain quarters and regions; thus security
and beauty will be combined.

Unlike Hippodamus and, as we shall see, Manhattan's grid planners,
Aristotle grasped beauty's integral importance to a city.

Regardless, like long linear streets seeking the horizon, the
"Hippodamian plan" spread through the urbanizing ages, especially
and most significantly throughout the Roman Empire. Gridded military camps evolved into rectilinear colonial cities, far-flung symbols
of order and subjugation.

Medieval European cities generally started differently, without
grids and inside defensive walls. As European cities matured—
destroyed or devastated by fire, flood, warfare, or disease, and then
rebuilt and repopulated, again and again—many emerged with
modern plans that seem like evolved forms of the original: the old
city as nucleus, the new city beyond the originally confining walls as
expanding organism. Amsterdam, Paris, Karlsruhe, and other cities expanded slowly but with increasingly planned growth, generally
under the orders of autocratic rulers. Often located on plains, these
cities radiated from their core, spreading over readily available land
with artificial boundaries instead of natural borders. Nowhere in the
flowering of European cities was the planning choice an unbroken,
rectilinear grid. But then, nowhere was a major European city confined to a long, narrow island.

"We Europeans live on the myth of the large city we constructed
during the nineteenth century," observed Sartre, who understood
modern cities as well as any professional urbanist. "The Americans'

myths are not ours and the American city isn't our city." The round cities of Spain, Italy, Germany, and France produced a particularly European dynamism. "Streets run into other streets. They are closed at each end and do not seem to lead out of the city. Inside them, you go round in circles. They are more than mere arteries: each one is a social milieu. These are streets where you stop, meet people, drink, eat and linger . . . They are alive with a communal spirit that changes each hour of the day." This is not gridded Manhattan.

As the grid was attractive to Roman conquerors, so too was it the choice of Spanish colonialists in the New World, making (or remaking native) cities under the evolving town planning prescriptions of the Laws of the Indies. Lima was the herald of American hemisphere grid building, laid out in 1535 with a rectilinear grid of blocks 400 feet square and streets forty feet wide. The Spanish had a sense of style, though: within Lima's original thirteen-by-nine-block grid was a large square with a fountain in the middle ringed by the major government and religious buildings. The Spanish built this way from Buenos Aires to Mexico: order with beauty. Santa Fe and Albuquerque, founded in the early 1600s and 1700s, respectively, in what is now New Mexico, are Laws of the Indies cities. So is Los Angeles, the current downtown of which was founded in the 1780s at a mandated invasion-safe distance from the sea and along a river, with a rectilinear grid a bit off (at thirty-six degrees) from the mandated forty-five-degree axis, which pointed the corners of the central square at the cardinal points of the compass.

Most Dutch and early English colonial cities in what became the United States were founded on no particular plan, just a random sprawl from the waterfront. New Amsterdam and Boston are the most prominent examples; while New York eventually straightened itself out, Boston couldn't be bothered. Its streets "simply grew with the population," scolded the *Engineering News* in 1891: "They are very irregular, running in all directions and totally without system, and as a rule are narrow and unsuited to the demands of modern civilization." Somehow, Boston, the jumbled incarnation of true believer John Winthrop's ideal "city on a hill," has survived.

Against New York and Boston are Philadelphia and Savannah, gridded cities by the original design of a founding individual, established in the 1680s and 1730s, respectively. William Penn's "green country town" was the first grid in English America, but its 400-foot blocks, intended as an antidote to haphazard London's congestion, proved too large for urban living in modest houses: over time a patchwork of smaller streets intervened. James Oglethorpe's Savannah had a tight grid of much smaller blocks, leading to a different problem: development that remained small-scale, which today makes Savannah charming but passive. Still, what both grids had in common was variation: in street widths and the placement of public squares and park space. In each plan, the developer was concerned as much with form as function.

Whatever softness Penn and Oglethorpe were seeking in their grid designs, in the broader scheme of things, when the colonies became a nation rectilinear became the rule and nature became the exception. It started with the territory west of the original colonies that the new nation began to acquire immediately after the Revolution, initially westward-stretching land ceded by the former colonies to the new national government.

Generally, the first boundaries of unmapped terrain are rivers, lakes, mountains, or valleys. Not so in the new United States. In 1784, the Continental Congress decided that new states (when the land was formally obtained in whatever manner from the natives) would be rectangular, two degrees of latitude—120 miles—tall, width to be determined. The northern and southern boundaries would be surveyors' straight lines, not the earth's natural features; often enough, the eastern and western boundaries would be as well. In 1785, starting with the Northwest Territory, Congress decided that the best way to settle these lands quickly—in order to generate much-needed revenue and discourage squatters and their rights—was to divide everything up into rectangles: from "open" land into townships six miles square into sections one mile square and ultimately down to lots 60 by 125 feet.

Under the extraordinary Land Ordinance of 1785, the first Geographer of the United States, Thomas Hutchins, started work where Pennsylvania met Virginia at the Ohio River. Hutchins was pretty much overmatched for the task, even in the relatively flat portions of Ohio, but rudimentary tools, drunken assistants, and native attacks didn't help. After three years, he completed only seven columns of thirty-six-mile-wide ranges. The results were more like an approximation of the accuracy needed. The first sales, at auctions in New York City in 1787, were equally disappointing. Still, the shape of the future had been seen. Rectangles large and small would come to dominate the American landscape. In a sense, rectangles *are* the American landscape that Americans have fit themselves into. As surveying historian Bill Hubbard Jr. writes, in much of the country "the boundaries were drawn before the cultural patterns arose. Before anybody had a sense of what it meant to be a Nebraskan and what Nebraskans might share in common, there was a place marked on maps with clear borders called Nebraska." This is also true of Philadelphia and Savannah: there were no Philadelphians or Savannahans before their developers created them.

Whether created from empty flatland by developers or imposed by early settlers inspired by the Rectangular Survey, Philadelphia, or New York, it's no surprise that rectilinear grids are the framework of most American cities, from Miami to Anchorage, from Sacramento to Erie, Pennsylvania, in all (rectangular) block shapes and sizes. As Lewis Mumford lamented:

> If the older cities of the seaboard were limited in their attempts
> to become metropolises by the fact that their downtown sections
> were originally laid out for villages, the villages of the middle west
> labored under just the opposite handicap; they had frequently

acquired the framework of a metropolis before they had passed out of the physical state of a village. The gridiron plan was a sort of hand-me-down which the juvenile city was supposed to grow into and fill.

The most popular grid size seems to have been the 300-by-300-foot block, with sixty- to eighty-foot-wide streets; this was the original grid pattern of Missoula, Bismarck, Phoenix, Tulsa, Mobile, and Anchorage, among others. Carson City, Nevada, claims the smallest urban grid, a mere 180-foot square with sixty-foot streets. Perhaps this tight pattern served well for shootouts during its Wild West days. By far the largest grid in the nation (and probably in the world) is Salt Lake City, with 600-foot-square blocks—ten acres!—surrounded by 120-foot-wide streets, reputedly the turning dimension of a Mormon oxcart.

Manhattan's largest blocks are half the area of Salt Lake City's and their average size is fairly normal, but the ratio of length to width is beyond all other urban measure. The 1811 grid's east-west dimensions are far larger than Salt Lake's, while the 200-foot north-south lengths are barely larger than Carson City's. While New York's grid brought order to the place, it also made it a place of extremes.

"THEYR STREETS ARE Nasty & unregarded," snorted Boston doctor Benjamin Bullivant. He was visiting New York in 1697. Generations of residents and visitors before and after, dodging hogs and goats and their evacuations, agreed.

New Amsterdam, established in the 1620s at the southern tip of Manhattan as a fur trading outpost of the Dutch West India Company, was not a pretty place: its existence was commercial, its dirt or badly cobbled streets were haphazardly laid, mostly narrow, crooked, and ill-maintained. Few if any of the eventually 1,500 New

Amsterdam residents much cared. Most were strivers for profit and survival at the frontier of European civilization. Many were traders, some were pirates and privateers, not a few were slaves, prostitutes, brewers, farmers, carpenters, bakers, tailors, blacksmiths, or sailors. They practiced many religions and spoke many languages. They built their eventually three hundred or so houses (and many taverns) of wood harvested from the island's ample forests and brick that arrived as ships' ballast. Household waste, by law to be collected and dumped outside of town or in the tide-flushed rivers, in practice mingled with animal waste in the streets.

Of the eventually dozen nasty New Amsterdam streets, most materialized the natural way: in service to where people chose to build homes, that is, on nothing like a plan. There were exceptions. At a natural inlet on the east side of town, the Dutch company characteristically dug a long canal that nearly bisected the entire town, allowing access at high tide by small boats, with roadways on either side. The canal was later filled in; it became and remains Broad Street. Intersecting "the Ditch," as it was called, was a shorter canal draining off a stream-fed marsh; it later became and remains Beaver Street. The main street, on the west side of town, was the Heere Straat, the high street that in time led up the island's spine as Broadway.

Civic virtue was yet unborn in 1664 when his merchant subjects compelled peevish governor Peter Stuyvesant to surrender the Dutch company town to an English fleet without a disruptive fight. The subsequent English century spawned a greater sense of urban purpose, but the town expanded slowly up Manhattan on no unified plan, with no model or style, unlike elegant rival Philadelphia. New York had no aspirational founder like William Penn.

Like Philadelphia, New York grew between rivers, on land that passed mostly peacefully on a similar timeframe from Lenape to Dutch to English occupation and control. Unlike Philadelphia, with its lovely grid of varied densities, broad central streets, and open squares, New York had a jumble of old pathways and new streets laid according to the whims of the owners of the land beneath them, with nothing like a proper public boulevard or square of urban celebration. The lullaby of Broadway was far off.

By the late 1600s the defining longitudinal roadways of the island, growing out of native paths, were taking shape: the Albany Post Road comprising various segments that eventually became Broadway on the west, the Eastern (or Boston) Post Road comprising various segments on the other side. Within the settled city proper, New York gained legal control of its current and future streets in 1686 under its second charter, bearing the name of provincial governor Thomas Dongan. The city's first English charter, of 1665, had established an English-style municipal government of mayor, aldermen, and sheriff but did not address streets, among many other subjects. The Dongan Charter reorganized the government as a Common Council of mayor and recorder (the chief legal officer), both annually appointed by the governor, and aldermen and assistants, annually elected by each ward (originally six, eventually two dozen). This basic structure continued through the 1800s, modified over time with longer terms and direct elections of the mayor and recorder. Among other things, the Dongan Charter gave the Council "full power . . . to establish, appoint, order, and direct the establishing, making, laying out, ordering, amending and repairing of all streets, lanes, alleys [and] highways . . . in and throughout the . . . city of New York and Manhattan's Island . . . necessary, needful and convenient for the inhabitants . . . and for all travellers [sic] and passengers there."

The only vague check on this broad power was that it could not be exercised if it took away any person's property without consent or "by some known law" of the province. Five years later, a new law authorizing the Common Council to appoint a surveyor to regulate buildings, streets, and docks specified that the value of any private ground taken by the city for public streets was to be fairly assessed and paid to its owner. "This was a noble provision," observed legal scholar James Kent, "and much better than the check on corporate authority contained in the charter." Thus was established in New York the principle that private property can't be taken for public use without just compensation.

This "noble" control of the city's streets was continued in the charter signed by Governor John Montgomerie in 1731. The landmark Montgomerie Charter, merging and greatly expanding the various provisions of the important Dongan Charter of 1686 and the lesser Cornbury Charter of 1708, guided New York up to and beyond the Revolution, so effectively that its form and spirit were largely retained in the state constitutions of 1777 and 1821 and intervening laws were based on it.

As with many aspects of municipal life, the 1731 charter was clear about the city's once and future streets. The Common Council would "have full power . . . not only to establish, appoint, order and direct, the making and laying out of all other streets, lanes, alleys [and] highways . . . not already made or laid out, but also the altering, amending and repairing" of them. As before, per legislative statute, the taking of private land required compensation, and the city could apply to the legislature for laws that clarified or expanded the city's power consistent with the general intent of the charter. Five times during the colonial years (in 1741, 1751, 1754, 1764, and 1774) acts were passed regarding Council authority over roads on the island and streets in the city, while a 1787 law (under the 1777 state constitution) conferred substantial powers on the Common Council as commissioners of highways.

So there's a long history of the colonial and early American city being empowered to control its streets. The history of the city actually exercising that power is much shorter. In fact, there really isn't much history until 1807. The Common Council was annually elected, subject to substantial turnover, unsupported by any standing bureaucracy, and thus admittedly shortsighted in most matters.

It was perennially uncertain if it needed provincial or (later) state legislation or could act on its own to construct public streets or close privately made ones. Indeed, on practically all important matters, the Council habitually doubted its charter rights even though they contained, in Kent's view, "a grant of ample powers, sufficient for all the purposes of . . . the good government of the city in its complicated concerns."

In practice, when the city wanted to exercise an important power, it went to the state for explicit permission in the form of a law. The city was the state's oldest child but it behaved like a timid adolescent, asking permission to use the car when it had a set of keys in its pocket. Regarding the streets themselves, the city rarely troubled the state. The Council was content to let landowners make streets and then do its best to regulate and clean them. "It is a matter of considerable surprise," observed the exasperated official nominally in charge of the city's streets in 1806, that the city had "made use of so little coercion" for so long "that individuals *even at this period* continue to project their streets in their own way and dispute with the Common Council upon their uncontroulable right to do so."

While the city effectively ceded its street-making rights for generations to private owners who generally laid streets on their lands as they chose, some owners did have good design sense. Harnessing the natural tendency of humans to proceed from randomness to order, Trinity Church in the early 1750s laid out a portion of its wedge of land between Broadway and the Hudson River into a small neighborhood of several rectangular blocks around its newly chartered King's College, at the town's then suburban fringe between Barclay and Murray Streets, west of Church Street. This marked the birth of both a great school (now Columbia University) and the idea of rectilinear planning on Manhattan. And this little grid was to feature another first: the first First—that is, the first Manhattan street named 1st Street. And a 2nd Street and a 3rd Street, all running north-south on lines that today are where Greenwich,

Washington, and (just east of) West Streets run. The thing is, though, these numbered streets were never laid. They appeared on a plan, but the plan imagined Hudson River landfill that didn't happen until New York was American, by which time the original plan had been abandoned.

Manhattan's first actual 1st Street in an actual grid, featuring a half dozen numbered streets, came into existence a bit later as part of what could be called Manhattan's first rectilinear land development. On the other side of the island from the college, the powerful DeLancey family decided to put their 340-acre estate to work in the 1760s, beginning with the layout of streets in the southwestern part of their property. Their plan centered on a spacious square bearing the family name, with 1st through 6th Streets running north-south and forming a grid with several cross streets. The DeLanceys had little time to develop their property, though. Being royalists, they were forced into exile after the Revolution and their land was confiscated by New York State. In subdividing the estate for sale, the state Commissioners of Forfeiture left the DeLancey grid but eliminated the grand square by running Grand Street through it. To avoid the confusion of numbered streets running north-south after the 1811 grid was announced, all of the DeLancey numbered streets were eventually given names, all of them but Orchard for War of 1812 dead, none of them particularly distinguished: Chrystie, Forsythe, Eldridge, Allen, and Ludlow, the major north-south routes of the modern Lower East Side.

Just after the Revolution, another landowning family developed a second grid, again with numbered north-south streets. Unlike the DeLanceys, the Bayards were patriots and prominent locals from way back: Judith Bayard was Peter Stuyvesant's wife; they emigrated from Holland to New Amsterdam in 1647 with his widowed sister Ann Stuyvesant Bayard, who had been married to Judith's brother, and her four children. Ann's son Nicholas, benefitting greatly from the patronage of Stuyvesant and others, established a farm that

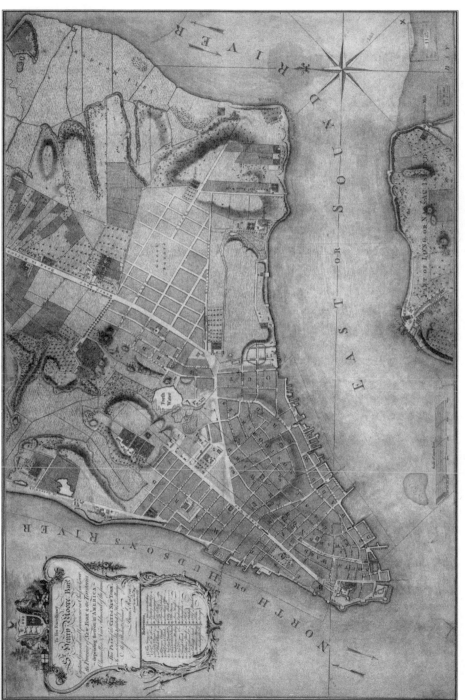

This highly accurate map of 1767 New York by British army officer Bernard Ratzer conveys the beginnings of pre-grid rectilinear order, along the Hudson River in the vicinity of Columbia College and, most importantly, the suburban development newly laid out around a great square by the DeLancey family. Compare with the 1796 map on page 19. (*Library of Congress*)

eventually spread to hundreds of acres between what is now Canal and West 3rd Streets, from the Bowery to Sixth Avenue, including modern Soho, Noho, and the southern reaches of Greenwich Village. After the Revolution, Broadway was extended north through the farm, sundering it east and west. The western portion was a hundred entirely undeveloped acres that presented opportunities— necessary ones, in that the financial disruptions of the war had compelled Nicholas Bayard III to raise cash through a heavy mortgage on the property, which had been much abused by the city's defensive military works.

In 1788, the Bayards hired Casimir Goerck (much more about him later) to survey and lay out West Farm into real estate: the hundred acres was converted to thirty-five whole or partial blocks within seven east-west and eight north-south streets in a convenient rectilinear grid (with irregular edges where the Bayards' property met others'). All of the Bayard streets survive and in their original locations, some widened from their original fifty feet. All of their original names are gone but one, named for Nicholas III's daughter Mary's husband, a prominent Georgian named William Houstoun. Time has made off with his ultimate vowel, but not the "HOW-stun" pronunciation that eludes tourists. Like those of the DeLancey grid, the north-south streets were numbered, in this case from 1st through 8th, but they had a very short run as numbered streets. Within a decade or so, the numbers had been exchanged for names, in this case those of mostly high-ranking Revolutionary War officers: Mercer, Greene, Wooster, Laurens (now LaGuardia), Thompson, Sullivan, MacDougal, and Hancock (now a short stretch of Sixth Avenue). But the Bayard Farm grid remains as today's Soho, with blocks from 350 to 500 feet long on the north-south axis, and a uniform 200 feet wide.

There was something else about the numbered, rectilinear Bayard Farm grid. Its blocks were subdivided by plan into some 1,200 lots, typically with eight lots on the narrow north and south

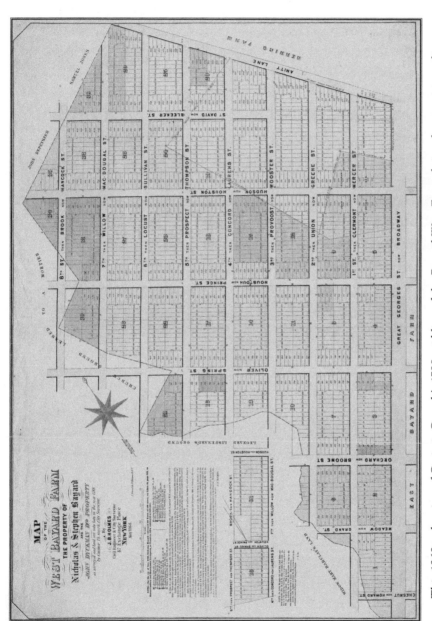

This 1868 redrawing of Casimir Goerck's 1788 gridding of the Bayard West Farm shows the transition of its north–west streets from numbers to the names of modern Soho and the original subdivision of its blocks into twenty-five-by-one-hundred-foot lots, a sizing that was not part of the 1811 Commissioners' Plan but would naturally evolve within its block dimensions. (*Museum of the City of New York*)

ends of each block, and from six to twelve lots along the east and west middles. Do the math and that makes the typical Bayard lot twenty-five feet wide and one hundred feet deep. While twenty-five-foot-wide lots already existed in Manhattan (more about that later), the twenty-five-by-one-hundred-foot lot as a subdivision within a rectilinear street grid, the dominant lot size of gridded Manhattan, debuted on the Bayards' West Farm.

The DeLancey and Bayard grids (and the Trinity intention) were the first attempts at rectilinear street order in New York City. They were all done by private interests: landowners seeking to make money from the subdivision of their land by laying streets in a pattern as they chose. Though it had been empowered for generations to make streets, the city government wasn't ready yet to assert its will over private property. But it was, with Casimir Goerck's help, ready to assert itself in a rectilinear way over land it owned, albeit far from the city proper.

CHAPTER 2

FIVE ACRES AND A RULE: THE GREAT GRID'S COMMON ORIGINS

The Surveys made by Mr. Goerck upon the Commons were effected through thickets and swamps, and over rocks and hills where it was almost impossible to produce accuracy in the mensuration.

—Street commissioner John Hunn, 1808

AFTER THE REVOLUTION, New York set about becoming the new nation's leading city. From the long colonial shadows of Philadelphia and even Boston, New York emerged on top by the opening of the first American century. It finally surpassed Philadelphia in population and was positioned to become the new nation's commercial center. It finally began to organize itself. The first city directory was published in 1787. The first regular street numbering, ordered by the Common Council in 1793, appeared in the directory of the following year, the same year that the city began changing the names of streets with royal associations. Also in 1794, the main road that went by various names as it proceeded through the town and beyond was named Broadway for its then entire length, all the way out to the suburbs that now are Astor Place (though it was not paved that far for another generation). The city streets themselves, all ninety or so of them by now, remained mostly a hodgepodge of private creations, with bits of rectilinearity, the Bayard and DeLancey grids, established at the city's northern fringes. The Common Council, meanwhile, caught some of the rectilinear bug, though not anywhere near where anyone would object.

The city government did not have a substantial revenue stream yet, primarily from taxes. It did have land that it thought it could sell. Three years before the Bayards had the idea of doing something rectilinear with a portion of their land and profiting from it, the city attempted to do something similar with the land it owned, the 1,300 or so acres of central Manhattan generally known as the "Common Lands." These were the remainder of what may originally have been twice as much "waste, vacant, unpatented, and unappropriated" land first granted by Dutch provincial authority to the government of New Amsterdam in 1658; the English charters of 1686 and 1731 confirmed city ownership. There's no map of the original Common Lands, which over the generations apparently were whittled down by grants and transfers. In any case, the 1,300 remaining acres in 1785 were not insubstantial, equaling about 9 percent of the island's total area.* The southern tip of the Common Lands in 1785 was the rural intersection of Bloomingdale Road (now Broadway) leading up the west side of the island and the Eastern Post Road up the other side, now the intersection of Broadway and Fifth Avenue at 23rd Street. From there, the lands broadened out irregularly as wide as what are now Second and Seventh Avenues, but the bulk was centered

---

* Manhattan's land area has grown with landfill over the past four centuries, with valuations varying by who's measuring and when. In 1626, the Dutch West India Company believed its sixty guilders (mythically equal to twenty-four of the dollars that didn't exist then) had bought them an island of 11,000 morgens, or 22,000 acres. Not that the Lenape were counting, but they beat the Dutch by double: modern estimates put early 1600s Manhattan at about 11,350 acres. The most generous measure of Manhattan today is about 14,600 acres, an increase of over 25 percent.

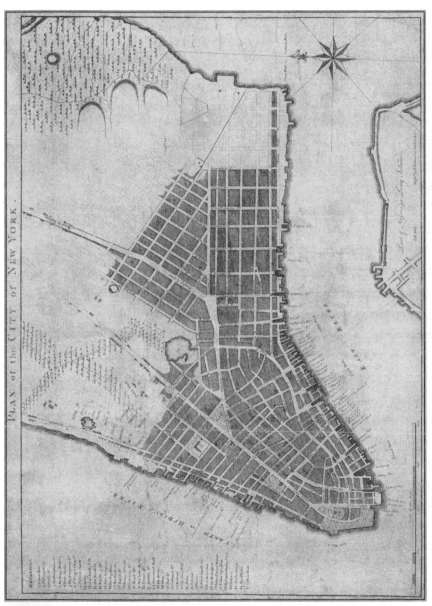

This very rare 1796 map (engraved by Peter Rushton Maverick, father of the 1803 Mangin-Goerck map engraver) depicts the effects of post-Revolutionary royalist land forfeitures: the DeLancey grid's great square is gone, the Rutgers estate to the south has been sold off and laid out in a fairly regular grid, and the presumed extension of each is depicted with dotted lines. (*Image provided by www.RareMaps.com—Barry Lawrence Ruderman Antique Maps Inc.*)

well inside the meandering, relatively level courses of the Post and Bloomingdale Roads, up to the village of Harlem's boundary with the Commons. (Originally a Dutch farming settlement along the Harlem River, Harlem was formally delineated by the English and remained a small, mostly autonomous village until it was subsumed by the city expanding northward under the 1811 grid plan.) The border between the city's Common Lands and Harlem's Commons was a diagonal line angling from what is now Second Avenue and 79th Street to the Common Lands' northern tip at what would have been Seventh and 93rd if Central Park hadn't been planted there. By odd chance, the Commons Lands of the 1780s, with its narrow tips and lanky, lumpy bulk, roughly approximates the shape of Manhattan itself, at 1:11 scale.

The problem with the Common Lands is that while it was a lot of land, it was also a lot of lousy land: alternately high and rocky or low and swampy without much level in between, and tangled with often impenetrable overgrowth. It was difficult land to farm and undesirable land for a proper estate. This is why the Bloomingdale and Post Roads started as native paths well clear of the difficult terrain that became the Common Lands. The Common Lands were also landlocked, at a time when only the island's long shorelines offered access and attraction to up-island residents. For their owner, the rugged, remote Common Lands would be a hard sell, but the cash-strapped government of the newly American city hired Goerck in June 1785 to survey them into sellable parcels.

Not much is known today about Casimir Theodor Goerck. He was of Polish (or possibly Germanic) origins, born around 1755, and came to America to serve as an artillery officer with the winning side during the Revolution. In the waning days of the war he married Elizabeth Roosevelt, of the prosperous Dutch merchant family of New York that would produce two presidents. They had a daughter (Henrietta) who might have been born a bit too soon for complete propriety and a son (Theodore), by whom the family name continued for several generations. After the war, Goerck quickly established himself, no doubt with his in-laws' influence, as a surveyor, one of a handful of "city surveyors" officially authorized by the Common Council to conduct public and private surveys. Anyone could survey land but a "city surveyor" was in effect certified and commanded higher fees. The status was prominent and Casimir Goerck was good. His name is on numerous important New York surveys conducted during the 1780s and '90s. Goerck is obscure now but unfairly: from his Common Lands work sprung Manhattan's grid.

Goerck was instructed to survey, divide, and map the bulk of the Common Lands into lots "as near as may be of five Acres each" to be sold at auction. Why five acres is unclear, but it proved prophetic. For access to these rural plots, Goerck was to lay a road of unspecified width through the middle. Nothing specific is known of his surveying techniques and tools but they likely were typical for the times, that is, like the contemporaneous national Rectangular Survey, not especially accurate. From certain map markings, we do know that Goerck used a Gunter's chain, a then standard length-measuring tool developed a century and a half earlier by English mathematician Edmund Gunter that is composed of one hundred links making a chain of sixty-six feet. Additionally, Goerck likely used a compass, other linear measurement tools like wooden or metal rods of specified lengths, and perhaps a device for measuring angles. It's interesting to note that Goerck was doing what he could with the inhospitable interior of Manhattan at precisely the same time that much maligned Rectangular Survey leader Thomas Hutchins was doing what he could with the inhospitable interior of the nation. For the next century, Manhattan would fill at about the same rate as the nation: the island city as a microcosm of continental frontier opening and closing.

By December 1785, Goerck had done the best he could. Given the rudimentary tools, relatively brief surveying period, and the unforgiving landscape, it's no wonder that the 140 or so lots of 1785 turned out hardly uniform and, though it was not a requirement, not especially rectilinear. Following directions, Goerck split the triangular lower section—from its southern tip to a mile north at Cross Road, a country path also known as Low's Lane and Steuben Street (now roughly 42nd Street) that linked the Bloomingdale and Post Roads—with the mandated middle road angling from the Post Road at today's 29th up to the midpoint of Cross Road. From there, Goerck fashioned two columns of forty-five somewhat cock-eyed lots each, with the middle road between, sixty-six feet—one chain—wide by Goerck's convenient choice, running north along the island's axis. Two large Commons tracts, at the wider northwest and central eastern portions that would have been in columns on either side of the central ones, could not be divided because there was no access from the middle, Post, or Bloomingdale roads. Importantly, in order to provide as many accessible lots as possible along the middle road, Goerck oriented his central lots on the opposite axis from his Bayard grid, that is, the shorter dimension on the north-south axis and the much longer dimension on the east-west axis. In time the middle road would be widened to one hundred feet and, unacknowledged, serve the 1807 Commissioners extraordinarily well as their Fifth Avenue. Likewise, those five-acre lots, after some further refinement, would serve the Commissioners quite nicely as an unacknowledged template for their five-acre blocks. But let's not get ahead of ourselves.

The anticipated bull market in these imperfect Common Lands lots did not materialize. Regardless of how it was marked up, the land was still unappealing and the middle road provided only limited access at the center; the outer edges of most of the lots bordered on private lands. Even the southernmost of the lots were over two country miles from the northern limits of the settled city; the northern lots were another four miles distant. In the long shadow of the recent war's disruptions, few New Yorkers had the cash or the confidence to speculate in bits of central Manhattan that had been avoided even by the natives.

The unattractiveness of Common Lands lots in the 1780s can be seen in the unfortunate case of Pierre Charles L'Enfant. The young French sophisticate had spent most his twenties as a military engineer for the Americans during the Revolution. In 1788, three years before he famously designed the nation's permanent capital, L'Enfant designed and, with four other publically appointed commissioners, oversaw extensive repairs and alterations to New York's aging second City Hall, opened in 1702 on Wall Street. These renovations were to transform it into a suitable Federal Hall for George Washington's inauguration (April 1789) and Congress's temporary home (1789–1790) until the scheduled moves first to Philadelphia and eventually to the new capital city. Whether L'Enfant was supposed to be paid for his Federal Hall work was unclear. There was no contract, and L'Enfant, an otherwise fervent patriot, could be a terror regarding compensation. In October 1789, with Congress happily functioning in its handsome refurbished quarters and the substantial £13,000 cost successfully raised by a special tax, the Common Council began paying off accounts "for work done . . . & Materials provided." L'Enfant was not on its list. The following week, the Council resolved that L'Enfant had furnished his plan "at the Request of the Citizens" and had "generously" overseen the work with "a highly distinguished Degree of Skill and Taste in Architecture" and completed it with "uncommon Zeal and Industry." In what it considered ample thanks, the Council graciously offered him "the Freedom of this City" and ten acres of its recently mapped Common Lands, location to be determined. The symbolic freedom was nice (though the modern equivalent at least comes with a collectible key) but, like most New Yorkers then, L'Enfant considered a piece of the Common Lands pretty much worthless.

A flurry of sales that summer—175 acres in thirty-three lots to nine buyers at an average price of about seventy-one dollars per acre—had suggested to the Council that its lands were becoming worthy. Few sales, though, had preceded these and few would immediately follow. And all but six of the thirty-three sold lots were at the Common Lands' extreme southern tip, the wedge of lots bounded and easily accessed by the Bloomingdale and Post Roads. The market for the bulk of Common Lands lots remained weak.

In April 1790, the Council formally offered L'Enfant ten acres at the northeasterly corner of the Common Lands, roughly between today's 68th and 70th Streets east of Third Avenue. Remote as it might have been from the city, this land did border the well-traveled Post Road and was just up the road from the Dove Tavern, a popular public house established in 1763 (and the locus of Nathan Hale's hanging in 1776) at today's 66th Street and Third Avenue. Regardless, L'Enfant did not bite: it "is perfectly agreable with my Sentiments & Disposition to refuse the Gift."

There the matter lay for another eleven years, until L'Enfant, by then short on cash and design commissions, revived his claim. In January 1801, an entirely new Common Council (but for perennial mayor Richard Varick) offered L'Enfant $750 cash. He asked for more. The Council declined. Another *nineteen* years passed before L'Enfant, sixty-five years old and practically destitute, petitioned yet again. The 1820 Council was not much disposed toward accommodating the old man, who appeared "to value his services far above what they were deemed to be worth" by prior Councils. Concluding now that "whatever his services were, they were rendered voluntarily & without stipulation for or expectation of a reward," the Council offered L'Enfant nothing.

The imported patriot seriously miscalculated. These days, undeveloped land in Manhattan goes for around $300 per square foot, or $13 million per acre, and L'Enfant's rejected ten is now prime Upper East Side real estate. Even if he had taken the land offered in 1790 and held it for just a few years, L'Enfant might have had a substantial windfall, thanks to the effects of Casimir Goerck's second mapping of the Common Lands.

By 1794, the city's economy was rising and its rapid northward spread was beginning. During the 1790s, the city's population doubled to 60,000 and the assessed valuation of property nearly quadrupled to $20 million. The Common Council, frustrated with the slow pace of Common Lands sales but encouraged by the indicators of future prosperity, hired Goerck to make a new Common Lands survey and map.

This time, Goerck was charged with laying out more uniformly rectangular five-acre lots and adding access roads on either side of and parallel to the middle road. For access on the opposite axis, he was also to lay off sixty-foot-wide east-west streets running along the northern portion of each lot. Thus were conceived the East and West Roads that the 1807 Commissioners, without acknowledgment, would use as guidelines for their Fourth and Sixth Avenues, and the cross-island routes that the Commissioners, again without acknowledgment, would turn into their numbered streets.

It took Goerck two years to complete his surveying and staking, and produce a map, which he presented to the Council in March 1796. With the additional north-south roads and intended east-west streets, Goerck was able now to map out the entire Common Lands into 212 numbered lots, the vast majority of which were relatively close to five acres, and all of which had—at least on paper—street access on at least two sides. Again, his work was difficult and understandably imperfect. "The Surveys made by Mr Goerck upon the Commons," observed sympathetic street commissioner John Hunn in 1808, "were effected through thickets and swamps, and over rocks and hills where it was almost impossible to produce accuracy in the mensuration." His East and West Roads turned out pretty straight: a consistent sixty feet wide and a consistent thirteen chains and ninety-four links—920 feet—distant from his existing Middle Road. (Yes, this is exactly the same distance between the 1807 Commissioners' Fourth and Fifth, and Fifth and Sixth Avenues.) As to the cross streets, "Goerck, no doubt, intended the streets laid down by him should be at right angles to those Roads," a later Common

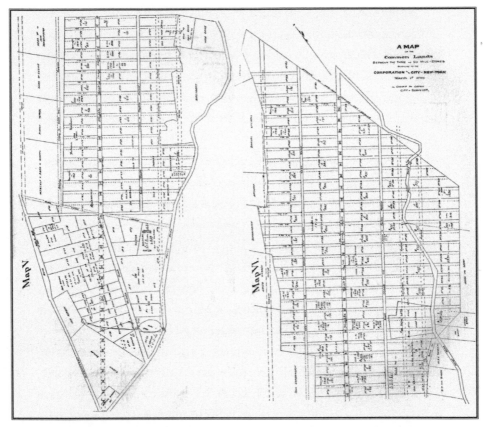

This 1891 redrawing of Casimir Goerck's 1796 Commons Lands survey illustrates how his map was a template for the 1807 Commissioners: their central avenues align perfectly with Goerck's three north–south roads (solid lines) and their streets align more or less with his intended streets (solid and dotted lines). The Manhattan grid is Goerck's Common Lands writ large.

Lands surveyor gently noted, "but they were not so laid out on the ground." In fact, very few of the streets that "were intended to be Sixty feet in width and Two hundred feet from each other" ever materialized. Without even a cleared path marked with fencing, purchasers of these lots would come to believe those sixty-foot strips were theirs, that is, that their 200-foot lots were 260-foot lots. This would cause problems later.

In the meantime, consider the numbers. Goerck intended two central columns of lots 920 feet by 200 feet, with sixty-foot crossing streets from Cross Road up to their boundary with the Harlem commons. Even though his east-west streets existed almost entirely on paper only, Goerck's 1796 Common Lands map is the genesis of the 1811 grid, whether its makers acknowledged it or not. As today's Landmarks Preservation Commission put it, almost as an afterthought in a footnote within its detailed 2010 report on the extension of the Upper East Side Historic District, "The Commissioners' Plan borrowed heavily from Goerck's earlier surveys and essentially expanded his scheme beyond the common lands to encompass the entire island." Indeed, for generations after the Commissioners' Plan appeared, land sales within the old Common Lands that ostensibly should have been defined by the 1811 plan's streets and avenues were more likely to be identified by their 1796 lot number.

In fact, the great grid is not much more than the Goerck plan writ large. The Goerck plan is modern Manhattan's Rosetta Stone (the decoding of which began in the years between the Goerck plan and the Commissioners' Plan). Goerck's embryonic grid was the shape of things to come. And it was all so inadvertent. The shapes grew by chance from the need to give street access to as many five-acre lots as could be squeezed originally along a single road. Goerck did not explain why he chose 200 feet and 920 feet in 1796. We do know that the 200-foot dimension didn't have anything to do with anticipated subdivisions, say into the twin rows of 100-foot-deep lots that now populate Manhattan, because in the late 1700s those five-acre (or so) lots were very cheap and clearly intended for occupation or other use by single owners. But if we analyze his options, we can see that Goerck didn't have much of a range to work with. Given a mandate for a five-acre lot size and only two new north-south roads on either side of the middle road, if he placed his new roads too far apart, the lots would become very thin and the mandated sixty-foot streets between them very many. He couldn't place his roads so close together as to fail to provide access to the full breadth of the Common Lands. Given the restrictions—three roads, five-acre lots, and sixty-foot streets—920 and 200 feet were reasonable dimensions. And from these constraints spread, a decade and a half later, the "great grid."

Meanwhile, back in 1796, the Common Lands seemed a more reasonable and proximate investment to certain New Yorkers than they did a decade earlier, especially as a speculation for rising merchants with cash. Sales in 1796 averaged £66 ($165) per acre, more than double the prices of 1789. The ten acres that L'Enfant might have had were part of over thirty acres sold in 1800 to John Jones, the owner of a large farm adjoining to the east. Jones paid a hefty £5320 ($13,300), exactly $400 per acre. Sales in 1801 of lots in the immediate vicinity also went for an average of $400 per acre. If L'Enfant had taken his ten free acres in 1789, he might have sold them for $4,000 a decade or so later, making him reasonably wealthy instead of increasingly destitute. As the historian of municipal landownership wrote approvingly a century later of the 1796 mapping and lucrative sales it generated, "A far-sighted policy could hardly fail to suggest itself as to the commons." Sadly, L'Enfant let pride cloud his foresight. Unlucky Pierre died in 1825 with some bits of jewelry and surveying tools worth less than forty dollars, instead of land worth a hundred times more.

CHAPTER 3

THE CITY TO BE OR
NOT TO BE?

My plan . . . is not the plan of the City such as it is but
such as it is to be.

—Surveyor-architect Joseph François Mangin,
December 1798

A YEAR AFTER his second Common Lands survey, Casimir Goerck took up a greater challenge. It would kill him.

In 1797, the city hired Goerck and another city surveyor, a French émigré named Joseph François Mangin, to create the first official map of the city since the Revolution. The partnership was convenient—they had made competing offers before joining forces—but brief.

A bit more is known today about Mangin than Goerck. He was born on December 17, 1764, in Châlons-sur-Marne in the Champagne region of France. His father was a prominent obstetric surgeon; his mother also was from a prominent family. After an education focused on engineering and architecture, Mangin, accompanied by his wife Theresa, served with the French military mapping the island of Saint-Domingue (now Haiti) beginning in early 1789. The slave rebellion there in 1793 and the ongoing revolution at home left him, Theresa, and possibly by then their young son Charles, nowhere to go in 1794 but New York.

A sophisticate with monarchal sentiments and Caribbean seasoning, Mangin naturally came into the New York orbit of Alexander Hamilton, who became his influential mentor. At Hamilton's behest, the federal government quickly hired Mangin to design New York harbor fortifications. By 1797, Mangin had also designed the city's first purpose-built theater (1795) and the state's first prison (1796), on the Hudson at what was then the village of Greenwich, to which convicts were sent "up the river" from the city. By the end of his twenty or so American years, Mangin's major New York City works included the First Presbyterian Church on Wall Street (1810; dismantled and moved to Jersey City in 1844), the first St. Patrick's Cathedral (1815; rebuilt after a fire but still standing in what is now Little Italy), and his 1802 masterpiece, New York's landmark third City Hall, the graceful locus of city government for two centuries and counting. The City Hall project, as we shall see, was closely tied to Mangin's fate and the city's planning fortunes.

We know nothing of Goerck's thoughts or vision, if he had any, about his adopted city; no writings, if there were any, have survived. But we know Mangin had been thinking deeply about the city since his arrival. "The city of new york appears to Be designed as the future center and metropolis of commercial world," he wrote in 1796 (in his permanently imperfect English), "as lying at the mouth of two large and Beautiful rivers, on which are imported from the remotest interior parts the productions of fertile and daily improved countreys, and commanding an extensive Bay the Safest and most strongly defended in the union." Mangin understood the lay of New York's land.

Mangin was generally unafraid to express his opinions, most comfortably in French, as at length in January 1799 to the fluent Hamilton (here in translation):

I was born French and would have died French if the disgusting
cruelties that befell my family and made me detest the country
of my birth had not forced me to search out elsewhere the peace
and happiness that I could no longer find at home. I examined
this country; its mild and moderate government pleased me, and
I was naturalized. I swore by this act to maintain its laws to which
I submitted myself, to support its government, and to defend my
adopted homeland against any enemy whatsoever. This I swore
and I will keep my word: I am an American and the last drop of
my blood will be shed in the service of my country.

At the time of Mangin's letter, American-French relations were
severely strained by their naval Quasi-War. Mangin, who been
granted American citizenship in 1796, was making his allegiances
clear to Hamilton, who feared and despised post-royal France.

Mangin was also seeking to resolve a dispute over money owed
to him for his harbor fortifications work; Hamilton and two other
men made up the War Department committee that had hired
Mangin. Such disputes were not unusual for the time: the young
government sought and accepted many services it didn't have the
money to pay for. Mangin gave full throat to his qualifications:

The minor projects that I have so far executed in Newyork cannot allow you, sire, to fully judge of my abilities; because it is only
by his work that one can know the worker. You can only have
been informed that I have honorably acquitted myself of the
enterprises that I have undertaken; this knowledge, however, may
leave you in some doubt as to whether I am capable of undertaking larger projects; I do not believe it is being arrogant to assure
you, sir, that I have always been considered a good builder mostly
due to my correctly combining and applying reason to all of these
works, joining as I do my knowledge with a Theory which does

not allow me to be wrong. I also believe, sir, that I know how to combine all kinds of defenses and that I know how to adapt them to local and other various conditions: just as I know how to approach all types of construction, I have the ability to present my projects in a clear manner to allow managers to examine them, to respect or accept them on the basis of my knowledge. Because I never speak beyond the basis of known principles.

Had he overspoken? "I am perhaps, sir, going on too long about myself. I beg of you to believe that I do not do so vainly, but in order to straightforwardly describe what my conscience dictates." And it was only because he aspired higher:

I was named City Surveyor; I must admit to you, sir, that I don't like this situation, it appears to me that it is well below my station; although I earn enough to live honorably, the responsibilities are so limited and so petty that they scarcely please me.

However, with what zeal would I not gladly fulfill my functions were I honored with a military-grade appointment; with what pleasure would I not pursue the type of occupation for which I was destined, and which has always been my ruling passion.

One can see how he might have rubbed certain people the wrong way. In any case, there was nothing Hamilton could do for his protégé. It was not a time for the appointment of Frenchmen, no matter how patriotic or qualified, to American military positions. Mangin remained an honorable surveyor and occasional architect when opportunities arose, and would gain a measure of greatness with his City Hall design a few years later.

In the meantime, Mangin wanted to make a map. As early as July 1796, he suggested to Mayor Richard Varick that the city could use an official survey and plan of its existing streets, the first since the Revolution. In early 1797, members of the Common Council let it be known around town that there was interest in proposals for such a map. Mangin and Goerck, two of then five city surveyors, each jumped in. In March, Goerck offered to make a "general and accurate" map "as far as the City is laid out into Streets and Lots," which was barely beyond Chambers Street. Promising elevations marked at every intersection and other information, Goerck estimated his price at £600 ($1,500), a not insignificant claim on the city's annual budget of $130,000. In April, Mangin submitted something even grander. He would produce a master map six feet square, and give half-size personal copies to the mayor and the fourteen Council members. He would mark the position of every house, lot, street, square, wharf, and ward, and indicate elevations by his own calculations throughout. All of this information would be recorded in an accompanying field book that would also contain the names of every property owner and the many "wrong levels" calculated by previous mappers with a correction method: "in order to make this map I cannot use the plans already made to avoid the errors and mistakes." Mangin said his work would take at least two years to complete. He doubled Goerck's price, asking $3,000, to be paid in advance. "I demand only this sum because I reserve for myself the right of raising a Subscription in which I will give a Share" to the city to cover the advance. Each subscriber would get a three-foot-square map with a field book facsimile.

While the Council took its time chewing over this fairly extraordinary proposal, plus Goerck's and others, Mangin and Goerck decided to join forces. In November, they submitted a joint proposal, in Goerck's superior English, on Mangin's superior terms, and much broader in geographic area. The partners offered to make a detailed map of the island out to "Sandy Hill Road at the two Mile Stone," which sat squarely in what four decades later became Astor Place. With Mangin's previously offered elevations on a six-foot master map and the detailed field book of streets, levels, and distances, the Mangin-Goerck map would offer greater breadth and depth than any previous map of the city and its outlying regions. The surveyors shortened delivery to eighteen months but held firm to Mangin's $3,000 price, reached by equally sharing with the city subscription revenues for three-foot-square maps until the fee was met. It was an offer from the city's two most prominent surveyors—one who'd laid out the Common Lands, the other who'd designed harbor fortifications and already two prominent buildings (the theater and prison)—that could not be refused. The Council promptly made a contract with Mangin and Goerck and started making payments to them on their account, $200 in December, another $1,000 by May 1798. By then, they were well along in their work.

During the spring and summer of 1798 they ranged all over the city and beyond, surveying by day, computing and drafting by night. By midsummer, though, theirs had become a dangerous occupation: the city's worst epidemic of yellow fever had started killing New Yorkers by the hundreds. This was no surprise. "The present sickness will subside and soon be forgotten," wrote newspaper editor and health reformer (and future dictionary maker) Noah Webster, "and men will proceed in the same round of folly and vice . . . piling together buildings, accumulating filth, and destroying fresh air, and preparing new and more abundant materials for pestilence, which will continue to assume greater virulence and to prove more destructive to human life, in proportion to the magnitude of our cities."

New York was cramped and filthy, and a spectacular breeding and hunting ground for virus-bearing mosquitoes that, unknown at that time, spread the deadly fever with their bite. Before a freeze in late November 1798 killed them, mosquitoes delivered death bites to two thousand of the sixty thousand New Yorkers. Casimir Goerck, who spent long days tramping the filthy streets, foul docksides, and swampy outskirts, was among them, early in the month.

Mangin survived. The Mangin-Goerck map, pursued now by Mangin alone, quickly became a very different project from the originally intended "general and accurate" map of the city and its environs.

A few weeks after Goerck's death, another surveyor, Charles Loss, working on an official map of the harbor, showed up at Mangin's house on Greenwich Street near Chambers, "to demand of me the map of the City," ostensibly to see how the harbor and city maps might mesh.

Loss was well known to Mangin. Here's a bit about Mr. Loss, who is important to us in two regards to be detailed later. Despite the Anglo name, Charles Frederick Loss—originally Lauss or there-abouts—was actually a Saxon and arrived in New York around 1796 with his wife and inexplicably good references. Probably in response to Goerck's death, the Common Council on November 5, 1798, named Loss one of two new city surveyors "whenever they become naturalized Citizens of the United States." Over the next few months, Loss become a citizen and, already under contract to do the harbor survey, gained city surveyor status. Not that status implied ability in his case. Loss would stumble through a dozen years of surveying, including "several errors of a serious nature," until the city relieved him of his duties in 1811. He was reappointed nine years later, apparently as something of a courtesy and with a proviso from then street commissioner John McComb Jr: "The Street Commissioner would suggest the propriety of the appointment being made under the impression that a greater attention to accuracy will be expected." Loss, then fifty-five, didn't cause too much more trouble because he died two years later.

One reason why Loss is important to us is that he is an associate of Aaron Burr. Why *that* is important, later. For now, some background. Burr first became acquainted with Loss and his wife after their arrival in New York and, Burr noted many years later, "we have ever since continued in habits of great intimacy." Loss mapped Burr's Richmond Hill residence, a large colonial estate reduced by the time of Burr's leasehold to twenty-six acres at what is now the southeast corner of Varick and Charlton Streets, at the southwest corner of Greenwich Village. In 1805, Burr included Loss in his assemblage of adventurers out west, seemingly as the benign surveyor for a possible canal around falls on the Ohio River but in all likelihood for illicit surveying duties related to Burr's notorious "conspiracy" (more about that below). "He is universally and justly esteemed for his integrity, fidelity, and honour," Burr lied in 1810 to a German friend whom Burr asked to convey the false particulars to Loss's parents and in-laws, especially if they had some money. "Should they be in good circumstances, I would wish to induce them to send some aid to their amiable children in America. A sum in money would be of great use to them, and no man in America is more capable of placing money to advantage than Charles Loss." Loss, of course, was soon to be removed from his position as city surveyor and was evidently on the edge of ruin, as happened to many Burr associates, especially those who grew dependent on him. "Neither Mr. nor Mrs. Charles Loss had the remotest idea that I should say anything to their parents about pecuniary aid. But having, since our first acquaintance, enjoyed their entire confidence, I know that a competent sum would just now be of the utmost importance to them, and might greatly advance the permanent respectability of their family." In fact, whatever respectability Loss might once have achieved was by that point unattainable.

It was this so-destined Charles Loss who turned up at Mangin's door in early December 1798 seeking a peek at his map. "I was singularly surprised with this demand," Mangin reported to the Common Council, "but without making him sensible of the motives I answered him that that map was not yet finished but that if it was I could not dispose of it without the consent of the Corporation according to the terms of our contract [and] that moreover I was occupied in making a Copy at which I had worked without intermission, to finish it as quick as possible."

Perhaps something in the German Loss irked the Gallic Mangin. Maybe it was political sensibilities: Mangin had been nurtured by Hamilton, Loss was already Burr's boy. Still, just a few months earlier they had worked together on the survey of a merchant's newly acquired farm at what today is Union Square, and they would work together in the future. New York was still a small town that made strange bedfellows, like political enemies but occasional legal cocounsels Hamilton and Burr.

When Loss reappeared at Mangin's door two weeks after his first visit, though, Mangin had had enough. Loss repeated what Mangin considered his unreasonable demand and Mangin again refused, prompting Loss to whip out a document from the Council that Loss said was an order for Mangin to show his map but that Mangin recognized as only a request. Now fully incensed, Mangin ordered Loss out, this time with a vow to write to the Council to prevent further incursions. This Mangin did, on December 17, 1798, in his French-infused English.

> How does he come to have the right to put off one day a plan which is . . . between the Corporation and me? it is useless that he should persiste in his demande which would hinder me in my work since it would take him at least five days to copy what is necessary for him[.] it is too precious that I could permit myself to loose it[.] moreover that it is right for him to come to put off a work which is the result of the fatigues of M. Goerck and me[?] No Gentleman your interest is mine[.] dont permit this conde-scension since it is not necessary for the completing of his maps.

That is, Mangin's map was "useless to the object of the Harbour" because Mangin's map, he asserted, "is not the plan of the City such as it is, but such as it is to be." Wait, what? Mangin's was "not the plan of the City such as it is, but such as it is to be"?

These appear to be the first written words about city planning in New York: "the City . . . such as it is to be." Mangin, it seems, was not making a map of the existing city and environs as he and Goerck had been hired to do; Mangin was making a map of what he believed New York should look like in the future: a plan of the city "such as it is to be." Before December 17, 1798, no New Yorker had written, or perhaps even thought, about such things.

The Common Council, perhaps not fully comprehending what he was doing, sided with Mangin nonetheless and told Loss to refer to East and Hudson River water lot maps in the city clerk's office. Mangin continued at his drawing board. Two months later, in February 1799, the city dutifully paid a $500 installment due Goerck to his estate. Two months after that, and a month before his eighteen-month deadline, Mangin gave his draft to Mayor Richard Varick, who, on April 10, as the first order of business, presented to the Common Council "the new Map of the City."

If there was any alarm about Mangin's city "such as it is to be," it's not evident from any record. Since it was just a draft and not yet public, let's wait a bit for its details. The map was committed to a committee "to examine & to correct as to the Names of the Streets," which suggests some possible consternation, but at the same time, the committee was "also to report a Mode for obtaining subscribers to the Work." In other words, all was moving forward per the contract. One member of that review committee was alderman Richard Furman, a logical choice in that for a number of years he had served as the city's Council-appointed street commissioner. Another order of Council business on April 10 was the appointment of fellow alderman John Bogert as a second street commissioner, joining Furman in that rapidly evolving office. The street commissioner office matters because a future holder of that office soon determined the fate of Mangin's plan.

Back in 1793, when there was no street commissioner, Furman was appointed by the Council to oversee certain street maintenance, a position that seems have matured into more formal oversight of the city's streets over the next few years, until Furman's three terms as alderman, beginning in 1797, when it's still unclear who's in charge of the city's streets generally and how. In June 1798, a Committee on the Duties of the Street Commissioners reported certain revisions and additions to the office. The commissioners now were to evaluate all applications (by landowners) "for the Regulating, Paving or other wise improving of Streets [and] Roads" and determine if surveys or plans were required in each case. They were also to enforce Council orders "for the regulating, digging, filling, paving or repairing of Streets or Roads" and prosecute offenders, and "take the general Charge of viewing and determining from time to time whether any and what Improvement or Repairs are necessary & can be made to any of the Streets or Roads." It's unclear when this street commissioners committee was appointed and who served on it. Only in the few weeks prior are there any references in the Council minutes to street commissioners. Who they were, what their prior responsibilities were, and whether there actually was more than one is also unclear. Indeed, after the committee report was noted, the minutes make reference to "the Street Commissioner," unnamed but clearly singular.

Some clarity arrives seven months later, in January 1799, when, a recent appointee "having declined to execute the Office," the Council decided that one street commissioner was "sufficient to do that Business," that commissioner already being alderman Furman. Apparently, the arrival of Mangin's plan in April 1799 suddenly transformed street policy from something casual into something of pending urgency, and fellow alderman John Bogert joined Richard Furman. One result of all this is that, like other new and evolving city offices, the street commissioner began to acquire more authority and influence.

For the time being, if Mangin needed friends in the street commissioner office, he had them. Bogert and Furman were Federalists, the party of Mangin's mentor, Hamilton. Bogert was related by marriage to Mangin's late map partner, Goerck, and Furman was an executor of the estate of Goerck's brother-in-law Cornelius Roosevelt, whose will of November 12, 1798, provided for Goerck's two newly fatherless children.

The formation of the committee to examine and correct street names on Mangin's plan seems to have been nothing more than standard practice. In those pre-bureaucratic times, the Council routinely formed committees to deal with new or special business. With no apparent concern and all apparent support, the Council went ahead with developing a subscription plan and preparing for publication. In July 1799, the map review committee reported that it was seeking an engraver, naming the highly regarded Peter Maverick as a preference. At this point, the map had been seen by many Council eyes, all apparently approving. Meantime, a subscription plan had been adopted, and by December enough subscription money had been collected that the street commissioners, Furman and Bogert, were authorized to advance another one hundred dollars to Mangin.

Then all was quiet on the map front for over a year, during which Maverick, who was indeed hired, presumably was busy with his engraving work, no easy task for a map six feet square. A better engraver could not have been found. A future cofounder of the National Academy of Design, Maverick had been a professional since executing the frontispiece of a 1790 Bible when he was nine. Among many important Maverick engravings is the published version of the plan that succeeded Mangin's, the 1811 Commissioners' Plan. In selecting the expert Maverick to engrave Mangin's plan, the Council effectively ratified Mangin's work.

Maverick was still working on the engraving in October 1801, when the Council voted to extend Broadway by ordinance a half mile or so, until it met the Bowery (at today's Union Square) "agreeably to the present Map of the City." That is, even in draft before its formal engraving, Mangin's plan of the city "such as it is to be" had become the authority for proactive Council street decisions without state legislative approval. The rarity of such Council action suggests how empowered the Council felt by Mangin's plan.

A month later a blip seems to appear. In November, the Council notes "great inconvenience is sustained in consequence of having several Streets designated by the same Names" in the actual city and on Mangin's plan, which nevertheless is still referred to as "the new Map of the City." Street commissioner (and alderman) Bogert is ordered, somewhat obliquely, "to attend to the completion" of the map, with Furman, now an ex-alderman and apparently ex–street commissioner as well, to assist him. Ultimately, though, they were untroubled by the street names because there is no further word about it. Indeed, there is nothing further about the map in the Council record for the next fifteen months. Evidently Maverick continued with his engraving work, overseen by Bogert and Furman. Mangin, meanwhile, remained very busy with various survey jobs, even working again with fellow city surveyor Loss in the summer of 1802 on improvements to the Broadway roadway, which was being lengthened per Mangin's plan. The main preoccupation for Mangin during this quiet period for the map was City Hall.

As a city centered on commerce, not government, New York in the early years didn't sweat its government seats. Dutch colonial administration was conducted initially out of a tavern, which was converted into an official city hall of sorts in 1653 and served the Dutch and the English until 1703. The building on Wall Street that L'Enfant later spiffed up for the brief stay of the federal government served for the next hundred years. In February 1802 the Common Council finally decided it needed a proper, purpose-built structure commensurate with the rising importance of the city. A design competition was announced.

Twenty-six entries were received, of which the names associated with only five remain known. Of those five, sets of drawings survive for only three, including those of the top two entrants: that of Benjamin Henry Latrobe Jr. and the joint entry of John McComb Jr. and Joseph Mangin.

Latrobe, the young, rising, English-born, Philadelphia-based architect, offered a handsome, compact Greco-Roman building that recalled his recent Bank of Philadelphia design, employing the latest neoclassicism of young English architects. The Mangin-McComb design was pure Louis XVI French neoclassical; in a style unknown to McComb, a prominent but very local architect, but known intimately by Mangin, the building was clearly Mangin's design.

There's a fair amount of scholarship comparing the two very different but well-conceived designs of Mangin and Latrobe. Unbiased opinion always comes down on the side of Mangin for his building's appropriate and well-rendered grandeur. Latrobe's authoritative biographer puts it best: "No one can study the two designs candidly without realizing that in spite of the economy, the organization, and the reticent distinction of the Latrobe design, the committee members made the correct choice."

Regardless, Latrobe expected to win. Indeed, his New York sponsor had guaranteed it: all the votes "save one" were sewn up. A Latrobe win was essential to his sponsor's intention to induce Latrobe to become a New Yorker. When the Council voted in October, the winner with "a large majority of votes" was Mangin-McComb. Latrobe had lost badly to what he bitterly but mistakenly denounced as the "vile heterogeneous composition . . . of a New York bricklayer & a St. Domingo Frenchman." For better or worse, the future "Father of American Architecture" would never design a New York building, much less relocate to the city. His sponsor, Aaron Burr, did not take losses like this lightly.

Burr was then Jefferson's vice president but directed northern Republican politics from New York.* He had orchestrated the overthrow of the Federalists that gave Jefferson the presidency in 1800

---

* Political party names in the nation's early decades are no simple matter. There were no formally organized parties per se before the mid-1790s; after that, Federalists were opposed by variously named factions that by 1800 became known as Democratic-Republicans, or just Republicans, as I will call them in this book. In the late 1820s, these Republicans morphed into today's Democrats, while the Federalists died off, were reborn as Whigs, and eventually emerged in the 1850s as today's Republicans. Any attempt to find continuity to the present between party names and party policies would be snipe hunting.

and, in the twilight of Federalism, was turning the Common Council Republican too. The 1801 Council, elected in 1800, was ten to four Federalist; four years later, with the addition of two wards, it was fourteen to four Republican.

But there were other, less evident but more durable local victories of special interest to the story. After the devastating 1798 yellow fever epidemic, health reformers targeted the city's foul water supply: public street wells polluted by animal and proto-industrial waste and private yard wells sunk next to privies. Neither had much to do with the as yet unknown mosquito-born virus, but cleansing water was the passionate notion of the moment. Burr, sensing opportunity, got his own private water company chartered in 1799 by the state legislature, in which he was then an assemblyman and leader of the city's Albany delegation: Burr as legislator managed the incorporation of his own company (in those days, companies could be incorporated only by the legislature and for a specific business purpose). Important to the process, he secured the essential support of Hamilton and other city Federalists for what appeared to be a civic enterprise that would bring abundant pure water from the then pristine Bronx River. Instead, once incorporated as an effective monopoly water supplier and capitalized at an unprecedented $2 million, the Manhattan Company abandoned the Bronx and created a meager and impure supply from wells behind Chambers Street, then the limit of dense habitation. The water was sent around the city in undersized, leaky wooden pipes, for the laying of which the company habitually tore up streets and left them for the city to repair. At the same time, the company opened a bank, as uniquely allowed by a powerful clause of Burr's devise that was quietly inserted at the last moment in the legislative proceedings. This appears to have been Burr's intention all along: to get a politically motivated bank inside a nominally public-spirited water company. This gave Republican business interests their first New York City bank, a wealthy lender to counter the only other local bank, Hamilton's Bank of New York, which only loaned to Federalists. While the water company hobbled along but prevented better urban health (and fire protection) until a permanent public supply was finally created forty years later, its corporate dependent, the Bank of the Manhattan Company, flourished and is known today as JPMorgan Chase.

Managing politics and self-interest as he did with the Manhattan Company was Burr's forte. Losing smaller battles, like the City Hall design competition decision that snubbed Benjamin Latrobe, displeased him. How to avenge it?

Five months after Mangin won the design competition, Peter Maverick finished engraving Mangin's map. It was presented to the Common Council on February 14, 1803. Now it was officially clear for all to see just how Mangin had not made a plan of the city as it was but as he thought it should be.

It was remarkable, in two ways. Mangin had idealized the city proper, in particular by enlarging the island's tip and smoothing the irregular waterfront with blocks of river landfill and new streets, out to South Street along the East River all the way up to Corlears Hook east of the old DeLancey grid, and West Street on the Hudson all the way up to the state prison Mangin had built at the foot of Christopher Street in Greenwich. No wonder Mangin refused to show his early work to harbor mapper Charles Loss. In time, West and South Streets would come to exist as waterfront perimeters exactly as Mangin prescribed, but that's getting ahead of the story.

Bolder still was Mangin's vision for the island beyond the settled city limits, for two miles up nearly to the southern tip of the Common Lands, a half mile beyond his contracted obligation. Here, where there were only farms, homesteads, and undeveloped land, he had mapped out numerous segments of rectilinear grid, in varying sizes with varying street densities, set at acute angles to each other. Each rectilinear segment started from a separate base: shorelines, or the different angles of the lines of the Bowery, Broadway, and other established roads. In the irregular meeting of the various grid segments were countless opportunities for small parks, prominent

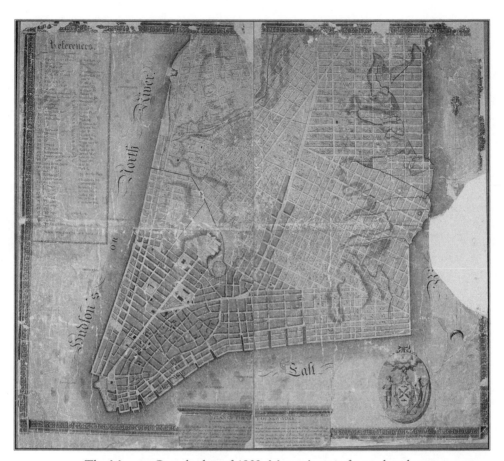

The Mangin-Goerck plan of 1803: Mangin's city of varied grids as it was not to be. The six-foot-square original disappeared long ago; this is one of the few surviving half-size copies, itself the worse for age, with the notorious "warning label" pasted at the bottom. Compare with the detail of the Commissioners' Plan on page 61. *(New York Public Library)*

buildings, or other urban display or public space. Linking everything were numerous north-south roads, some new, others extensions of existing roads, like Broadway out to the Bowery, as already approved back in 1801. It was a layered picture of order and ornament, urban function and natural form: the complexity and grace of a European capital adapted to the limits of a narrow island.

Two particular grid segments stand out. In the middle of the island, Mangin extended the Bayard West Farm grid. From the northernmost cross street of the existing Bayard grid (now Bleeker Street), Mangin extended the grid northward eight blocks, through the existing Amity Lane and Art Street up to what he called Cornelius Street (now roughly 13th Street). Amity Lane was a country road, opened in the 1750s, angling between what are now Bleeker and West 3rd Streets from Broadway to MacDougal. Art Street was originally a country lane running roughly along the line of today's Astor Place and Washington Square North to Waverly Place. Extended northward through these existing and proposed streets were six of the Bayard grid's north-south streets, Mercer through Sullivan, creating blocks of similar size and orientation to the Bayard blocks. Like Mangin's South and West Streets, all of these street extensions would come to exist as Mangin prescribed, but again, that's getting ahead of the story.

As Mangin laid things out, the eastern edge of his extended Bayard grid would run north along Broadway until it merged with the Bowery, and then narrow as Broadway angled to the northwest. On the opposite side of the Bowery and Broadway, Mangin had different ideas in mind. First, he extended the former DeLancey grid east and north. To the east, as landfill into the river he added three short north-south streets, one named Goerck and another Mangin. Greater honor (and calculated flattery perhaps) went to current Council members Mangle Minthorne and Andrew Morris and prominent physician Benjamin Romaine, whose land Mangin was proposing to subdivide for him. Romaine, Minthorne, and Morris Streets, in that order, would run parallel to North Street, then the northernmost street in the DeLancey grid, for over a mile from the Bowery to the East River, intersected by extensions of all the existing north-south streets. This bit of northern extension wasn't extraordinary. Romaine, the owner of land that had been part of the forfeited DeLancey estate, was already in discussions with the city about ceding some of his ground for the extension of streets into the developing neighborhood. Mangin's plan simply pushed it forward.

More bold is what he proposed north of Morris Street. Here he cantilevered the DeLancey grid about twenty degrees to the west and, after filling in the resulting wedge with an assortment of short streets, created an entirely new grid aligned with true north. The island itself—like Goerck's Common Lands grid and the forthcoming 1811 grid—is on an axis of about twenty-nine degrees east; the DeLancey grid axis is about nine degrees east. (The Bayard grid axis, if you're wondering, is about thirty-two degrees; that is, slightly overrotated from the island, Goerck, and the 1811 grid.) In the space between the Bowery Road and Broadway on the west and the river on the east, Mangin placed a grid of six truly north-south streets running off the northern limits of his map and twenty-one truly east-west streets, the northernmost called Spruce Street at what today would be about 16th Street. With a ratio of three and a half east-west streets to one north-south street, this grid reversed the orientation of the DeLancey (and the Bayard) blocks: here on the east side of Manhattan, Mangin made blocks oriented like the Common Lands lots of his late partner Goerck—long on the east-west dimension, short on the north-south.

Mangin did not create this grid wholly out of his imagination. Its nucleus had been laid back in 1788 by Petrus Stuyvesant, successor to the vast *bouwerij* (Dutch farm) established by his great-grandfather, Peter. Petrus, looking to make a country village of sorts, mapped out a nine-by-four-street grid, with Stuyvesant Street as its central east-west street. That street had been laid (and remains Manhattan's closest approximation of a true east-west street) but few others had by the time Mangin expanded Stuyvesant's plan into a grid connected to the city: on the south to his expanded DeLancey grid and on the west to his expanded Bayard grid across the Bowery and Broadway.

Mangin's extended Stuyvesant farm grid leads boldly northward off his map . . . to where? In a mile or so, it would collide, at a

twenty-nine-degree angle, with the central portion of his late partner's Common Lands lots, aligned on the island's axis. That impact
we will never know. But one thing we do know: Mangin's extended
Stuyvesant and Bayard grids together have a total of ten streets
leading north off the top of the page. Eight years later, in a broader
space, the Commissioners who made the 1811 grid would find it in
their rectilinear hearts to provide only six, now routinely congested
avenues.

In sum, Mangin's plan of the city "such as it is to be" was a
synthesizing of patterns already establishing themselves at the suburban fringes of the city and, in the city proper, an orderly filling in
east and west with linear streets out to continuous roads along the
waterfronts. The city government hadn't asked for it, but it seemed
to be just what it wanted.

As the Council looked over the six-foot-square engraving by
Maverick, a committee of three aldermen, the city comptroller, and
the new street commissioner was appointed "to examine the New
Map of this City, now nearly ready to be published and to take such
measures as will be the most proper to indemnify this board, and
the persons who have executed the same for the expense that has
been incurred." ("To indemnify" here means nothing more than "to
repay.") Thus, exactly as it had in July 1799, when it sought Maverick to engrave Mangin's work, the Council now nearly three years
later considered it "the New Map of this City." Just two weeks earlier, the Council had shown its continuing faith in its mapmaker by
reappointing him one of four city surveyors. And yet the map of the
city "such as it is to be" was headed for trouble.

CHAPTER 4

THE CITY NOT TO BE

The Map of the City lately printed and ready for sale . . .
would be improper to adopt.

—Street commissioner Joseph Browne, 1803

M ANGIN'S PLAN, CONCEIVED by him in 1798 as "the plan of the
City . . . such as it is to be" and considered by the city from
1799 into 1803 as "the New Map of this City," was to be neither.
There was a troublemaker on the five-man review committee named
in February 1803. It was not one of the three Federalists—two current aldermen and a former alderman who recently had been named
the city's first comptroller—or the one Republican alderman. It was
the one member with no explicit party affiliation and no record of
public service until five months earlier, when he was elected on a
close Council vote to replace John Bogert as street commissioner,
making him the first non-Council member to hold the office. His
name was Joseph Browne Jr., a handsome English-born, French-
fluent military surgeon who had a newfound interest in the city's
streets. Just who was this Joseph Browne?

Among other things, since 1799 Browne had been the superintendent of the Manhattan Company waterworks, which made a habit
of tearing up and not repairing streets where it laid its wooden water
pipes. The previous year, before the yellow fever epidemic, Dr. Browne

had suggested in a published pamphlet that the Bronx River could answer the city's longstanding water supply needs. Browne had a farm on the then rural and pristine river and knew it well. In his pamphlet, he argued strenuously for a city-owned public water supply using the Bronx and claimed that no water sources on Manhattan were adequate or clean, especially the "disgusting" groundwater in the swampy and already polluted fringes of the city just beyond Chambers Street. A year later Browne was the superintendent of a private water supply company taking its water from wells behind Chambers Street. This is what happens when you are the devoted, dutiful brother-in-law of Aaron Burr.

Browne and Burr were as close as any two brothers could be, unfortunately for Browne. Near the end of the Revolution, in which both had served, they met through and married half-sisters, Catherine De Visme and the newly widowed Theodosia Bartow Prevost, in a double-ring ceremony. After the war, Browne lived with his wife Catherine and the first of their eventual eight children at 9 Little Queen (soon deroyalized as Cedar) Street. Burr lived with Theodosia and her children at number ten across the street. In 1786, Browne purchased his farm along the Bronx River as a summer escape from the city's annual fevers; the Burrs got a summer place nearby in 1790. In 1793, Browne named his third child Aaron Burr Browne. In 1794, Burr's deeply loved wife died, quickly but painfully of what was probably uterine cancer. Burr remained devoted to their only child together (daughter Theodosia, who would be lost at sea in 1813) and his wife's surviving children, but her death left an emotional void that Burr increasingly filled with increasingly reckless sexual, financial, and political intrigues and adventures. Browne stood close by. In 1801, he sold his farm and moved his family to property conveyed to him by Burr near his Richmond Hill mansion. By then, they were involved together in the sham water company, Browne having forsaken all principle in serving as superintendent.

Once he came into Burr's orbit, Browne rarely did anything without his brother-in-law's instruction. In all things remotely political, if Burr was the devil, Browne attended to whatever details he was assigned. This would play out tragically for Browne, in Burr's not yet and perhaps never fully understood "conspiracy" of 1805–1806 to claim lands bordering the newly acquired Louisiana Territory. After Burr killed Hamilton in their infamous duel of 1804 (making him the first of two sitting vice presidents to shoot someone), Burr lit out for the territories, so to speak, with many of his people already in place. Among them was Browne, appointed "upon the special and single recommendation of Aaron Burr" by President Jefferson as the first secretary of the Louisiana Territory, based in St. Louis, a frontier town then of a few hundred buildings, to which Browne, with wife and children, relocated and awaited instructions. "Browne will obey any orders you may give him," Burr advised alleged coconspirator James Wilkinson, whose appointment as the territory's governor Burr also had arranged. The orders never came. The supposed plot blew up (thanks to Wilkinson's treachery), Burr was tried for treason but acquitted, and he treated himself to a five-year exile in Europe. Browne, meantime, remained in St. Louis with no place to go, broken and increasingly despairing, abandoned and terminally tainted by his Burr association. He died around 1810, leaving his once prosperous family impoverished.

Before meeting Burr, Browne had served with distinction as surgeon to a Pennsylvania regiment during the Revolution; a War Office report of 1780 attests to "his good character and the sacrifices he has made." As late as 1786, Browne was the adept translator into English of a French military medicine journal, the first medical journal printed in America. By then, he had forsaken medicine and tied his fate to Burr.

In February 1803, Browne was the city's new street commissioner, chosen by the Council five months earlier through Burr's influence. And he attacked Mangin's plan, an assault that damaged if not destroyed "the new map of the city." Was Browne acting on Burr's orders? Was this Burr's revenge for the City Hall design loss, which came a month after Browne became street commissioner? As Burr scholars know, he rarely if ever left a decipherable mark on his various manipulations. He got his bank disguised as a water company by numerous sleights of hand, including the solicited and unwitting support of Hamilton and other political opponents. Did Burr conspire to create a personal empire in the remote American southwest, or was he acting patriotically and secretly to curb Spanish influence in territory the United States coveted? Even the modern editors of Burr's available papers threw up their hands at "the sequence of events known, for better or worse, as Burr's 'conspiracy'. . . . Readers must judge for themselves the true nature of Burr's goals and motives." Likewise, readers in the relatively lesser affair of Mangin's plan must judge for themselves. There's no smoking gun, but there is Burr furious at Mangin's City Hall victory and pliant in-law Browne's relentless effort a few months later to discredit Mangin's plan, which the Common Council had endorsed for the past four years.

The trouble seemed to start innocently enough. Browne already had been examining the proposed cession of portions of Benjamin Romaine's land for streets to extend the grid started by the DeLanceys before the Revolution. In comparing a recent survey for prospective streets in the area by city surveyor Evert Bancker Jr. with the "General Map of the City as lately made by Messrs Goerck and Mangin," Browne observed that they did not jibe. "The Streets as laid down in the general Map which make the Blocks and house Lots nearly square [is] an arrangement certainly to be desired, but unfortunately it deviates so much from the Streets as laid down by Banker [sic] that the adoption of it would create great difficulties from its total derangement of a great number of the Lots . . . now owned by a variety of proprietors." This, of course, was true. Bancker's survey, like so much of the city to date, sacrificed regularity of possible streets for conformity with existing land ownership; Mangin's plan—like the Commissioners' Plan to come—did the opposite, and the Council had embraced it for four years. Browne's suggested resolution at this time was to adjust Mangin's map, not

Bancker's, by changing the widths of various streets continuing into the area from the south. At its February 14 session, the Council agreed. And it agreed to the review committee featuring Browne, which by April the Council was calling "the Committee appointed to publish the new map."

And publish it, it did. On June 23, the Council officially deposited with the city clerk "A Plan and Regulation of the City of New-York, Made from actual survey by Casimir Th. Gorrek [sic!], and Joseph Fr. Mangin, City Surveyors, by order of the Common Council, and protracted by Joseph Fr. Mangin Anno Domini 1800." Beginning July 12 and continuing through October, newspapers ran advertisements for copies of the map at four dollars apiece. Then the ads stopped. And Browne's hand was revealed.

For months, and with greater intensity during November, Browne had been busy working his case against Mangin's plan. November 1803 was a fairly chaotic month in the annals of the Common Council and a good time for subversion.

To begin with, the Council was a locus of the dramatically changing state and city politics that Burr was engineering. Indeed, the "extreme violence of party politics in those times was exhibited in this city beyond all other places." Stalwart Federalist and long-serving mayor Richard Varick was gone and the state legislature had appointed DeWitt Clinton, a Republican of varying factional alliances, on November 1. Strange as it may seem today, Clinton had resigned as a U.S. senator to take the more lucrative (through various fees) job of mayor. Clinton had an arm's-length association with Burr politically but a close relationship with Burr's nefarious Manhattan Company, initially as a major shareholder, then as mayor, ordering the deposit of all city funds into the company's thriving bank, and later, after banishing Burr from the company for fiscal malfeasance, as influential board member and lawyer fortifying its corporate existence. The city recorder in 1803 had an even closer relationship to Burr: John Bartow Prevost was the late Theodosia Bartow Prevost Burr's oldest child from her first marriage and was treated as a son by his stepfather. Prevost's appointment as recorder in 1801, the first Republican after three Federalists, including soon legendary legal scholar James Kent, was Burr's doing. Predictably, Prevost would resign as recorder soon after Burr killed Hamilton in 1804 to become the first federal judge in the newly acquired Louisiana Territory, an appointment made, like so many others, by President Jefferson at Burr's strategic request.

As to the elected members of the Council, the annual balloting in the first week of the month was an historically contentious political affair, especially in the northern wards, including two new ones, with a younger and more liberal electorate. It was late December before numerous and substantial voting irregularities were resolved and the full Council roster was completed, two weeks after the normal swearing-in on December 5, with a then record six Republicans. In the midst of all this, Mangin's plan met its fate.

On November 7, Browne was asked to report which streets through private land shown on Mangin's plan had been named and opened prior to April and which had been opened but not ceded to the city since then. This apparently was an attempt to clarify the status of streets in Mangin's extended Bayard, DeLancey, and Stuyvesant grids. At the Council's next regular session a week later (in those days, the Council met regularly only once or twice a week), Browne submitted his report but, for reasons unclear, consideration was postponed. The Council did, though, pay Mangin the remaining one hundred dollars due him "for making the large map of the City." Another week later, on November 21, the Council received another report from Browne, which was submitted to the map review committee together with his previous report. The contents of both of these reports is unknown, beyond that they were "in relation to the laying out and regulation of new streets." What we do know is that on this date the committee was recomposed to include assistants Caleb Riggs and Robert Bogardus in place of aldermen John Outhout and Joshua Barker, who had not stood for reelection, even though they remained Council members until December 5.

Riggs and Bogardus, lawyers both, were members of the outgoing and incoming Councils. Arguably, Riggs and Bogardus, as Federalists, were more inclined to be supportive of Mangin than Republican Barker. On the other hand, informed committee members who may have been resisting Browne were replaced with new committee members who had little time to get up to speed. A week later, the Browne-dominated committee devastated the Mangin plan.

"The Map of the City lately printed and ready for sale," reported the committee on November 28, "contains many inaccuracies and designates streets which have not been agreed to by the Corporation and which it would be improper to adopt, and which might tend to lead the proprietors of Land adjacent to such Streets so laid down into error." This, of course, was no truer in November 1803 than in April 1799, when that year's Council was first presented with Mangin's plan and embraced it as "the new map of the city."

The Council's response to the committee was firmly supportive: "that the Street Commissioner be authorized to return the money paid by each subscriber [and] requested to endeavour to recall as many of the said maps as have been sold." Anyone who wished to keep or obtain a copy of the map would have it pasted with what in effect was a warning label, devised by Browne:

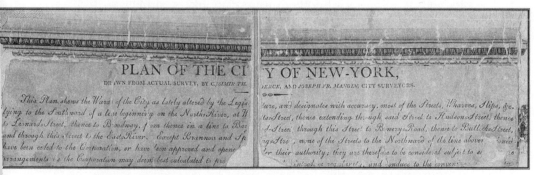

The warning label, devised by Mangin plan wrecker and Aaron Burr operative Joseph Browne, specifying the line beyond which streets were "to be considered subject to such future arrangements as the Corporation may deem best calculated to promote the health, introduce regularity, and conduce to the convenience of the City." (*New York Public Library*)

This Plan . . . designates with accuracy most of the Streets . . . lying to the Southward of a line beginning on the North [Hudson] River at Watts Street, thence extending through said Street to Hudson Street, thence to Leonard Street, thence to Broadway, from hence in a line to Bayard Street, through this Street to Bowery Road, thence to Bullock [now Broome] Street and through this Street to the East River. Except Brannon and Spring Streets, none of the Streets to the Northward of the line abovementioned have been ceded to the Corporation or have been approved and opened under their authority; they are therefore to be considered subject to such future arrangements as the Corporation may deem best calculated to promote the health, introduce regularity, and conduce to the convenience of the City.

The few scholars of Mangin's plan have taken this action to be its complete demise, which today makes it a fantasy or a curiosity. Browne, and Burr, may have felt they had accomplished that. But a closer look suggests that it didn't really die but lived on with a reduced authority. Having been considered "the new map of city," it was too important just to disappear—which is what makes Browne's actions against it so important. With his action, as we'll see, the city finds itself needing another future plan and eventually, in 1807, turns to the Commission that gives the city its great grid. Without Browne's action, Mangin's plan remains in full effect, the varied grids he mapped are extended, the need for the 1807 Commission never arises, and the great grid never happens. If we accept that Browne was only acting on his brother-in-law's instructions, then we can give thanks for the great grid of Manhattan to Aaron Burr.

Let's go back. There is a lot going on in the label pasted on Mangin's plans and the associated Council actions, not quite the simple rejection of the Mangin plan that Browne (and Burr) seemed to be aiming for.

First, and remember this for later, the warning label concludes with the first use of a phrase that, with variations, will resonate for

years to come: that the Council was interested in street arrangements "best calculated to promote the health, introduce regularity,
and conduce to the convenience of the City."

As to the map itself, the Council formally acknowledges that
Mangin's plan was okay below the specified exclusion line, which
at that time was roughly the limits of the settled city. In not taking issue with what Mangin laid out below that line, the Council
effectively endorses it, including the several blocks out to the as yet
unlaid South and West Streets. As we'll see later, the Commissioners' Plan of 1811 *below* its grid uses and is identical to Mangin's plan
below the line, which is to say that at least this portion of Mangin's
plan became and remained the new map of the city.

In warning that none of the streets north of the line—primarily consisting of Mangin's extensions of the Bayard, DeLancey, and
Stuyvesant grids—"have been ceded to the Corporation or have been
approved and opened under their authority," Browne's label asserted
an authority over prospective streets that the city government had
rarely been much concerned about. But the map above the line is
not so much rejected as deferred: the streets there had not been
approved or opened but were only "to be considered subject to such
future arrangements" as the city government might choose—which
is to suggest that the streets above the line might well be approved
or opened some day in the future. Which perhaps explains why map
copies were subject to recall but not destruction. The street commissioner was merely "*requested to endeavour* [italics added] to recall as
many of the said maps as have been sold, and either return the person the purchase money and keep the map or return him two dollars
thereof, and deliver him back the map" with the warning label, which
was also to be affixed to "such copies of the said map as may hereafter be sold or distributed." In other words, with much less urgency
than, say, an automobile with a safety defect, the Council only asked
Browne to try to recall as many copies of Mangin's plan as he could.
The Council did not itself order the maps recalled or destroyed; in
fact, it anticipated that more could be sold, making the label akin to

warnings on today's cigarettes, alcohol, mature video games, spray paint, and toys with small parts: use but understand the risk.

So what exactly was the official status of "the new map of the city" at the end of November 1803? It seems that the Council had no idea. Nor, it seems, did the Council have any idea what its authority was over any streets, whether actual and approved, actual and not approved, or merely proposed in Mangin's plan, whose status was uncertain. Two weeks later, Browne provided what passed for answers in his five-man committee's final report. It carried only four names—Browne, Riggs, Bogardus, and Philip Brasher—suggesting that committee member Selah Strong, the Federalist city comptroller, was not involved in its preparation, and by specific reference the report was largely based on the recommendations in street commissioner Browne's own reports of November 14 and 21, the contents of which are not available. In sum, this report "upon the subject of new streets" of December 12, 1803, is Browne's official word on whatever he was trying to accomplish. It was deemed important enough by the Council to have fifty copies printed.

That something needed to be done was clear. "It happens in this, as in most other cases, to be much easier to discover and point out defects, than to digest and apply suitable remedies." Browne grumbled about landowners who made streets that gradually became part of the city without any planning agency by its government, yet he also was openly contemptuous of Mangin's plan: "the maps exhibit a view of streets by name, neither opened, named, nor approved of by the Common Council; unless the mere act of causing the smaller maps to be published, and a few copies of it sold, shall be deemed opening, naming or approving thereof." We don't know if "few copies" was an honest appraisal or a disparaging snark, but Browne was barely less contemptuous of the Council itself, which "nevertheless . . . with their accustomed liberality, have paid the consideration money." After tracking through the various actions and resolutions of the Council in support of "the new map of the city," from its April 1799 presentation in draft through its February 1803 presentation in six-foot engraving, "the Common Council may judge how far they have a binding influence on this board, in respect to shutting up certain streets, and opening, or laying out new ones on a different plan." As far as Browne was concerned, the Council was at least legally unbound. "It is taken for granted by your Committee, that *something* [italics added] has been transacted . . . but they are unable to state *what* [italics added] has been so transacted or when." The Council minutes contained no committee reports or other acts formally endorsing the map "unless the references to them are sufficient to bind" the Council. Clearly, Browne thought not: "In all the preceding resolutions of the board, the Committee do not perceive any one which appears to recognise any street as laid down in the New Map, except the one for continuing Broadway to the Bowery Lane." The Council, in Browne's view, was free to proceed with making new streets as *it* chose, without the constraint of Mangin's plan. As a legal argument, Browne was possibly on solid ground, but in practice the Council often acted with the same caution, uncertainty, and ambivalence as it demonstrated in matters involving the city's streets.

Then Browne made an extraordinary recommendation. If the Council believed it was within its rights, it should order him to make

> a plan for opening new [streets] and especially in those parts of the city, where the present state of buildings an improvements will render it practicable to extend them from river to river, in an easterly and westerly direction, and others to intersect them at right angles, as nearly as may be so, and also, the most suitable places for the Corporation to obtain grounds, or make use of those they have, for public squares or pleasure grounds, and the necessary quantities for those purposes, and how the same ought to be improved, and that such plan or plans be illustrated by drawings or otherwise.

In other words, the Council should empower Browne not only to do what he had prevented Mangin from doing but also to plan on an even broader scale, indeed one that seems enticingly like what the Commissioners appointed in 1807 would come up with in 1811. Which is to say that Browne did not.

Back to Mangin. His map is, if not legally ineffective, seemingly put aside. The six-foot-square original engraved by Maverick is not a treasured document in the city's or any other archive. It is lost and presumably was destroyed at some point. But given that the lower end of the island as depicted in the 1811 Commissioners' Plan is nearly identical to Mangin's 1803 plan of streets that did not yet exist, it seems reasonable to assume that the Mangin original or an official smaller copy was on hand for John Randel's reference. It is unknown how many of the smaller copies were printed, but fewer than a dozen exist today, and none in very good shape. Though there was no prohibition on sales of the smaller labeled maps, there's no record of any. Mangin was fully paid his $1,500 share for producing the large map, but he almost certainly was denied any further profit from subscription sales. Perhaps this was enough for Browne and Burr.

If Mangin's plan above the line was put aside, though, why did so many streets there soon come into being exactly as Mangin planned? In fact, practically everything he laid out became actual city streets, many with his chosen names, but for the upper portion of his expanded Bayard grid and his expanded Stuyvesant grid with its near-true east-west axis. What seems to have happened is that, regardless of whatever its official status might have been, without another plan, Mangin's became the de facto plan—if not "the new map of the city," the sort-of map of the city.

Below the line, along the Hudson, West Street, making a linear edge with the shore, was fully built by 1830. On the East River, South Street followed in similar fashion by 1835. Today, the waterfronts at the tip of Manhattan remain West and South Streets, exactly as Mangin planned.

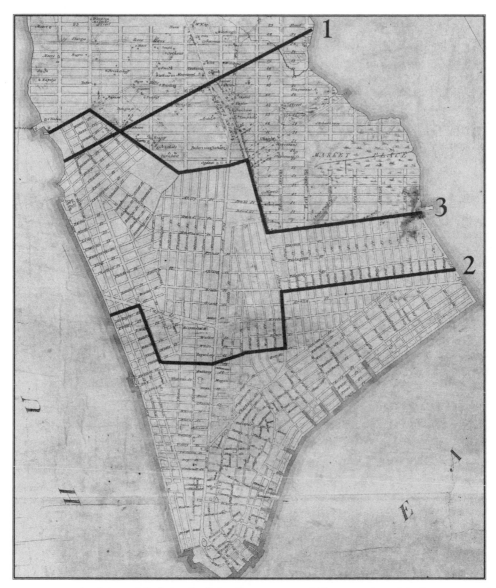

In this modified detail of the Commissioners' Plan map, line 1 is the northern edge of the Mangin plan, line 2 is its supposed limitation by the Browne warning label, and line 3 is the southern boundary of the Commissioners' planning authority. Compare with the Mangin plan on page 45, and note how the Commissioners effectively ratified the entire Mangin plan below their boundary. (*New York City Municipal Archives*)

Above the line, up at Corlears Hook, Lewis Street was in place by 1808, Goerck and Mangin Streets by 1817. At what is now the eastern fringe of the Lower East Side, a block of Lewis Street remains from Grand to Delancey Streets, between massive postwar housing developments. On the north side of Delancey, the sprawling Baruch Houses swallowed up Goerck in the 1950s, but two bits of Mangin remain. One is directly under the Williamsburg Bridge, a cacophonous no man's land. The other is tucked inside the northeast corner of the Baruch footprint, where an existing school campus was preserved. The school building opened in 1920 as the P.S. 97 Mangin School. When that grade school closed in 2001, the Mangin name went with it, but not the one-block street on the building's eastern border. The building now houses the Bard High School Early College, whose smart, college-bound kids have daily proof in their little bit of street that the Mangin plan was no fantasy.

Just prior to the map trouble, Mangin had another curious bump in the road. In the spring of 1803, after some Council-ordered revisions to the City Hall design that Mangin may not have agreed to, his competition partner, McComb, was put in charge of the construction, with his name alone on the cornerstone as "Architect." Newspaper editorials and letters howled at Mangin's apparent removal from the lucrative construction of the building that he clearly had designed. If Mangin himself protested, there is no record. Over the generations his connection to City Hall was deeply obscured, helped along in the 1890s by a McComb descendant who erased Mangin's name from the original competition drawings in hopes of increasing their sale value as a McComb design. By 1915, even the *New York Times* would acknowledge only Mangin's "reputed" association with the building. Not until 2003, after the erasures were revealed and the true history rediscovered, was Mangin officially recognized as the principal designer of City Hall, in a ceremony unveiling a new stone with his name. If Burr had anything to do with the severing of Mangin from City Hall in the months before Browne took care of the map, it would not be surprising, but there appears not to be a connection. Likeliest is that Mangin was (easily) offended by the design changes and was happy to step aside.

Nor does there appear to be a Burr connection to a February 1804 bastardy proceeding against Mangin, which was dismissed two months later. One especially wants to find lawyer Burr in dirty business like this, but, as with the City Hall construction, if Burr was meddling here he covered his tracks without even a scent.

Despite these problems and the map troubles, Mangin's career was not dramatically affected. He was busy for many years with important surveys in the city, New Jersey, and upstate, where he purchased a large tract of land and moved to for a brief period before returning to the city and finishing his career with the celebrated design and construction of the first St. Patrick's Cathedral.

CHAPTER 5

NOW WHAT?

Individuals *even at this period*, continue to project their streets in their own way, and dispute with the Common Council upon their uncontroulable right to do so.

—Street commissioner John Hunn, 1806

THE STREET COMMITTEE that did its best to decertify Mangin's plan remarkably proceeded to fret about the city's lack of just the sort of plan that Mangin had proposed. "The evils daily experienced from the want of an uniform plan, in relation to streets and roads are innumerable, and will doubtless encrease in number and magnitude, so long as the Common Council shall want power, or neglect to exercise it, to prevent individuals from forming plans of their own." No faith should be placed in landowning planners, like Petrus Stuyvesant, "as such individual arrangements will generally be calculated only for their private advantage, without a just regard to the welfare of others, and to the almost total neglect of public conveniences and general usefulness."

A few weeks later, in an early January 1804 session, the Council gave street commissioner Browne the opportunity to fill the void he and his committee had created. He was to report "with all convenient speed" a plan to "have new streets laid out and opened in an easterly and westerly direction and in straight lines or as nearly so" either from river to river or from either river "to any intermediate line or lines running Northerly and Southerly." The north-south streets were to intersect the east-west streets "at right angles, or as nearly so as circumstances will permit." Mangin had planned only a mile or so beyond the settled city; Browne now was asked to plan only so far north as he "found practicable and deemed expedient."

There were no reference points in his instructions, no baselines, no specific guidance on whether the street directions were to be true or magnetic, whether they were to align with the island's axes or the compass, or whether they were to intersect at some point with the rectilinear Common Lands lots. It was really very vague, even to the point of straightness and rectilinearity being only "as nearly so" as Browne could manage. Still, he was asked to indicate, as he had generally suggested, "what grounds ought to be retained or procured by the Common Council for military parades, pleasure grounds or other public uses or for ornamenting the City in its future growth and extension." As we will see, this ancient notion of urban beauty, ignored by Hippodamus but treasured by many, from Aristotle to Spanish colonizers of the Americas, would be an ideal of little value in modern New York.

As to the city's authority in all this, a succession of state laws asserting the city's ownership and power over its streets had been passed since 1793 but had prompted no action by the city. All of the several laws, which nominally gave the city title to and legal control of its streets, had been primarily health-related, focused on the city's authority to make or keep itself clean, with streets of secondary focus to wharf and slip cleaning. Each law was of limited duration, tending to expire before a new one conveying similar powers was eventually passed. The most recent health law that included streets, passed in April 1803, had a duration of only three years, an inadequate foundation for a long-term street-making strategy that the Council recognized as such. The instructions in January 1804 to Browne were premised, with a mix of hope and assertion, on an 1801 health law that may or may not have actually contained enough authority for what the city was asking of Browne, even though of course the city had long possessed power over its streets through it charters. Regardless, the Council now seemed to believe it could act through ordinances and bylaws without specific state action. One gets the sense that Mangin's plan had given the city a vision of what it might do and now, after Mangin's plan had been damaged, a boldness to press on regardless.

In fact, the Council remained quite focused on Mangin's plan. Among the many things it demanded of its street commissioner in January 1804 were reports "from time to time and as expeditiously as possible" recommending any "improvements by straightening, widening, or being extended" any streets in the thickly inhabited part of the city—that is, the sort of improvements that Mangin had included in his plan.

It was against the backdrop of the health-based laws that included streets that Mangin's plan had surfaced and been sub-merged. But even in January 1804 it was not altogether drowned. In addition to its instructions to Browne, the Council resolved to ask Mangin for his field book, which by his contract of 1797 he was required to provide but hadn't, either the original or copies with official copies of his map. Nor had Mangin provided the elevation and other details on the original map as specified in his contract. Now, months after he'd been paid in full, he was "required to insert as far as is practicable on the large map made for and furnished to the Common Council the descriptions and specifications" under his contract. So the Council still wanted Mangin to complete his map. Browne was charged with gaining Mangin's compliance.

The city was asking a lot of Mangin and Browne. There's no evidence that Mangin ever complied—it's hard to imagine him not crossing the sidewalk muttering French epithets when Browne approached—and the city eventually stopped asking, though evidently it held on to his big map for some period of time.

It should come as no surprise that Browne failed in every request put to him. Six months later, Burr killed Hamilton and close Burr associates like Browne knew their New York days were numbered. In January 1805, after Browne's increasing neglect of his street commissioner duties generally, the Council removed him. Two months later, he was appointed secretary of the Louisiana Territory at Burr's behest and was off to his sad fate in the west.

The street planning mantle passed to Browne's successor, John Hunn, elected by "the greatest number of votes" of the Common Council. Hunn was a lesser Burr crony, having served in the key positions of bookkeeper and second teller at the bank of Burr's Manhattan Company. His qualifications regarding streets were limited or none—he moved directly from teller at the bank to the city position—but even in New York after the Hamilton duel, Burr's influence was large. Hunn, already in his forties, put a bit of effort into the job, mostly in the form of exasperated reports about the physical condition and legal limbo of the city's streets, but he was no more effective than his predecessor in doing anything about it. He lasted five years in the job, until he was replaced (by Samuel Stilwell) amidst "a rapid succession of [financial] misfortunes" and moved upstate as cashier of a new bank in Newburgh.

A month into his tenure, the Council asked two things of Hunn: to estimate the cost of making a map of the island showing all its real property and roads, and to have a map made of the city proper. There's no evidence that Hunn did anything about the latter request, further suggesting that Mangin's plan remained the city's quasi-official guiding map. As to the new idea of an island map, a project conjuring large but vague notions far beyond even what Mangin had planned, nothing happened under Hunn's guidance.

In his two years in office before the great street Commission was appointed in 1807, Hunn concerned himself not at all with planning out where Mangin had dared to go and Browne had not. But Hunn became something of an ardent and articulate voice for change. Possibly this was through the influence of his brother-in-law, the Revolutionary poet and Jeffersonian polemicist Philip Freneau; Hunn's wife was Freneau's youngest sister and Hunn was close to the family, caring for Freneau's unmarried oldest sister in her later years despite his own financial troubles. It was Hunn who observed in January 1806 that the city "made use of so little coercion" in regard to street policy "that individuals *even at this period*, continue to project their streets in their own way, and dispute with the Common Council upon their uncontroulable right to do so." Hunn lamented, "Where do we see two proprietors of any considerable property who have agreed either in the width or direction of their streets?" Hunn recounted how the Council had in 1804 adopted a plan to widen a narrow, crooked city street (Maiden Lane) but, after a landowner in 1805 rebuilt structures in the portion of the street to be widened, the Council decided its own plan was "unjust," allowed the encroachment, and "virtually abolished [its own] laudable resolution." Hunn was outraged: "The dangerous and powerful influence of individuals frequently interfere to thwart the laudable intentions of the common council, and procrastinate, if not prevent, desirable and useful alterations." Hunn was an ineffective administrator but a surprisingly lucid critic who hoped his city would one day "widen, straighten, and beautify the streets and . . . render them more convenient and healthy." Here again, amongst the more mundane objectives, was the idea of beauty, soon to be ignored. "It can never be presumed," Hunn continued, that the Council "will adopt a useless plan very extensive in its operations, or consent to injure any citizen, by unnecessary arrangements. Why then cease to exercise the power and discretion delegated to them by law?" Why indeed?

A few weeks later, in late January 1806, the Council created an island map committee that did not include Hunn but seemed to be a step toward acknowledging his call to arms: "It is highly important that a correct Survey and map be made of the Island of New York, laying down as well the individual as the Corporation property, and also the heights, valleys, roads, and wharves." Another few weeks later, that committee proposed something far beyond what might have been expected: a draft state law for the appointment of "commissioners to regulate and lay out the streets in this city beyond certain limits"—that is, something that sounds a lot like getting state authority to do what Mangin's plan had proposed. The bill was referred to another committee, this time one that included street commissioner Hunn. Another month later, in March, the Council voted to . . . do nothing, until the next meeting of the legislature, whose current three-month session was ending in a few weeks.

In the meantime, the Council moved forward on the matter of an island map. In June 1806, they arranged for the services of Ferdinand Rudolph Hassler, a sophisticated Swiss geodesist who had worked on a pioneering topographical survey of Switzerland until the invading French had made that work impossible by 1803. Two years later, at age thirty-five, Hassler had immigrated to Philadelphia with his wife Marianne and most of their eventual nine children. Hassler was not an easy character. As a math professor for a number of years at West Point and Union College, his salary and his opinion of himself far outstripped his teaching abilities. His wife, a bon vivant, eventually tired of his ego and peripatetic and often impecunious career, moved out, and saw him only once in his final twenty years. Hassler eventually would find his American fame as the leader of the first Coast Survey: he was the chartmaker of the young nation's coastal waters. But in early 1806 he was desperate.

Hassler had arrived in Philadelphia to find that the Swiss-American land company he had organized and invested in had failed; to support his large family, Hassler started selling off artwork and volumes from the large library he had brought with him. In the spring of 1806, a Philadelphia merchant friend made contact with friends in New York and arranged Hassler's first substantial American employment: an accurate survey of Manhattan, which presumably would be the basis of a plan for its development. "A correct Map of this Island is a matter of very great importance," observed the Council, which made a very liberal contract: five dollars a day for Hassler, four dollars for his assistant, plus a dollar a day for personal expenses and money for an ample surveying crew. The survey was to start in July and take three months.

But Hassler never showed. All that arrived in New York were his regrets, in October, when it was too late for surveying. It seems that his wife and he both, bags and instruments packed, had "taken ill" in the office of his Philadelphia mentor on the very day of their scheduled departure to New York back in July. It is curious, to be sure, that Hassler, who certainly needed the work, did not recover after a few days and find his way to New York, with or without his wife, who possibly preferred the then superior sophistication and comforts of Philadelphia. It is curious as well that the city, which so desired his services, apparently made no inquiry before his regrets arrived in October. In any case, Hassler soon earned the first of his important presidential appointments from Thomas Jefferson, and a few months later New York pursued an entirely different course.

Its passive response to the rejection by Hassler was like so much of the city's behavior in exercising rightful authority over its dominion. It was like a proverbial slumbering giant that couldn't be bothered to stamp its foot. For generations, the Common Council was reluctant or just indifferent to exerting its interest—the public interest—over private rights. Many of the city's revolving cast of aldermen and assistants were either landowners themselves or associated by family or friendship with landowners. But the effects of Mangin's striking plan, Browne's zealous rejection of it, Hunn's exhortations, the city's rapidly expanding and diversifying population, and a sudden shift in the composition of the Common Council would soon coalesce into the bold action that gave Manhattan its grid.

CHAPTER 6

THREE MAN ISLAND

From the respectability and talents of the gentlemen employed on this important and long contemplated subject public improvement, we have no doubt that the execution of their trust will do honour to themselves and the community.

—*New York Evening Post*, June 1807

Men of genius were needed. . . . Unhappily, they were . . . men devoid of all imagination.

—Jean Schopfer, *The Architectural Record*, 1902

THE COMMON COUNCIL that finally found the nerve to take charge of its city's planning was an unlikely creature. After three annual Councils dominated by Republicans, the election of November 1806 had returned a large majority of Federalists, to be presided over by Republican mayor DeWitt Clinton only until the state Council of Appointment replaced him in the spring of 1807 with a Federalist. The new Council was seated on December 1, 1806, which was a perfect time and opportunity for Sir James Jay to send them a letter. In most things there was little reason to pay attention to what Sir James had to say. But not this time.

James Jay was the less patriotic and long estranged older brother of John Jay, Gouverneur Morris's old friend, who by 1806 was the former chief justice of the country and former governor of the state. James was a curious character, to be sure. A New York native, he went to England for a medical education and returned to the city to become an unsuccessful physician: "haughty, proud, overbearing, supercilious, pedantic, vain and ambitious," to say nothing of an overcharger, Jay had a patient list that quickly dwindled to relatives. He spent his thirties and most of his forties back in England, where he obtained his knighthood, but returned to New York in 1778, was elected to the state senate, and actively supported and participated in patriotic activities for four years, notably distributing to various prominent revolutionaries quantities of an invisible ink he developed. He also made a substantial loan to Congress for military clothing that a committee featuring Gouverneur Morris refused in 1781 to repay. After denouncing Morris and others in the press under a pseudonym, Jay secretly arranged his capture by the British and his return to England as a supposed prisoner. Nearly a quarter century of unfettered British existence later, he returned again to his birth city, and at seventy-four hoped to be seen as a repatriated New Yorker who, as he explained in his letter to the Common Council, "ardently wishes to render his native city healthy, happy, and great."

Jay was a recently self-proclaimed Republican (his Founding Father brother John, an author of *The Federalist Papers*, most ardently was not). This and the fact that, though a native, he'd mostly been English since the Treaty of Paris were reasons enough for his letter, when presented to the newly Federalist Council, to be politely referred to street commissioner Hunn and quickly forgotten.

But, as often happened with ostensibly private communications, the letter became public three weeks later. It was printed across half of the editorial page of the *Evening Post*, Hamilton's Federalist mouthpiece that was then turning into a nationally influential voice of editorial reason (and survives perhaps less so as the *New York*

Post). Here, Jay's interesting ideas, artful phrasings, and aggressive opinions had a public airing, for all New Yorkers to contemplate.

Jay noted that, compared even with Paris and London, randomly built New York, with its narrow, crooked streets and few and shabby public buildings, was "the ridicule of strangers and all persons of taste." The familiar cause: "the narrow or avaricious views of selfish individuals" who laid streets on their lands as they chose. New York could be "large, healthy, convenient and beautiful." Jay, like Aristotle and John Hunn, was big on beauty. New York's leaders could be "the founders of the finest city in the world." If they acted promptly.

Jay recommended that a comprehensive survey with elevation details be made of the island northward of the settled city. It is unclear if he was aware that the Council had been attempting just that when Hassler had failed to show. Regardless, Jay continued,

> from such a map, and a careful personal examination of the ground, a person of judgment and taste will find no difficulty in laying out streets, squares, crescents, circusses [*sic*] and other figures, according as the local circumstances of particular places or spots of ground shall be fit for the one or the other. These forms of building, when judiciously laid out, not only embellish a city, but increase the value of the ground on which they are erected.

This is what makes Jay's letter important. In another four years or so, his words would be repeated nearly verbatim, without attribution, by the grid-making Commissioners in their pointed rejection of beautifying embellishments.

After prescient suggestions about the city's future water supply—he specifically named the mainland Croton River a quarter century before anyone else—and a strange offer to make "our" harbor "impregnable to the united nations of all Europe," Jay concluded by repeating his primary message: "In laying out a city, the great objects to be kept in view, are health, convenience, and beauty."

When it petitioned the legislature in February 1807 for a state law empowering a planning commission, the Common Council cited three reasons for its own failings regarding street planning: being annually elected, one Council's accepted plan could easily be the next Council's abandoned plan; there was no agreement in any case within the current Council on a particular plan; and any plan that had come up met with paralyzing landowner opposition. The Council recognized that state law had the power to overwhelm any opposition and achieve the city's purpose: "to unite regularity and order with the public convenience and benefit and in particular to promote the health of the City." The language was very similar to the language on the Mangin map warning label, and similarly lacking in the objective of beauty.

The city's memorial was signed by Mayor DeWitt Clinton for delivery in Albany to . . . Senator DeWitt Clinton, the head of the city's legislative delegation and the most powerful politician in the state. His will was being and would be done.

It would be terrific if the record, printed or manuscript, indicated anything substantial about Clinton's role in the city's evolving street policy. His role a few years later in the beginnings of the state's Erie Canal project is amply documented. We know that the technologically radical and politically risky canal idea was not his—it originated with pioneers in the state's undeveloped west—but that when it was brought to him as the person best situated politically to move it forward with a state commission, he embraced the idea as sound and good for the nation, the state, the city, and especially himself. In Clinton's correct judgment, the long-term political benefit of a successful canal far outweighed the safer course of opposition or abstention. Making order of Manhattan was seemingly a lesser challenge with lesser political risk or reward, which arguably is the reason for the more slender paper trail. For all his power in the state during the first quarter of the 1800s, Clinton was, like his cousin Simeon DeWitt, not much of a thinker, and driven more by ego and will than wisdom and political organization. A city plan, like the state canal, was something that fell into Clinton's lap. He embraced it, or at least chose not to oppose it, as something long overdue.

But the memorial had gone upstate with three blanks: the names of the men the city wished appointed as Commissioners. Two weeks later, and with Clinton's implicit approval, the city named Gouverneur Morris, Simeon DeWitt, and John Rutherfurd as the "fit and proper persons." We can speculate about why and how these three, and not any number of qualified others, were deemed "fit and proper," but we will probably never know. If nothing else, it makes sense that a Federalist Council would pick fellow traveler Morris and, with a lesser passion, Rutherfurd. In any case, no one could argue that sophisticated Founding Father Morris, landowning Rutherfurd, and Surveyor General DeWitt were unfit or improper for mapping Manhattan. Unless, that is, the city had wanted deep commitment and well-debated design, like the state got for its canal from Morris, DeWitt, Clinton, and others a few years later.

Of the three men commissioned to plan Manhattan, John Rutherfurd (1760–1840) was the only one born on the island, but he brought the least experience and interest to the work. Trained as a lawyer, Rutherfurd lived in the city as an adult for only three years, from 1784 to 1787, when he moved to Tranquility, the family estate in Sussex County, New Jersey. He spent the rest of his life on various family properties in New Jersey, attending to vast, mostly inherited landholdings; at his death, he was the state's largest land-owner. He served briefly in the New Jersey General Assembly and represented the state in the U.S. Senate but resigned in 1798 during his second term, retiring "to the more agreeable pursuits of private life." He probably was tapped for the street commission through the influence of Morris: Rutherfurd was married to a daughter of Morris's half-brother. In Rutherfurd, Morris had a pliant ally. Ruth-erfurd was a Morris chauvinist; after Morris's death, Rutherfurd claimed that Morris had originated the idea of the Erie Canal, an assertion never made by Morris or by others for him. In his diary, Morris repeatedly frets about Rutherfurd's absences from or lateness to meetings of the street Commission. Still, he did spend the winter of 1808–1809 in the city, at his father's home, presumably to fulfill Commission duties but possibly also in connection with his daughter Helena, who in May 1809 married Peter G. Stuyvesant, son of the late Petrus, who initiated the gridding of the family farm.

Rutherfurd spelled his name that way. Some contemporaries, prompted by the vagaries of cursive and pronunciation, mistakenly spelled it Rutherford and it is usually misspelled that way today, bringing sighs to generations of the family. After seventy-nine healthy years, John Rutherfurd got sick on a sea voyage home from England, suffered for five months with an increasingly painful chest edema, and finally succumbed at his New Jersey estate. Of the 1807 Commissioners, Rutherfurd had the most money in his pocket and the least investment in the project.

Simeon DeWitt was born in Ulster County in 1756, descended from early Dutch settlers of the mid-Hudson region. Trained in surveying as a youth, he gained early distinction making maps for George Washington during the Revolution, ultimately becoming Geographer and Surveyor of the Continental Army. After the war, DeWitt settled in Albany, where he served for a half century, until his death in 1834, as the surveyor general of New York State. In 1796, Washington nominated him to be surveyor general of the United States but DeWitt declined the appointment. Immediately after the Revolution, DeWitt had tried to interest the Continental Congress in a national mapping project. Washington had promoted his mapmaker to Jefferson: "I can assure you, he is extremely modest, sensible, sober, discreet, and deserving of favors. He is esteemed a very good mathematician." Jefferson "was happy to learn from you something of the man," but not enough to include the New Yorker in the national land policies that the Virginian was then developing. In Jefferson's cautious hands, DeWitt's petitions went nowhere; he retreated to New York and never seriously considered national service again. Despite what some careless authorities suggest, DeWitt had nothing to do with the federal rectangular policy that Jefferson oversaw. While it is attractive to imagine that DeWitt later did for Manhattan what he had set in motion twenty years earlier for the nation, it's as true as Al Gore inventing the Internet.

New York, meanwhile, happened to be a good place for a mapmaker. It was one of the few states that had a surveyor general and ample funds committed to the office. During his extraordinary tenure in New York, DeWitt oversaw the state's transformation from a largely unsettled wilderness to a widespread commercial and industrial power. Among other excellent work, his "meticulously drawn" 1802 state map set a standard for American cartography; it is still considered "the most important map ever made of the Empire State." It shows some subdivided and gridded territory but mostly it is uninhabited space, that is, uninhabited yet by white people, the long and continuing habitation by native peoples conspicuously absent from the depiction. The city map DeWitt would put his name to in 1811 was the reverse: a dense grid that blotted out a landscape of natural features and nonurban settlement.

DeWitt had nothing to do with Jefferson's national grid, but he put plenty of rectilinear grids all over New York, on numerous state land developments, on Albany, which he laid out with an extensive, prospective grid in 1794, and on land at Ithaca, which he founded, laid out, and developed through the early 1800s.

DeWitt was an imposing presence. Nearly six feet tall, robust, with what his proud son considered "a noble, serious face, resembling in some respects that of Genl. Washington." Well-behaved in society and a devout Christian, DeWitt was everything that his commission partner Morris was not, in domestic life especially. DeWitt was widowed three times. After the death of his first wife, he married Jane Varick Hardenbergh, the sister of longtime New York City mayor Richard Varick and widowed herself. After her death in

April 1808, DeWitt married a third time in October 1810, to Susan Linn, literary-minded daughter of theologian William Linn; brother John was a poet, sister Elizabeth married novelist Charles Brockden Brown, and Susan herself published fiction and poetry. If the death of one wife and marriage to another during his service on New York's street commission was a distraction, there is no record of it. Widowing was nothing unusual in those days and rarely the occasion for extended mourning, especially among people of faith like DeWitt, who saw death as God's will and remarriage as his desire.

Unlike his in-laws, DeWitt was not much of a writer or scholar. Outside of his numerous maps and a few brief published letters on scientific topics, he wrote a short, fairly standard treatise on perspective drawing (1813) and another arguing for a state agricultural college (1819), something that didn't happen for another half century. Not surprisingly for someone who left a limited scholarship, very little has been written about him. A eulogy on his "life and services" published shortly after his death doesn't even mention his street Commission service, nor do any of numerous brief newspaper obituaries. On the other hand, biographical material always points out his service on another commission: in 1810, while serving on the Manhattan street Commission, he eagerly accepted a position on the first state commission exploring a cross-state canal to Lake Erie; surveys he ordered proved the transformative Erie Canal possible.

DeWitt never lived in New York City and did not relish his Manhattan days. The only Commissioner compensated for his services (Morris and Rutherfurd, both rich, waived the four-dollar per diem), DeWitt sought additional payment for days spent traveling from and to Albany and for the Sundays he had to remain, apparently unhappily, in New York. The Common Council grudgingly approved his travel expenses but rejected Sabbath pay. Simeon DeWitt was just short of seventy-nine sturdy years when he caught a violent cold on a tour of his upstate New York properties and died at home in Ithaca.

Like many of the Founding Fathers, Gouverneur Morris was an exceptional soul. In life, he was brilliant but often out of bounds, a fusion of reactionary political opinion and unfettered personal conduct. "He went through life eating the sunny side of the peach, but not throwing away the stone, a mixture of self-indulgence and self-control, of warm blood and of cool brain, dashing, enterprising, aristocratic, and always in positions of trust." To pious Roger Sherman, Morris was "an irreligious and profane man." Exasperated George Washington warned his friend that "the promptitude, with which your lively and brilliant imagination is displayed, allows too little time for deliberation and correction." Today Morris is often forgotten, having failed to achieve great things in his own name. Of all his accomplishments, Manhattan's iconic street grid is perhaps his most lasting, yet none of his many biographers have accorded it more than a few perfunctory sentences at best. It is entirely ignored in a biography by Theodore Roosevelt, who knew New York and understood history.

Morris was born in 1752 at Morrisania, the sprawling family estate at the southern end of the mainland along the Harlem River opposite upper Manhattan; once rolling Westchester countryside, Morrisania survives as a downmarket slice of the urban South Bronx.

Morris served in the Continental Congress (among numerous field and government positions during the Revolution) and was a leader of the Constitutional Convention; he penned the final draft of the Constitution and alone crafted its lyrical preamble. He served courageously as our man in Paris during the Terror, the only foreign minister who remained but was later criticized back home by revolutionary Francophiles like Jefferson for negotiating (secretly and unsuccessfully) to save the royals' heads.

Morris lost an extremity of his own—his lower left leg—in a 1780 incident involving either a moving carriage or a leap from a lover's window (the latter is likeliest). Generally sober John Jay, with whom Morris had written New York's 1777 constitution, offered consolation: "a certain married woman after much use of your legs [has] occasioned your losing one." Morris's peg leg was no hindrance in his vigorous public and private affairs; the latter, often with the willing wives of others, especially during his European years, were reportedly enhanced by his special appendage. "Gouverneur's Leg has been a tax on my Heart," Jay sighed just months after the accident. "I am almost tempted to wish he had lost *something* else." That he did not lose. On Christmas Day 1809, Morris happily married a much younger "reduced gentlewoman" from Virginia (an orphaned Jefferson relative who was cast out decades earlier after allegedly birthing and disposing of a child sired by her brother-in-law) with whom he promptly had a son, stunning and embittering expectant heirs of the aging inveterate bachelor.

Regardless of his virility, Morris's later years were plagued by urinary blockages, gout, and other painful afflictions that limited the time and effective effort he could commit to his final projects. Coming long after his national relevance had faded, Morris's street Commission service has remained largely unexamined, especially compared with his contemporaneous and controversial service, with DeWitt and others, on the first Erie Canal commission. Indulging a characteristic intractability, Morris insisted against all reason that the canal should be built as a massive inclined plane, effectively spilling Lake Erie water 360 miles east to the Hudson River; only after Morris's death in 1816 did the canal project move forward, under then governor DeWitt Clinton's guidance, from visionary scheme to buildable project, with traditional locks and levels. Little has been written on Morris's grid work and Morris himself, usually a voluminous correspondent, wrote almost nothing about it. One almost has the sense that Morris, especially after throwing himself into the Erie work, wasn't especially proud of or interested in what he did to Manhattan. Many have credited Morris with running the street commission, including eventual chief surveyor John Randel, who considered Morris its "President." He was not officially that, but in effect, he was in charge. When it came time in 1811 to write the remarks that would accompany their plan, Morris was the only Commissioner around who could have done it.

With Senator (and as of mid-March, ex-mayor) Clinton in control of drafting the 1807 law, the legislature wasted relatively little effort on debate and amendment, except over how much the Commissioners should be paid. The Assembly rejected five dollars a day and settled on four; the Senate, remaining above that fray, quickly concurred.

On April 4, 1807, the last day of the three-month legislative session, fifteen bills received their final procedural approval and became state laws, including "an act relative to improvements, touching the laying out of the streets and roads in the city of New-York, and for other purposes." It had a few substantial flaws that would later be corrected, but as an expression of government power over its citizens twenty-five years after the Revolution, it was a ripper. Depending on your point of view, it was extraordinarily prescient and urgently necessary city planning or a land grab of unprecedented compass.

In law, Morris, DeWitt, and Rutherfurd were designated "Commissioners of streets and roads in the City of New-York." In reality, they were autocrats of the bulk of the island, from their southern baseline to the remote northern reaches thirteen rural miles away, a domain of some 11,000 acres. None of them would have been intimidated by the size. Morris and Rutherfurd each owned substantially more than that, while DeWitt, who owned only 2,000 acres, mapped the development of the entire state.

The law gave the Commissioners "exclusive power to lay out streets, roads, and public squares, of such width, extent, and direction, as to them shall seem most conducive to public good." It was all broad discretion, narrow obligation, and absolute power.

The Commissioners were given four years to survey the island and produce three copies of a map on "an extensive scale" showing where future roadways were to be built. The "leading streets" and "great avenues" were to have a minimum width of sixty feet; other streets were be at least fifty feet wide. The law said nothing about the length or maximum width of any street or avenue, how many of each there might be, or how they ought or ought not intersect each other, whether at right angles or not. Nor were the number, configuration, location, or any other details specified about the public squares, except that the Commissioners were to lay them and the streets "of such ample width as they may deem sufficient to secure a free and abundant circulation of air" after city had risen up around them. In the field, the Commissioners were required only to "erect suitable and durable monuments at the most conspicuous angles" and take elevations at as many intersections "as they may think sufficient."

The Commissioners' authority was explicit. They could order closed any existing road that interfered with whatever plan they chose. They or their surveyors could enter any land or building "in the day time" to conduct surveys; the relatively brief language on this point would soon cause issues. In case anyone didn't quite get the Commissioners' "exclusive power" to lay out everything as they saw fit, their plans and related surveys were deemed "final and conclusive" with respect to the mayor, the Common Council, landowners and land occupants, and "all other persons whomsoever."

The city's authority to build and pay for the Commissioners' new streets was also explicit: the city would assess and pay damages to owners of houses or land that would have to be removed or bisected by new streets; owners dissatisfied with their compensation could appeal to a panel appointed by the state supreme court. At the same time, the city could make appealable assessments on owners whose property was enhanced in value by the accessibility resulting from the new streets. This manner of funding civic improvement was not new for New York (or elsewhere): back in the 1680s, the city started building public street wells and paying for their construction with assessments on the neighborhood residents whether they

CHAPTER 7

INTO THE WOODS

The *time* within which the Commissioners were limited
by the Statute to make their *Plan* of the streets, avenues,
and public places on Manhattan [was] barely *sufficient* to
enable them to comply with the *letter*, although not fully
with the *spirit*, of the Statute.

—Surveyor John Randel Jr., 1864

THREE DAYS AFTER Mayor Clinton officially qualified the Commissioners for their duties, Gouverneur Morris wrote in his
diary: "Meet with DeWitt one of the Comm[issioners] and do
business." It might seem remarkable that for this first meeting of
the three-member commission, one of them wasn't there. As the
weeks, months, and years passed, John Rutherfurd's absences would
become unremarkable.

It is also remarkable that business was done but we have no
record of what. The law empowering the Commissioners required
them to report nothing for four years. Even the constitutional con-
ventioneers at Philadelphia twenty years earlier, Morris prominently
among them, were more transparent. New York's Commissioners
were at liberty to keep their deliberations private; for four years,
they kept no official records, and the gleanings from their personal
writings—only Morris kept a diary—can be maddeningly opaque.

We know Morris and DeWitt met on June 29, 1807, to "do business" but we have no idea what business. Likewise, for example, the following June: "Go immediately after Breakfast to attend the Board of Commissioners—A pretty long Sitting." And, if long, likely important, but Morris doesn't tell. Finally, on Thursday, March 28, 1811: "Raw damp and NEast Wind. Go to town on Business of the Comm[ission] to lay out Manhattan Island. Dine with Mr. Rutherford [sic] and execute the Maps—Much indisposed [from gout]." So, on the very day that the Commissioners sealed their John Hancocks on the copies of the map that gave birth to a new city, Morris had as much to say about the weather and his well-being.

Among the things we do know is that the surveying got off on a very bad foot, so to speak. That is because the Commissioners' first chief surveyor was none other than Charles Loss, the same Charles Loss then in the midst of the incompetence that would get him removed as city surveyor in 1811.

Why the Commissioners selected Loss is another mystery. There were city surveyors with better reputations and deeper knowledge to choose from, such as Benjamin Taylor, then the longest-serving city surveyor, or Samuel Stilwell, successor in 1810 to John Hunn as street commissioner and first in a long familial line of skilled Manhattan surveyors.

The most skilled local surveyor wasn't around, though arguably, given his history, he would have been an interesting choice. In the spring of 1807, Joseph Mangin had sold his considerable properties on Greenwich Street and acquired a mile-square tract of land at Madrid in far upstate St. Lawrence County, a popular area for French expatriates that was developed by Hamilton associates whom Mangin knew. "I leaved the residence of the City of New York," he wrote (in his Frenglish) during his family's first deep winter, "in order to pass the residue of my life . . . on my farm Seate." By the residue of winter, though, Mangin's northern idyll was done and he was back in the city seeking commissions; his unmarketable farm seat would prove a crippling saddle on his financial health for the residue of his life. Mangin was immediately reinstated as a city surveyor and soon got two major church contracts. He sought (and didn't receive) military jobs, but there's no indication that in the spring of 1808 he was interested in becoming the street commission's chief surveyor, or that they wanted him, though by then Loss's position was in jeopardy and the whole project seemed to be lagging.

Back in October 1807, four months into the Commission's work and with one of four summer surveying seasons gone, not much had happened. Important decisions arguably had to wait for the completion of Loss's work, but there's no indication that the Commissioners in the meantime were even exchanging thoughts about what their options might be. DeWitt as usual was in Albany. Morris had been confined at Morrisania for weeks with physical infirmities. When "my Health permitted of my Attendance" at decision-making meetings requiring two Commissioners, Morris found that "Mr. Rutherford's [sic] Affairs called him to the Mountains of New Jersey, wherefore a Board cannot be made until his Return." For a commission on a timeframe, its members seemed fairly disengaged. This stands in sharp contrast to Morris, DeWitt, and the other Erie Canal commissioners, who leapt to their work immediately after their appointment in 1810.

If Morris could not get a quorum for street Commission meetings, he could at least check in on his chief surveyor at their field office, a rented room in a carpenter's house in the village of Greenwich, at the northeast corner of what are now Bleecker and Christopher Streets. "I attend at the Office occasionally," Morris informed DeWitt by letter, "and my Arrival being uncertain makes it inconvenient to Mr. Loss to absent himself." Worse than Loss avoiding work was Loss doing work:

> On my first Visit I found him protracting from old Maps and new Surveys without verifying the Variation of the one or the Courses

of the other. I directed him therefore to see that the Compasses of our Surveyors were immediately compared with the Meridian, believing (and so it has turned out) that they would not only vary from it but from each other. I desired him also to take the Courses of some Streets in the City and comparing them when corrected according to the Variation of his Compass with the old Maps see if they were correct. It turned out again (as I apprehended) that the old Maps are erroneous and that his Work from them must be done over.

Loss was in over his head.

His first assignment was to make a map of the island—a city objective since 1804—and get accurate positions of certain existing streets. The map would provide a framework in which to orient and locate whatever plan the Commissioners decided; existing street positions would enable projections of future streets. Morris, highly educated and with a lifetime of experience in land issues, knew much better than Loss how to proceed. While other surveyors were busy determining the island's meridian, a tedious but necessary business, Morris had the idea that a long baseline should be established from Manhattan across the Hudson to Hoboken. This line could be measured by basic trigonometry using two points on Manhattan, the distance between them, and the angles between them and the Hoboken point. With the long Manhattan-Hoboken baseline, clearly viewed across the river, other very accurate triangles using different points on Manhattan could be generated, and eventually enough and smaller triangles to get an accurate map. The key was Morris's idea of going across the Hudson for the long baseline. Because measuring angles over long distances is highly accurate, the cross-river triangulation would "assist also in ascertaining the Correctness of Work done by our Surveyors."

Morris was also concerned about the accuracy of his surveyors' compasses. He suggested that magnetic variation should be measured every six months at various spots on the island: "the Pre-vention of Law Suits and Security of landed Property are Objects of such Magnitude as to justify and I almost permit myself to say require the Attention of Government."

But his chief concern was the risk of continuing with Loss: "We cannot indeed remedy what is past but Mischief may be prevented in future. Will you my dear Sir pardon me for suggesting that an official Represent[ative] from the Surveyor Gen[eral] might not be improper."

Nothing would happen though "till next Season when you can Attend," a concession that distance already was preventing DeWitt's regular participation, in this case from the fall of 1807 to the spring of 1808. Meanwhile, Rutherfurd was no easier to corral. In Septem-ber 1807, he had been "absent three weeks in Sussex County." Ten days after writing to DeWitt on October 2, Morris was supposed to meet with Rutherfurd at their office but he didn't show. The next day, Morris again went to the office "and again I am disap-pointed." Rutherfurd finally appeared the following day to "do Busi-ness," the details of which Morris as usual did not record in his diary A week later they were supposed to meet again but a "very high Wind" apparently detained Rutherfurd; Morris waited at the office for two hours, before heading back north by carriage. Demonstrat-ing unusual perseverance, Rutherfurd caught up with Morris at the bridge over the lower Harlem River (the first such bridge, opened in 1798, the site of the current Third Avenue Bridge), where "We do the Business of the Meeting and I return Home." Again, what busi-ness they did on the road on a windy November afternoon is entirely unclear and presumably not substantial. They met only once more before the end of the year, during a December morning at the office.

No other diary entries or letters for 1807 make any reference to Commission business or decisions, except that the December Morris-Rutherfurd meeting might have begun to resolve Loss's status. In January, Morris wrote to DeWitt that the decision had been made that Loss, at his request, would forgo daily wages and attendance at the office and simply complete the island map for a fixed amount. "Not having the Materials before me I cannot, from Memory, ascertain either the Date or Amount," Morris confessed, "but it was I think to be ready about the Middle of May, and to cost somewhat less than by allowing his Wages." Morris, writing from Morrisania, was mostly concerned in this long letter and for much of the coming winter with proposals for additional bridges across the Harlem. His street commission was a distraction, even important details "vague." A month later, in a postscript to another long letter on bridges, Morris informed DeWitt that Loss was to get $500 and deliver his island map by May 13.

Morris believed that Manhattan could and should be connected to the mainland by bridges across the narrow Harlem River only. "The idle Projects for making Bridges across the North and East Rivers can never seriously occupy the Attention of considerate Men," he lectured DeWitt in January. "To say they are impracticable would be rash, but they certainly cannot be built but at an Expence infinitely beyond any Advantages they can offer." Morris presumably had in mind the recent proposal by local architect Thomas Pope to join lower Manhattan and Brooklyn with his "Flying Pendant Lever Bridge," a long, graceful single span technologically unbuildable with the proposed construction of wood, the only available material at that day. The century was three-quarters older before the steel wire suspension and other technologies of the Brooklyn Bridge astounded the doubting majority even then. In the long meantime, a dozen or more ferries made East River bridges as ridiculous as Morris imagined them.

Harlem bridges were not ridiculous, though, and the agitation by private interests—"the Bridge Men" in Morris's parlance—for the state to authorize more of them was relevant to Morris the Manhattan street planner. "I cannot shut my Eyes to the public Benefit of free and easy Access to the Emporium of American Commerce and Capital of the Northern and Eastern States. . . . it is evident to me that many Years cannot pass by without opening every Avenue to the City of New York which the Nature of the surrounding Country will permit." In this and many other letters from this period Morris is passionate about the city, bridges, and other topics related to the city's future, but never about the streets he was supposedly planning. After his September 1807 letter on surveying techniques, not one of Morris's many dozens of letters focuses any substantial attention on his street commission, even though, with Morris and DeWitt physically removed from each other, letters would have been their primary form of communication. Indeed, Morris apologized to DeWitt in a brief letter on May 12, 1808, for not answering a letter of DeWitt's from March 23!

By May, at least, Loss's Manhattan map was finished and his service was at end. In the meantime, very little commission business had been done. Morris hadn't been on Manhattan for many weeks, "prevented by Visitors and by Weather," and various travels. He anticipated further "Engagements which will occupy at least six or eight Weeks of my Time." DeWitt was preparing to come down from Albany for his first visit in many months but he would find neither Morris nor Rutherfurd, whose "Business will I fear prevent him from giving you much Assistance." Nevertheless, "I have however great Reliance as well on your Experience as on your Talents."

In the meantime, a chief surveyor was needed to replace Loss. "My Opinion of the other Persons employed are not more flattering than yours," Morris told DeWitt, "and I seriously apprehend Difficulties from erroneous Work when we come to lay out Streets according to the Survey & then cause such Streets to be designed on the Ground." Morris is not saying that they had any idea yet how they would lay out those streets because no surveying for streets had been done. There was no plan yet, but they needed a surveyor to move the project to that stage. Morris had an idea: "It will be well I think to bring Mr. Randell with you. I have always considered that

the Acquisition of that young Gentleman will be valuable to us."
Despite the misspelling, Morris was talking about John Randel Jr.
How Morris had always considered the Albany nineteen-year-old
valuable is unclear; the best guess is that Morris was aware of Randel's first upstate surveys through his mentor DeWitt. But this was
enough to launch Randel to Manhattan.

Of late, a myth has grown up as myths do that John Randel
was responsible for Manhattan's grid. "Gridlock? Blame John Randel Jr.," asserted the *New York Times* in 2013, and "Randel's matrix,"
said the paper in 2012, each time neglecting to mention the Commission he worked for and whose instructions he followed. Earlier
references, two centuries worth, either put Randel properly in his
place in service to the gridding Commissioners or don't mention
him at all. If the designers of the grid—the heavy greatcoat on the
land, the dense undergarment of the city—were the Commissioners,
John Randel was their tailor, though a skilled, dedicated, exacting
young needleman to be sure. And, at a time in America when land
surveying was often a professional apprenticeship on the way to civil
engineering, Randel failed at the transition and life generally.

Randel was born in Albany on December 3, 1787, a date we
know only from a mention of his birthday in one of his Manhattan surveying field books. Formally educated no further than primary school, he owed the start of his professional life to DeWitt.
The families were well known to each other in Albany; DeWitt's
brother had served during the Revolution with Randel's father, who
became a successful brass founder and jeweler. John Jr. may have
started working for DeWitt as young as age twelve, though probably more like sixteen. By 1807, he had been an assistant on two
small surveys in a frontier New York county and had mapped the
road between Albany and Schenectady. These were not unimport-
ant documents in their way, but they were not war maps for General
Washington, constitutions for state and nation, or escape plans for
Louis and Marie Antoinette. Morris and DeWitt had participated

in the largest events of contemporary American and European history—wars, revolutions, nation-building, destroying, and rebuilding, with their attendant horrors and rewards—and were intimate with the famous and the infamous. Their surveyor hadn't traveled much beyond Albany, population 7,500. In any case, Randel was long indebted to DeWitt: "I have always been in the habit of looking up to you," he wrote around 1823 to his mentor. "It is my pride to have it known that I was brought up under your eye."

After completing his service to the Commissioners in 1811, Randel was retained by the city for the next decade to complete a detailed atlas of the island, establishing with astounding precision and accuracy where all the Commissioners' streets and avenues were to be laid, essential details absent from the plan announced in 1811.

For Randel, it was pretty much downhill from Manhattan. Soon after completing his long years of service there, Randel imprudently and publicly accused the chief engineer of the half-completed Erie Canal of wasting time and money with political engineering decisions. Randel was on solid ground but his arguments were lost on politicians and the public and made a professional enemy of Benjamin Wright, the Erie chief. Two years later, Wright and Randel wound up working together on the Chesapeake and Delaware Canal as chief engineer and lead contractor, respectively, after Randel sought and failed to get the engineering position. Seeking vengeance for Erie, Wright got Randel fired, lying outrageously that Randel had abandoned his duties. Randel sued Wright and the canal company. "This J.R. is so full of his lies and schemes of trouble," grumbled Wright, who considered Randel "a complete Hypocritical, lying nincompoop (and I might say scoundrel if it was a Gentlemanly word)." Randel's supporters rightfully and publicly accused Wright and the company of "shocking oppression and injustice." Wright escaped prosecution but in protracted litigation that reached the U.S. Supreme Court, Randel eventually collected from the company an historic judgment of nearly a quarter million dollars, a staggering amount when it was finally awarded in 1834 that nearly beggared the company. With his winnings, Randel built Randalia, a spectacular estate looking down on the canal.

The victory was Pyrrhic. Wright went on to become the "Father of American Civil Engineering," while Randel's job offers and solvency gradually dwindled as his eccentric and self-righteous litigiousness escalated. Though his mind remained inventive—he devised (and unsuccessfully promoted) elevated railways decades before their general adoption—he died in debt, leaving his widow Letitia tangled up in plentiful lawsuits of his making.

"I am a ruined man," Randel confessed publicly when he was just forty-eight, irretrievably fallen from the youthful triumph of his Manhattan work and already obscure. Reports of his death in 1865 were hardly exaggerated: there were a couple of brief notices with conflicting dates and places; his grave has not been found. Shortly before his death, Randel called the grid "the pride and boast of this city." Not everyone shared or shares that opinion, but all would agree that his own life turned out less well.

In his relentless pursuit of recognition and fair treatment, Randel left a trail of newspaper correspondence, published writings, annotated maps, and legal testimony, in addition to his substantial field notes, but very little of it covers the three years of surveying prior to the 1811 grid plan. Of his nearly four dozen field books that have survived, relatively few entries in just two of the books refer to fieldwork in 1808 and 1809, with brief, nonsubstantive entries in another book for 1810, the final season of surveying before the Commissioners announced their plan the following March. This, together with certain other Randel materials and the Commissioners' reticence on the subject, leads one to wonder just how much thought and effort went into the plan before it was announced.

Randel officially joined the Commissioners as their chief surveyor in June 1808. It was a period of unusual activity for them, with Morris conducting meetings with at least one of his fellow

Commissioners at least four times in late June and early July. It seems possible, but there's no confirmation, that DeWitt and Rutherfurd had official meetings of their own in the days or weeks prior. As always, we don't know what they decided, but there's no indication from Randel's subsequent surveying that they had even thought about what their street plan was to be. They appear to have given Randel surveying orders that had nothing yet to do with a grid.

For a person whose attention to detail is regarded as his best trait, Randel seems not to have been particularly organized at the outset. In pencil on the second page of the field book numbered 68.2 in ink on the spine, he recorded possibly his first day of surveying: "Friday 9th July 1808 Begin at Oliver Waldron's Grocery." This was a reference to Oliver Waldron Jr., whose country store was located at the southwest intersection of the Eastern Post Road and the lower portion of Goerck's Middle Road (at today's west side of Park Avenue South between 28th and 29th Streets). The problem is that July 9, 1808, was a Saturday, not a Friday. The following week, he started again, in ink, in a different book, designated 68.1: "Wednesday 12 July 1808. Begin measuring with a chain from Waldron's Grocery." The problem here is that July 12 was a Tuesday. Perhaps it was just nerves that caused the twenty-year-old to start two field books at the same time and screw up the dates in both. In any case, his ensuing survey of the Eastern Post Road featured, along with various measurements, drawings detailing its course, including natural features and intersecting roads like Steuben Street (aka Cross Road or Low's Lane) running slightly northwesterly (from what is now 41st Street) toward Bloomingdale Road. Seven pages, in the second book, and two days later he was done: "Thursday 14 July 1808—completed surveying from Oliver Waldrons to James Beekmans with a compass & foot chain." In the process of arriving at what is now 50th Street near Second Avenue, Randel had gotten his calendar straight. He also seems to have arrived, in the increasing firmness of his hand and clarity of his drawing, as the confident surveyor of Manhattan.

The Albany boy, at age twenty, had become a Manhattan man, the provincial assistant surveyor turned professional mapper of a future island metropolis.

The tools that Randel used were fairly rudimentary. In 1808, he had a compass, a transit (a telescope for sighting compass headings), chains, and two ten-foot mahogany rods that had been fabricated in 1807 and used by Charles Loss. Randel soon found them inadequate. "Although they would answer very well for short distances on nearly level ground, they were found inconvenient for measuring long lines on rough ground." During 1809 and 1810, he had constructed a pair of longer, hollow, iron rods that, when used in tandem, did not expand or contract with varying temperatures. With these Randel "measured several lines in 1810." Several, not many.

What was he mapping in his 1808 march from Oliver Waldron's to James Beekman's? It was not the grid. It was the Eastern Post Road, which the grid of 1811 would eliminate. In the summer of 1808 there was not yet a grid plan. In fact, practically all of his surveying in 1808 and the following two seasons as well was related to existing roads, not to anything like the 1811 grid. During the rest of 1808, into late November, Randel did surveying of Greenwich Lane, Art Street, a developing village at Kips Bay, Manhattan and Albany Avenues (the evolving names of Goerck's Middle and West roads), and Steuben Street. What Randel was doing was getting the lay of the land as it existed, not the way it would be. He noted hills, rocks, ponds, streams, marshes, woods, underbrush, briars, foot paths, cleared fields, fresh and salt meadows, grasslands, property fences, stables, barns, the occasional house, and gardens planted with turnips, carrots, clover, potatoes. He marked no new streets.

One line that Randel ran in late July 1808 suggests he was looking for an alignment very distinct from the 1811 grid: "Exploring line run on a course (S41W) parallel to the Streets at Kips Bay from North Street to Bellevue." "S41W" means forty-one degrees west from a true north-south axis. Bellevue was an old estate recently converted into a hospital along the East River, east of what is now First Avenue and 27th Street; the site remains a city hospital. Let's take a moment with Kips Bay streets.

The Kips were among the oldest and most prominent New Amsterdam families, arriving before 1635. Their farm along the East River where two streams emptied into a rocky inlet eventually comprised about 150 acres, from the Post Road to the river, roughly from what is now 31st to 40th Streets. Starting in 1800, the family had the farm laid out (by Charles Loss) in a rectilinear grid of four by four streets, bearing the first names of various living Kip children. The little grid was cocked on an axis of forty-one degrees from north, roughly perpendicular with the property's north and south property lines, and precisely on the line that Randel was surveying in 1808, from North (now Houston) Street at the Bowery (we know from a diagram in his field book that he started at this intersection). Why was he surveying a line from North Street to Bellevue, about a mile and third, on a line parallel with the Kip's Bay grid? Randel didn't explain but it had nothing to do with the eventual 1811 grid aligned at twenty-nine degrees.

In September, Randel carefully measured a line perpendicular from Manhattan Avenue at Steuben Street (today's Fifth and 42nd) west. The line crossed Albany Road (now Sixth Ave), Bloomingdale Road, and Fitzroy Road, and various woods, grasslands, meadows, fenced property lines, and scattered houses, until it reached a Hudson River inlet at the mouth of a swampy creek (unnamed by Randel but well known as the Great Kill, which flowed from many sources at the center of the island). It is tempting to look at this line and shout: "West 42nd Street!" For Randel, though, in 1808 it was only a line that enabled him to place Manhattan Avenue, the Middle Road of Goerck's Common Lands, in the context of Manhattan Island. If Goerck ran his lines out to a Manhattan shoreline, there is no record. Goerck's Common Lands maps were just that; they were not maps of Manhattan showing the Common Lands. Now Randel was doing the survey work that might accurately place the Common Lands grid in the context of the island. Why? It would enable the Commissioners to know precisely where the Common Lands grid was. If accurately located, the Common Lands grid could become the basis for a larger grid.

One thing Randel didn't put into his 1808 surveying notes was that he was getting a lot less done than he might have hoped. Most landowners were not happy to have a team of surveyors on their land, uninvited and not at all clear on what their plans were, if any, and how they might affect the lands they were surveying.

Randel did not record the circumstances of surveying that brought him in August 1808 onto the farm of John Mills, in the vicinity of what is now Sixth Avenue and 9th Street. Mills did, by taking Randel to court. Mills, an otherwise upstanding citizen involved with various volunteer services (in a fire company and at the almshouse), did not want Randel on his land. He filed a lawsuit for trespass, claiming that Randel and his surveying crew with axes and other implements had damaged or cut down trees and trampled or otherwise ruined crops to the tune of some $5,000. The claim and the language of the allegations were, typically for contemporary trespass lawsuits, far beyond the damage that Randel actually had done—Mills eventually collected about $150—but the effect was real. Randel later recalled that Mills was not his only problem. "I was arrested by the Sheriff, on numerous suits instituted against me . . . for trespass and damage committed by my workmen, in passing over grounds, cutting off branches of trees, &c., to make surveys under instructions from the Commissioners."

The surveying was physically difficult enough given the island's natural state—rocky outcrops, swampy bogs, innumerable streams—but it had also been ravaged during the Revolution and worked over by generations of landowners. For example, the surveyors "encountered in our surveys extensive ancient and neglected hawthorn hedge-fences, then grown to saplings, extending along the east side of the Bowery, in front of the Stuyvesant estate, that were impassible without the aid of an axe."

Many likely apocryphal stories about physical aggression have been passed down through the years, perhaps founded in truth but embellished with time, such as the surveyors' supposed retreat from a barrage of cabbages and artichokes hurled by "an estimable old woman" who objected to men running a line through her kitchen. Randel, as we know, was not the sort to make a point of endearing himself to people who stood in his way, as this entertaining account suggests:

> He was opposed to offsets, and in order to run exact lines, insisted on cutting down trees, and disposing of things in a way disagreeable to the owners. At one time he sent, in advance of his coming, printed copies of the law, appointing the Commissioners, with a notice of his intention to remove trees and other obstacles to the survey. The people, who had not then been tamed by the collection of an income tax, refused to admit him within their enclosures until he modified his pretensions.

This anecdote comes to us in an 1877 account by surveyor Samuel Stilwell Doughty, great-nephew of surveyor and Randel contemporary Samuel Stilwell, who perhaps was in the habit of transmitting professional jealousy to his descendant along with most of his name.

The dates of many of Randel's surveying troubles were never precisely recorded, but by the end of the 1808 season they had become more substantial. Morris was out of the area from August into early October. Rutherfurd had been mostly elsewhere. But DeWitt apparently was in the city in early September to inform the Common Council of the "difficulties and impediments" facing the surveyors. Unless their surveyors were "protected from such vexatious interruptions," DeWitt warned, the Commissioners faced "the impracticability of their completing the duties of their appointment." Nearing the conclusion of the second of four surveying years and without a plan as yet, the street commission was in a startling predicament.

The 1807 law was very brief on the Commissioners' surveying rights: "It shall and may be lawful to and for the said commissioners, and for all persons acting under their authority, to enter, in the day time, into and upon any lands, tenements or hereditaments which they shall deem necessary to be surveyed, used or converted for the laying out, opening and forming of any street or road." In 1807, the relatively limited activities conducted under the authority of veteran local surveyor Charles Loss may not have offended so deeply or yet have carried as much import as surveys carried out the following year by brash, young, and unknown John Randel.

By mid-September 1808, a Council committee had developed language to strengthen the 1807 law. One would assume that the city that in April 1807 sought and won the appointment of a Commission with complete and final word to plan the city's future in four years' time, would continue to support that endeavor a year and half later. This would be a bad assumption.

Toward the end of its October 17 session, the Council took a vote on whether a formal amendment should be prepared and sent to the legislature. Without the amendment the street commission could not pursue its work and would effectively die. The vote was 7–7.

How could this be? The simplest explanation is politics. The Council that sought the 1807 Commission was overwhelmingly Federalist. The Council voting 7–7 in October 1808 (elected in November 1807) was overwhelmingly Republican. Federalists were unanimously in favor, 3–0; Republicans were overwhelmingly opposed, 7–4; four Council members, two from each party, were absent. Of the fourteen 1808 voters, only five had been on the 1807 Council, with all four of the returning Republicans voting no and the lone returning Federalist voting yes. The division on the original 1807 vote wasn't recorded, but the suggestion is strong that it was the Federalist majority that created the 1807 commission and the Republican majority in 1808 that wanted to undo it. Parsing the various affiliations and motives of the voters and nonvoters would be a narrative killer here, but it might be noted that among the absent was Federalist Ninth Ward assistant alderman and up-island land developer Samuel Kip, who presumably would have been highly interested in the street commission's future. For whatever reason he was absent that day.

What to do at 7–7? Is it possible that a revote would have been called, with the future of Manhattan planning in the balance? Certainly, except that the mayor hadn't voted yet. In those days, the mayor had no veto power or other executive authority, just the limited power of a Council vote. Republicans having regained a Council majority in November 1807, the state legislature the following February, per custom, had replaced Federalist mayor Marinus Willett with the Republican mayor he had replaced the year before: DeWitt Clinton.

Both of the 1808 Council members affiliated with Clinton's wing of the highly factionalized Republican party were among the seven "no" votes. But Clinton was the cousin and close friend of Commissioner DeWitt and still the powerful state senator who had guided passage of the 1807 law. And so, the Council "being equally divided the Mayor gave his casting vote in the Affirmative." By that slender margin, the city authorized itself to have its broken street Commission repaired in Albany. But for DeWitt Clinton, a subtle actor in the city's planning efforts, the great goal of bringing order to the future city might have been thwarted by its capricious government.

Though the Council acted in October 1808, nothing happened until March, when the state legislature was back in session and passing bills. Like the 1807 law, the 1809 revision passed with little debate; this was a city affair that roused no state issues. Employing language chosen by the Council, the revision provided that "where surveys or other necessary acts" could not be executed "without cutting trees and doing other damages," the Commissioners or surveyors were required to give "reasonable notice" to the landowner and with him view the property to be affected. The landowner was to present a bill for damages; if the city in thirty days paid "reasonable compensation," any subsequent lawsuit was expressly precluded. Of course, reasonableness often needed to be determined in court, but at least a mechanism was established that substantially cut down lawsuits, especially $5,000 claims for minimal damages, and generally allowed Randel to go about his business starting with the 1809 season.

But what was his business in 1809? As in 1808, the only recorded surveys are of, or connected to, existing roads that the 1811 plan would either eliminate or, without acknowledgement, make use of. Nothing in Randel's field books indicates any surveying for new rectilinear streets. He certainly must have been busy, but he still seems to have been surveying the land itself—its natural features and existing roads—without as yet any particular plan. In July, the field office was relocated from Greenwich up to Smith's Tavern, on the Eastern Post Road, at what is now Third Avenue and 77th Street. There's no indication that, before the move, Randel had surveyed anywhere near so far up-island. The likelihood of a plan at this time is still as remote as most of the island remained to Randel. In fact, his recorded surveys for the remainder of the 1809 season are all back south. Among them, in August, is a line extending along the line of the main section of Manhattan Avenue (Goerck's Middle Road) south from Steuben Street; that is, diverging from the southern portion of Manhattan/Middle that angled southwest to the Post Road. Five days and a mile later, Randel's line reached the junction of the Bloomingdale and Post Roads. Again, like the line Randel measured from the same starting point the previous September out to the Hudson River, the line measured here in 1809 is not a street. It is a line that helps locate the Common Lands' Middle Road. In the Commissioners' 1811 plan, this line will become Fifth Avenue from 23rd to 42nd Street, but there's no indication that in 1809 anything like such an idea had been born. In fact, in another August

1809 survey, as in 1808, Randel ran another line parallel with the Kips Bay grid southwest into the center of the island, suggesting that the Commissioners in 1809 were possibly looking to tie in Kips Bay with the Common Lands, the sort of grid pastiche that Mangin had been after.

The strongest pattern that can be discerned from Randel's late 1809 surveying is a focus on the alignment of Goerck's Common Lands roads. By then, Randel had run several lines run out to the rivers from Goerck's north-south roads, providing more of an idea of how the Common Lands grid related to the island generally. As we know, Goerck had located his Common Lands surveys in relation only to the Bloomingdale Road and the Eastern Post Road on either side, and the Harlem Commons to the north. Randel, by the end of 1809, again seems to be placing the Common Lands, again without explicitly saying so, in the context of the island as a whole. The once "waste, vacant, unpatented, and unappropriated" lands in the middle of the island, organized in a rectilinear fashion by Goerck in 1796, seem to be shaping up as central to the Commissioners' thinking. And who could blame them? With time beginning to run out, all those rectilinear 920-by-260-foot lots with parallel avenues along them must have seemed pretty attractive: a tin cup serving as the Holy Grail. But, again, there's nothing to indicate that the Commissioners had actually begun that quest.

It's disconcerting but hardly surprising that in late 1809, with just one surveying season plus another few months left to issue their plan, the Commissioners had not settled yet on what they wanted to do. They almost never wrote to each other about it and rarely got together. During all of 1809, Morris participated in just eleven meetings: portions of three days in June, three in July, two in September, two in October, and one in late November. Several of these meetings involved all three Commissioners; the November meeting included Morris, DeWitt, and Randel, presumably to discuss the results of the surveying season. It certainly is possible these meetings involved discussions of what their plan should be, but nothing in any of their papers or Randel's survey records explicitly or implicitly says so.

Randel did more surveying during the 1810 season, but we have little record of it. Only one of his nearly four dozen existing field books includes specifics of any 1810 survey, and those are not substantive. As noted earlier, Randel used his 1808 hollow iron rods to measure only "several lines in 1810," which is to say far fewer than the hundreds of lines he would run starting in 1811, after the Commissioners decided on their grid, which are highly documented in his field books.

DeWitt and especially Morris were highly distracted in 1810. On Christmas Day 1809, Morris surprised everyone who knew him by marrying his recently arrived "housekeeper" Nancy, formally Anne Cary Randolph. As we know, Morris was in upstate New York for nearly the entire period from August 1808 until February 1809. He was in the city just once during that period, on business entirely unrelated to the street commission: an interview in October at a modest boarding house on Greenwich Street with a woman he had last seen twenty years earlier, when she was thirteen, on her eminent family's Virginia plantation. Five years later Nancy was an orphan, widow, rumored lover of her married brother-in-law, and unproven infanticide (a dead white baby, possibly stillborn, was found by a slave on a trash pile). Cast out of genteel society, the "Jezebel of the Old Dominion," as her derisive relatives allowed her to be called, commenced a patient hegira in modest occupations until Morris heard that she was in New York. Seven months after their reacquaintance, she became Gouverneur's housekeeper, and eight months after that, his first, only, and truly beloved wife and active physical companion. He was nearly fifty-eight and suffering from various infirmities but still virile; she was thirty-five and eager. Three years later, she gave birth to Gouverneur's only heir, who after his father's death in 1816 and his mother's many years later built St. Ann's Church at

Morrisania, where Nancy and Gouverneur are buried in the yard of the stone church in what is now the urban South Bronx.

In March 1810, Morris and DeWitt were named to the state's Erie Canal commission, which became a principal activity for both of them, especially for Morris as its official head. Morris's days filled up with canal commission activities. On one day in June Morris, DeWitt, and Rutherfurd met as the Commissioners "for laying out the Island" for what appears to be the first meeting of that now secondary Commission since Morris, Rutherfurd, and Randel met the previous November. After their June meeting, Morris and DeWitt were off on an upstate tour of the canal commissioners (Morris famously brought Nancy with him for a highly companionable honeymoon). Morris didn't return home until late September. Not until the morning of November 29 did Morris meet, at Morrisania, with DeWitt and Randel about the "Manhattan Comm[ission]." It was that Commission's second meeting of the entire year, but it only lasted the morning; in the afternoon the business at Morrisiania was "the Navigation Comm[ission]."

So just when did the 1807 Commissioners, formally titled the "Commissioners of streets and roads in the City of New-York," become the "grid Commissioners"? That is, when did they decide that New York would get its single, rectilinear grid? At the end of November 1810 there were no surveying seasons left and only four months in which to make a plan and submit it. If no decision had been made before then, and nothing in the written record, from surveying notes to letters and diaries, suggests one had, it must have been on or after November 29.

In fact, it might well have been that morning. "I am directed to inform you," Morris wrote to the Common Council later that day,

> that the Commissioners for laying out the Manhattan Island
> have completed their work so far forth as depends on them; but
> much is yet to be done on the ground. It would be useless to detail

the causes, which have delayed their operations. The unpropi-
tious weather for the last and preceding season is not the least.
So much, however, is accomplished, that with tolerable success
in the operations now going on, it will be practicable, to make
within the time fixed by the Statute a report complying substantially, if not literally with the law, shewing all the streets to be laid
out and specially designating those, on which monuments have
not been placed.

The Commissioners had not met since June. The meeting
of November 29 featured the essential participants—Morris and
DeWitt—to make an official decision and Randel, the chief surveyor,
to understand it and map accordingly. No more Commissioner meetings followed, but December featured numerous meetings between
Morris and Randel, presumably to get clear on how Randel was to
draw his map and how Morris was to write his accompanying remarks.
"These Streets may hereafter," Morris continued, "without the
superintendance [sic] of Commissioners be accurately traced by a
skilful, practical man, possessed of suitable instruments. It is, however, proper to remark, that in order to establish points, which have
been ascertained by measurements already made, the course of operations commenced this year ought to be continued next year by the
surveyor now employed, after which, the work may be conducted in
such manner as the corporation may deem most expedient."
Morris wanted to be clear that the Commissioners had planned
the way forward. "I am directed to state, that only one surveyor can
be employed in what remains, and that the Commissioners have
been under the necessity of directing the construction of particular
instruments in order, that he might attain to that degree of accuracy, requisite in a work of this sort, where the difference of an inch
may afterwards be a source of contention."
Morris also wanted to be clear that very little of their plan,
which he did not announce, had been accomplished: "There are,

however, measured and to be measured with this extreme precision upwards of five hundred & fifty thousand feet, that is to say upwards of one hundred miles. A work so extensive, although enjoined by the statute was not, perhaps, contemplated, when it was proposed." Morris, in fact, was quite unfamiliar with the extent of the plan. The correct measure was over 700,000 feet (703,398 feet by Randel's later count).

The hundred miles of streets (actually just over 133 miles) was a clue about the plan; evidently, it would have many streets. And those streets evidently would run in an area smaller than the Commissioners' original mandate of the entire island:

> To place and take the elevation above high water mark of about three thousand five hundred monuments will also require as little time. Yet all this must be done to comply literally with the provision of the Statute in relation to so much only of the island, as may, in the opinion of the Commissioners, become part of the city in the course of ages. If the whole were embraced, the labour would of course be increased with a proportionate increase of expence.

Morris didn't indicate how much was "so much," but he showed that he was significantly unclear on how many monuments were to be placed. His projected 3,500 was over double what Randel would place. The point is not that Morris was wrong. The point is that even in late November 1810, the plan was new and either not fully evolved or not fully understood. Randel eventually placed monuments (or iron rods) at each of over 1,600 intersections in the plan formally announced in March 1811. Does Morris's estimate of 3,500 monuments mean that in November 1810 the plan then envisioned 3,500 intersections, with perhaps double the number of avenues and more streets than the final plan delivered? Or did Morris just goof on his monument count as he had on his street mileage?

Morris offered nothing more about what they had decided and no one knew until after Randel completed the ongoing work to which Morris alluded and drew the required maps, which were signed and presented four months later. In the meantime, as the Commissioners insisted, Randel was hired by the city to do the great amount "yet to be done on the ground," which would take him most of the next decade.

On December 11, Randel was out at Morrisania on "Manhattan Comm[ission]" business. He was back again on the fourteenth with an unnamed city surveyor, and again on the nineteenth, the twenty-first (possibly), the twenty-second, and the twenty-seventh, a rare session that proceeded from morning to night. This is more concentrated time than Morris spent in nearly four years with his fellow Commissioners or Randel (whose name in successive diary entries Morris wrote as Randall, Randal, and Randell before happening on the correct spelling). By then, Morris was happy to see Randel go: "I am and have been for some Days," Morris told his diary on the twenty-eighth, "indisposed by Indigestion and Constipation." In the opening three months of 1811, Morris was busy with canal and other business. He and Randel and either of the other Commissioners did not meet again until late March, when they officially submitted their map and accompanying remarks.

If the grid was chosen on November 29, 1810, how much information went into that decision? When the Commissioners' Plan and remarks were made public in late March 1811, only thirty of the then 1,600 intended monuments had been placed. Of those thirty, over half of them were below what would become 16th Street, the rest widely scattered but only as far north as 125th Street. The vast majority of the thirty were placed along existing streets, primarily the Bowery and the line of Manhattan Avenue that the Commissioners would call Fifth Avenue. All of these monuments apparently were placed after November 29, part of "the operations now going on" that Morris obliquely referred to in his letter to the Common

Council, further suggesting that when the Commissioners made their decision they hadn't decided very much.

Many years later, Randel incidentally provided some insight. In May 1857 he participated in a legal proceeding, not in his by then usual role as plaintiff or defendant but as expert witness. The case involved the valuation of a parcel of property the city was claiming for Central Park. Randel, then living in Maryland, had been a neighbor of one of the property owners a number of years earlier. In the course of his testimony over two days, Randel provided some details of his first three years of Manhattan surveying. Though it was nearly half a century after the fact and he was nearly seventy years old, Randel's testimony was clear and under oath. Randel by then had his lost his wealth but not his mind.

Beginning in mid-1808, Randel testified, he led surveys "with a view to ascertain the most eligible grounds for the intended Streets and Avenues, and with reference to sites least obstructed by buildings, roads, improvements, rocks, precipices, steep grades, and other obstacles." He submitted maps of his findings "for the use of [the] Commissioners at their meetings, from which, after examination, they gave me further instructions as to what should next be done. This proceeded until the fall of 1810, when the Commissioners began to decide as to certain Streets and Avenues, in the plan to be adopted." So there we go. For Randel's three surveying seasons, the Commissioners were contemplating a street layout that worked around natural and built obstacles. In the fall of 1810, quite possibly on November 29, given that their previous meeting was in June, they "began to decide" what to do. Randel continued: having "pretty much determined" their plan that fall, the Commissioners "ordered certain cross lines and lines for the Avenues to be specially examined and reported to them; and such of those lines as were adopted, were defined on the land by brownstone monuments, which were sunk in the ground by me." But we know that those monuments, the scattered thirty, actually defined very few lines. Counsel asked for clarification. "Witness says he means that only certain lines were adopted, which were experimental." Randel clarified: "The points only were fixed and indicated, so as to guide the surveyors, afterwards, in fixing and locating the Streets, on the ground, in accordance with the Commissioners' Report." In others words, the stones and the lines established before the Commissioners' map and remarks in March 1811 were nothing more than mere starting points for the real work during the coming decade. Only after Randel was done putting down those stones, presumably in December after the November 29 meeting, did an actual plan appear: "The Commissioners then decided that certain Streets and Avenues should be of certain widths, and the Avenues should be a certain distance from each other; and the Blocks between certain Streets should be of equal breadth." The great grid of New York, with its equally spaced streets, was born sometime in December 1810.

Even as their final decisions were made, the Commissioners knew their work was not really complete at all. As Randel observed in 1864, "The *time* within which the Commissioners were limited by the Statute to make their *Plan* of the streets, avenues, and public places on Manhattan [was] barely *sufficient* to enable them to comply with the *letter*, although not fully with the *spirit*, of the Statute." The italics are Randel's. Indeed, as he noted in 1816 in a field book, by 1811 "only a Plan of New York Island had yet been completed and not exceeding 30 monuments placed to designate upwards of 1600 intersections of Streets." Morris recommended to the Common Council that Randel be kept on after the expiration of the four-year Commission to make the soon-to-be-announced plan a reality. Randel made his contract with the city on December 31, 1810. So little actual work related to the plan had been completed that Randel spent the entire upcoming decade completing it.

Why does any of this matter? What difference does it make whether the Commissioners decided early in their tenure or in their final months what their plan would be? It matters when we add all the circumstances together, and determine how they arrived at the plan, to put a value on it. Was it the greatest grid, for which the Commissioners and their surveyor have been lauded (or condemned) for two centuries? Or was and is it an excuse for a plan, arrived at with little thinking and with time running out, based conveniently on an existing plan already on the ground, the Goerck Common Lands grid of 1796? Surely the Commissioners would explain this when they delivered their plan in March 1811.

CHAPTER 8

A GRID IS BORN

[A] City is to be composed principally of the Habitations of men, and . . . strait sided and right-angled Houses are the most cheap to build and the most convenient to live in.

—Remarks of the Commissioners, 1811

Such plans fitted nothing but a quick parcelling of the land, a quick conversion of farmsteads into real estate, and a quick sale.

—Lewis Mumford, *The City in History*, 1961

The street plan . . . had only the dubious merit of the most childish regularity and of devoting the maximum proportion of area to building sites. Every consideration of economy of intercommunication, future financial economy, sanitation, healthfulness and aesthetics was absolutely left out of the reckoning.

—Julius Harder, "The City's Plan," 1898

THE WINTER OF 1810–1811 was brutal for Gouverneur Morris. It began in December with indigestion and constipation and ended in March with gout, afflictions that kept him in bed, in severe pain, or otherwise indisposed for days on end. He also had to write an important report by a state commission of which he was the head. The report had to be carefully crafted, with extensive surveying and other practical details and reasoned, even passionate argument to engage public and political support. When Morris was done, it ran to dozens of manuscript pages, with the artful style and manifest wisdom for which Morris had been known since his work on the nation's Constitution decades earlier. It was, after all, a report eagerly anticipated throughout the state and the nation. This document was the first report of the year-old commission on the Erie Canal. Morris delivered it to the state senate on March 2. Three weeks later, he delivered to the New York City Common Council his report on the city's future street plan. Four years in the making, the report was eleven pages long. It was not so much a report as an excuse for one.

"The Commissioners of Streets and Roads in the City of New York," it began, "Remark on the Map hereunto annexed." Remark? The only words of explanation for their great grid plan were remarks, handed in along with the map, titled "A Map of the City of New York." The remarks were written by Morris but mostly devoid of his characteristic articulation. Half of them were merely geographic instructions that read as if prepared by someone else, perhaps surveyor Randel, as a key to the accompanying map. The meat of the remarks is contained in just a few paragraphs—not much explanation for what today is considered the iconic plan of American urbanism. Shortly after handing in the map and remarks, Morris was bedridden for three weeks with gout. Neither he nor DeWitt nor Rutherfurd ever commented on what they had done, as if they were happy to be clear of it.

The first remark of the Commissioners is a running excuse:

As soon as they could meet and take the Oath prescribed they entered on the duties of their office and employed persons to make Surveys of Manhattan Island, which they personally reconnoitered so as to acquire the general Information needful to the correct Prosecution of their Work, which has been much delayed by the Difficulty of procuring competent Persons on those oeconomical Terms which they prescribed to themselves and by Seasons peculiarly unfavorable.

I count four excuses here: the Commissioners met "as soon as they could" and their work was then delayed by incompetence, expense, and bad weather. It is true that it took the Commissioners nearly three months after the passage of the 1807 law to meet for the first time. It is also true that they hired the minimally competent Charles Loss as their first chief surveyor. Until these remarks, though, there had been no suggestion of compensation issues; the city had paid all surveying fees and associated costs. And, while the weather was often bad and Morris complained about it in his letter the previous November to the Common Council, there's nothing in weather records to suggest that the surveying seasons were "peculiarly unfavorable." In all, then, two excuses for the Commissioners' own actions and two of questionable validity. As Benjamin Franklin (supposedly) said, "He that is good for making excuses is seldom good for anything else."

The next remark, in one long paragraph, is the meat of the matter:

One of the first objects which claimed their attention was the Form and Manner in which the Business should be conducted; that is to say, whether they should confine themselves to rectilinear and rectangular Streets, or whether they should adopt some of those supposed Improvements by Circles, Ovals, and Stars, which certainly embellish a plan whatever may be their

Effect as to Convenience and Utility. In considering that subject they could not but bear in mind that a City is to be composed principally of the Habitations of men, and that strait sided and right-angled Houses are the most cheap to build and the most convenient to live in. The Effect of these plain and simple Reflections was decisive.

This morsel has been chewed over for generations by grid thinkers, like Chaplin's tramp making the most of his Thanksgiving boot. Without expressly saying so, the Commissioners were rejecting the sort of plan that L'Enfant had made for the nation's capital, opting for cheapness and convenience. "They even, by their own showing, rose to the height of considering the claims of what they believed to be the beautiful," wrote a later historian, "before they decided upon giving place to the useful alone."

Morris also, without saying so, was opting for the language of James Jay from December 1806. "[A] person of judgment and taste," Jay had written, "will find no difficulty in laying out streets, squares, crescents, circuses [sic] and other figures." Now, Morris, who was appointed just weeks later, rejected such "supposed improvements [as] circles, ovals and stars." Jay had insisted that "these forms of building, when judiciously laid out, not only embellish a city, but increase the value of the ground on which they are erected." Morris, as if working with Jay's letter in front of him, admits these forms "certainly embellish a plan" but concludes that value resides not in irregular building forms but in right angles only. It's hard to know why he thought so, but it certainly was convenient to use the rectilinear shapes of Goerck's Common Lands.

"Having determined, therefore, that the work in general should be rectangular," the Commissioners next considered if they should "amalgamate it with the plans already adopted by individuals as not to make any important changes in their dispositions." This "might render the work more generally acceptable" and less expensive.

It was therefore a favorite object with the Commissioners, and pursued until after various unsuccessful attempts had proved the extreme difficulty, nor was it abandoned at last but from necessity. To show the obstacles which frustrated every effort can be of no use. It will perhaps be more satisfactory to each person who may feel aggrieved to ask himself whether his sensations would not have been still more unpleasant had his favorite plans been sacrificed to preserve those of a more fortunate neighbor.

So the Commissioners considered fitting their rectilinear plan into existing plans, like the Kips Bay grid, but abandoned the effort "at last but from necessity." Morris deemed it unnecessary—"of no use"—to explain, and played neighbor off against neighbor. In fact, there were very few developments like Kips Bay, but there were hundreds if not thousands of property lines, and the Commissioners' grid violated every one of them, except, for the most part, the lines established by Goerck's Common Lands grid. The remarks do not mention the Common Lands, making the Commissioners' Plan seem like a bold creation of their own. Which it was not. In this important remark, Morris is artfully employing his craft. He had done it most famously a quarter century earlier with the Constitution, creating its lyrical "We the People" preamble from a clunky draft that presented the listed states, not the American people, as the Constitution's makers. Morris's preamble brought clarity to a unified nation. The fourth paragraph of his remarks explaining the constitution of Manhattan's future landscape threw a haze over the whole affair. The next brief paragraph spread it thickly: "If it should be asked why was the present plan adopted in preference to any other, the answer is, because, after taking all circumstances into consideration, it appeared to be the best; or, in other and more proper terms, attended with the least inconvenience."

So the plan was adopted because it was "the best," which is to say no more than it was the easiest. To say that the easiest was "the best" says very little and hardly answers the question why. It's like *(Founding) Father Knows Best*, or to the child asking "Why?" the parent replying, "Because I say so." For whom was it convenient to ignore every property line on the island (except most Common Lands' lines), erase the Post Road, Broadway, and every other of two dozen or so existing north-south and cross roads? Certainly not for their owners and users. The convenience was entirely the Commissioners', who had run out of time to concern themselves with the concerns of most everybody else.

And that's it for explanation of the plan generally. There were no explanations for the spacing of the avenues, none for the spacing of the streets, or for their sizing. The 1807 law asked for avenues not less than sixty feet wide and streets not less than fifty. The Commissioners delivered one-hundred-foot avenues and sixty-foot streets, with an assortment of one-hundred-foot streets. Goerck's Middle Road was one hundred feet wide, his streets sixty feet. How convenient! The Middle Road had a parallel road 920 feet distant on either side—convenient for the Commissioners' central avenues. To the east, more random spacing; to the west, regular spacing, none of it explained.

As to the fifteen wide streets—14th, 23rd, 34th, 42nd, 57th, 72nd, 79th, 86th, 96th, 106th, 116th, 125th, 135th, 145th, and 155th—there is also no explanation, and their locations have perplexed grid ponderers ever since. Though only three of them—57th, 72nd, and 79th—were laid through Goerck's Common Lands, those three did cause increasing inconvenience with the Common Lands model above 57th Street by throwing off owners' property lines. In fact, as we'll see in a bit, the opening of streets above 42nd (the old Steuben Street) would be delayed until 1836, when a law established a method for compensating Common Lands owners whose land was turned to slivers by streets. But still, for whatever reason, the Commissioners decided on fifteen wide streets. To place none of them within the Common Lands would have required explanation,

explanation that would have forced them to acknowledge their use of the Common Lands plan.

From 86th Street north, the wide streets are in two regular patterns—on the sixes and then the fives—so we can discern a certain, if seemingly arbitrary, rationale. Certain of the lower wide streets were tied to other aspects of the plan to be discussed shortly, and arguably to certain natural features, but others are seemingly inexplicable. Take 72nd Street, for example. It seems that 71st Street would have been a much better choice.

Much of what became 71st already existed as Harsen's Road, a country lane from the Eastern Post Road across the island all the way to its intersection with Bloomingdale Road at the settlement of Harsenville. Because Harsen's Road was a well-established cross-island route, no houses or other structures were built in its path, and it served as a dividing line between properties, through the Common Lands and further west. Instead, the Commissioners chose 72nd Street, a line that had over a dozen structures on it, including the prominent estate house of the late John Broome, just west of Bloomingdale Road. Nearly half of these structures would have survived if 72nd Street was sixty feet wide and not a hundred. For whatever reason, 72nd was convenient for the Commissioners and especially inconvenient for many others.

The 1811 plan was not an *entirely* unbroken grid. Under the 1807 law, the Commissioners were asked (but not required) to lay out "public squares," in number, size, and orientation as they saw fit. In 1811, having decided on the unitary grid, they scattered across it a grudging baker's half-dozen of public places, all rectilinear within the confines of the grid: a Market Place (7th to 10th Streets, First Avenue to the East River); a Parade for military exercises (23rd to 34th, Third to Seventh Avenues); Bloomingdale Square (53rd to 57th, Eighth to Ninth); Hamilton Square (66th to 68th, Fifth to Third); Manhattan Square (77th to 81st, Eighth to Ninth); Observatory (or Reservoir) Place (89th to 94th, Fifth to Fourth); and Haerlem Square

(117th to 121st, Sixth to Seventh). (The Commissioners also noted but left ungridded Haerlem Marsh, 106th to 109th, Fifth Avenue to the East River, a wetlands that defied filling and gridding until 1837.)

The total space of these public or purposed places claimed a very small portion of the future city's grid: less than 400 acres, or less than 5 percent of the grid. The Parade claimed 240 acres, and the six others just under 160 acres between them. "It may to many be a matter of surprise," Morris wrote in the remarks,

> that so few vacant spaces have been left, and those so small, for the benefit of fresh air and consequent preservation of health. Certainly if the city of New York was destined to stand on the side of a small stream such as the Seine or the Thames, a great number of ample places might be needful. But those large arms of the sea which embrace Manhattan Island render its situation, in regard to health and pleasure as well as to the convenience of commerce, peculiarly felicitous.

Felicitous perhaps for the Commissioners, who in the salty embrace of the island's bordering waters could spend little time and effort planning public spaces.

As the decades ensued, all of the Commissioners' would-be open places were overrun in whole or large part by the advancing grid. By 1815, the intended Market was legislated from fifty-one acres down to sixteen, the Parade from 240 to ninety. The Market was later whittled to today's ten-acre Tompkins Square Park, which with its boisterous recent history honors its namesake Daniel D. Tompkins, onetime governor and vice president who might have been president but for "his habits of intemperance." The Parade was eliminated altogether in 1829, though a vestigial then-undeveloped seven acres were rescued in 1837 for Madison Square. Its step-cousin, Union Square, did not exist in the Commissioners' Plan. The location was an "irregular trapezium" formed by the complicated intersection of Broadway, the Bowery, various new streets, and Fourth Avenue, whose origin was not down at the statutory baseline like the other new avenues but "lost in Union place." "Its central position," Morris wrote, "requires an opening for the benefit of fresh air; the union of so many large roads demands space for security and convenience, and the morsels into which it would be cut by continuing across it the several streets and avenues would be of little use of value." In other words, the Commissioners didn't quite know what to do about the intersection that over time evolved into the formal small park it is today.

Of the Commissioners' other open spaces, only Manhattan Square survives (today as the campus of the American Museum of Natural History), only because it was officially appended in 1874 to Central Park, the grid's originally unimagined saving grace.

After anticipating that people might be surprised at the few open spaces, Morris also acknowledged that indeed "it may be a matter of surprise" that the Commissioners had quit at 155th Street. He had given a hint of this back in November, that "only [so much] of the island . . . may . . . become part of the city in the course of ages." In earlier years, Morris had anticipated the entire island becoming city. Why quit three miles short now? Morris sought to explain. The Commissioners

> have in this respect been governed by the shape of the ground. It is not improbable that considerable numbers may be collected at [the village of] Haerlem before the high hills to the southward of it shall be built upon as a city; and it is improbable that (for centuries to come) the grounds north of Harlem Flat will be covered with houses. To have come short of the extent laid out might therefore have defeated just expectations; and to have gone further might have furnished materials to the pernicious spirit of speculation.

The Commissioners' Plan, of course, led to decades of *real estate* speculation throughout the grid; precisely such speculation made already wealthy fur merchant John Jacob Astor the richest

American by the 1840s. It's quitting their gridding at 155th that leads to a different sort of speculation. Did they stop counting at 155 because they couldn't imagine the need for 220, as there eventually would be? Or, with the clock ticking, did the Commissioners trim their sails and keep to the south of the island's rockiest highlands, which would require more thought than their simple grid?

And that's it for the Commissioners' remarks. Over half of the document simply describes street, avenue, and open space placements that are otherwise evident on Randel's map. The portion that purportedly offers explanation mostly generates questions, which none of the Commissioners or Randel ever answered.

As to Randel's 1811 map itself, it required another decade of surveys to turn into a reality. The 1811 map, for example, contains only sixteen elevations for the entire island. By comparison, his subsequent surveying, which generated over ninety maps that if laid together would measure fifty feet by eleven feet, derived some six hundred elevations. Of the original sixteen elevations, only four— along 34th Street at Third, Fifth, Eighth, and Tenth Avenues— survived on the later maps. Clearly, very little science went into the 1811 plan. This makes the revered map not so much a plan as a notion. Still, unlike the *Annie Hall* Hollywood partygoer whose reality was abstraction—"Right now it's only a notion, but I think I can get money to make it into a concept . . . and later turn it into an idea"—the 1811 map was real and legally binding. It just needed time to turn it into a city.

After the Commissioners signed off on their plan in March 1811, none of them had anything more to do with it, and in all of their remaining years they wrote nothing about it. Randel, as we know, would remain with it for another decade, and late in life would offer some commentary on it. He told us, as we've seen, that the time the Commissioners were allocated was "barely *sufficient* to enable them to comply with the *letter*, although not fully with the *spirit*" of their duties. He also told us, in 1864, a bit more about the plan's specifics as they were known in 1811. The plan indicated "the width of all the streets and avenues and the spaces between some of the avenues . . . *without locating* the whole of any one of the avenues permanently *upon the ground* and . . . establishing on the ground *only one point* in some part of 16 out of the 155 streets." In other words, sixteen streets had a single physical placement, but without a second physical placement for each, there was no actual line marked for any of those sixteen streets. The other 139 were supposed to fit somewhere in relation to those sixteen. Even 155th Street, which the Commissioners remarked was "the most northern of those which it was thought at all needful to lay out as part of the city of New York," was placed physically with no more specificity than it "runs from Bussing's Point [on the Harlem River] to Hudson's River." The northernmost physically marked street was 153rd, the southern side of which "touches the northern side of the ten-mile stone on the Kingsbridge road, at the surface of the earth." Which is to say, the location of 153rd Street had not been determined by Randel at all but by whoever placed the tenth in the island's first series of milestones along the Post Road before the Revolution (in 1769 to be exact)!

In fact, the northernmost street for which Randel by 1811 had obtained even a single physical position was 125th. No wonder that the best Morris could muster in his remarks is that the spacing between streets was "in general about two hundred feet." As Randel put it in 1864, all the Commissioners in 1811 could say was that the space between streets "should be of *equal breadth*, without specifying the breadth of any of those spaces, or *locating any of those streets permanently upon the ground*." Once Randel got down to actual surveying during the ensuing decade, the streets he physically placed would range in distance between each other, as they do now, from 181 to nearly 212 feet. The only streets below 125th that came out actually 200 feet apart were—surprise—the thirty from 42nd to 71st, that is, the segment of Manhattan laid out a generation earlier by Casimir Goerck!

The point here is not that the Commissioners were dramatically off in their 1811 estimate of 200 feet per block; the average of all the blocks *is* about 200 feet. The point is that it was an estimate, based on very little if any surveying that actually pertained to the grid. The plan announced in 1811 was simply not something that had been deeply thought out. It was "a quick solution to a difficult problem," one modern grid student has suggested, by "apathetic authors, who simply overlaid Manhattan with eight miles of uncompromising grid."

What if the "great grid" of Manhattan is not the enlightened vision of Founding Father Gouverneur Morris and surveying eminence Simeon DeWitt but their lazy aggrandizement of obscure Casimir Goerck? None of the Commissioners offered a word of explanation about their grid, but Morris did understand imperfect choices. "In adopting a republican form of government," he famously observed in 1803, "I not only took it as a man does his wife, for better or worse, but what few men do with their wives, I took it knowing all its bad qualities."

Among the many detractors of the Commissioners who rose up over the generations, local historian Thomas Janvier despaired of the "deplorable results" of "the excellently dull gentlemen." They simply had botched it. "Unfortunately, the promise of this farsighted undertaking was far from being fulfilled in its performance. The magnificent opportunity which was given to the Commissioners to create a beautiful city simply was wasted and thrown away," Janvier wrote in 1894. "Thinking only of utility and economy . . . in the simplest and dullest way . . . their Plan fell so far short of what might have been accomplished by men of genius governed by artistic taste." Yet Janvier, unlike many grid detractors, also recognized "they were surcharged with the dullness and intense utilitarianism of the people and the period whereof they were a part." This explains why the grid when it was announced seemed to shock few and only slowly made lifelong enemies.

CHAPTER 9

GETTING SQUARE WITH RIGHT-ANGLED LIVING

The whole island has been surveyed and framed into
extensive avenues and commodious streets, forming an
important legacy to posterity, from which the most solid
advantages may be anticipated.

—*Citizens and Strangers Guide*, 1814

And young New York, from that time on, grew like a
child in an orthopaedic corset.

—Jean Schopfer, *The Architectural Record*, 1902

THE YEAR 1811 was a fearful one in America. The nation stum-
bled toward an armed, ill-conceived rematch with the British, a
"Great Comet" aroused increasingly nervous fascination as the year
progressed, and in December the first in a series of massive quakes
along the Mississippi River ruptured confidence from Missouri to
the Atlantic states. Impressionable American minds were primed
for unsettling, extraordinary things. Many found it in "A Solemn
Warning to All the Dwellers Upon Earth . . . That the Certain
Destruction of One Third of Mankind, As Foretold by the Scrip-
tures, Must Take Place on the Fourth Day of June, in the Year of

our Lord 1812." That thirty-one page pamphlet was the product of visionary Virginian (and suspected horse thief) Nimrod Hughes. His warning was published in May 1811. By midsummer, it was a best-seller. By winter, newspapers were warning readers away from the obviously "false prophet." Early in 1812, Nimrod Hughes attracted his first lampooner, the presumably pseudonymous pamhleteer "Nicodemus Havens, cordwainer of New York City." In Havens's "Wonderful Vision . . . Wherein he was Presented with a View of the Situation of the World, After the Dreadful Fourth of June 1812 and Shewing What Part of New York Is To Be Destroyed," a great earthquake spawns a storm of smoke, fire, and flood that over-whelms the world and Manhattan. While Nimrod had been heavy on scripture and vague on logistics, Nicodemus mapped out the devastation from Paris to London and on to New York, where the convulsion lasted five hours and twenty-three minutes, and claimed 1,408 houses and 125,000 inhabitants (25,000 more than actually populated the city). "Whole families were enclosed within its horrid grasp, and whole streets in this flourishing city, swallowed together [and] fabrics which had stood the test of ages, where [sic] no longer to be seen; all had been engulphed in the dreadful ruin." Indeed, all of Old New York—streets and landmark structures—were swept away: from Broad Street to the Bowery and the newly completed City Hall, though the tumbling steeple of St. Paul's Church diverted the torrent, saving the lives of one Mr. John Edwards, scale beam maker, and one Mr. A. Broad, carpet weaver. Others benefitted as well: "The price of shaving actually advanced by a third" and "Law-yers and Doctors [saw] plenty of business, but no abatement in fees." They and other survivors then submit to a global theocracy and live happily ever after.

The "Wonderful Vision of Nicodemus Havens" is considered the first in the now long line of New York City destruction fanta-sies. Whoever the actual author was—there was no Nicodemus Havens, cordwainer or not, in New York—he (or she) wrote with a New Yorker's intimate knowledge of the city's physical and social geography. A person with such awareness would certainly have been aware in early 1812 of the then nearly year-old plan to lay out a new city beyond the limits of the old. Ironically or perhaps not, the first vision of New York's *destruction* comes at the same time as New York's great new plan of *construction*.

The greatest historian of Manhattan, I. N. Phelps Stokes, telling New York's story in a half dozen doorstop volumes published a century ago, arrived at 1811 sighing: "We have now reached the point where the old city, which had grown up at haphazard, with crooked streets, wooded hills, and fertile valleys traversed by streams and winding country roads, begins to be absorbed into a new city, in which antiquity and nature are no longer respected, with streets laid out in accordance with a carefully considered, symmetrical plan." Like many New Yorkers before and after, Stokes was not a fan:

> Unfortunately, this plan, although possessing the merits of simplicity and directness, lacked entirely the equally essential elements of variety and picturesqueness, which demand a large degree of respect for the natural conformation of the land. The new plan was entirely deficient in sentiment and charm, and with its gradual development, little by little, the individuality, the interest, and the beauty of one choice spot after another have been swept away [until] scarcely anything remains to remind us of the primitive beauty and the fascinating diversity of natural charms which we know Manhattan once possessed. The year 1811 marks the end of the little old city and the beginning of the great modern metropolis.

As if to cosmically pause and contemplate all these doings, the city and the nation suddenly took three years off for war. Together with the lingering effects of Jefferson's devastating 1807 trade embargo, this caused the city poised for greatness to have an episode of arrested development. From 1810 to 1816, its population increased by just 4,200, an average of seven hundred a year, after a decade in which the population had increased by nearly 4,000 a year. Yet the signs of urbanization were clear. In the depths of winter wartime stagnation, the city's first soup kitchen, organized by concerned citizens, not their government, opened on February 1, 1816, serving 1,200 people the first day and, by March, some 6,600 people daily. The numbers of needy New Yorkers has varied ever since but, emblematic of the city's transition from overgrown town to industrialized city, a permanent class of impoverished people had been born.

During the 1810s, the grid developed slowly. Avenues were opened—Third starting in 1812, Eighth in 1816—but few streets. As we know, the plan when it was announced in 1811 was a project with an overview diagram at best, with no construction plans. There was a gigantic map of the island overlaid with a grid, but there were no markers or practical maps showing exactly where each street was supposed to go and, equally important, which buildings, streams, ponds, marshes, hills, and valleys were in the way.

John Randel at twenty-three, with a battalion of assistants at his service, was now entirely in charge. After three years under the Commissioners, he would serve over three times as long for the city directly. The Commissioners selected the grid's design and Randel drew it up for them in 1811; now he prepared it for the market. By the time he was done nearly a decade later, Randel would mark exactly 1,647 intersections of future streets and avenues, 1,549 of them with three-foot-high, rectangular white marble monuments where the terrain allowed, and ninety-eight with iron rods where solid rock prevailed. And he would produce ninety-two small-scale maps that have obtained a near biblical place in the city's archival history. The so-called Randel Farm Maps record in exquisite color and detail every natural and artificial feature of the existing island, overlaid in a graceful but firm hand with the future grid that would

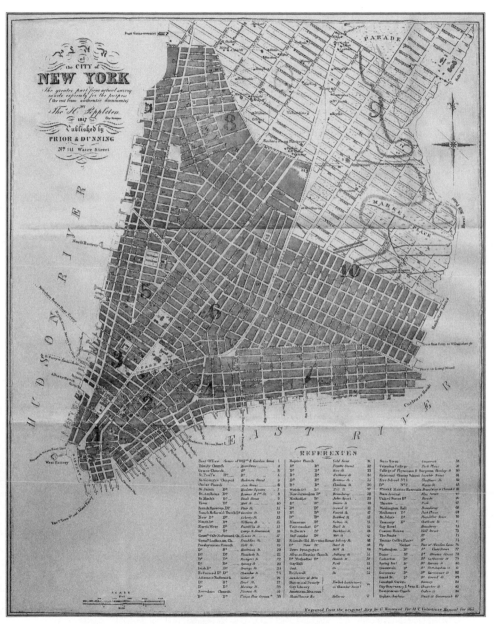

This 1817 map, engraved for the 1855 *Valentine's Manual* from the original drawn by city surveyor Thomas H. Poppleton, clearly depicts the southern boundary of the 1811 Commissioners' Plan. The shaded area shows the pre-grid city (more or less accurately); the unshaded area shows the avenues, streets, and public spaces of the lower portion of the intended grid plan, very little of which actually existed in 1817.

vanquish them. Randel's atlas reveals New York's transition from naturalistic variety to civilized unity.

Randel's decade creating the farm maps was essential for implementing the 1811 master plan because that plan was the most amorphous of great creations. It was not a proposed bridge or a canal with structural design images that communicated an anticipated finished appearance. It was a dense two-dimensional crosshatch of straight lines, with no third dimension suggesting either the varied natural topography or how structures might rise from it and give it texture and shape. It expressed the city's exclusive and total control over its island, but when it was announced in 1811, there was practically no public reaction. On paper and at first impression, the grid looked like an abstract concept, not a physical reality. Unlike a bridge or a canal, the grid was proclaimed in 1811 without a schedule for the building of its components or a completion date. In the beginning, it was just inked lines on a large page that very few people saw and scattered markers on the ground. At some undetermined time, enough of it would be built for people to begin to see a grid and understand that it would not stop until it had conquered Manhattan.

The people who felt it first were those whose lands Randel and his team entered for the definitive surveys and marking of future intersections. And much of that feeling was rising resentment: "In 1812 & 1813, several measurement and transit pegs were destroyed which he replaced by remeasuring," Randel reported (in the third person) in 1816. "In 1814 pegs were destroyed to a considerable amount. In 1815 the pegs were destroyed to such an alarming degree as almost to discourage him from ever completing the work." Not just temporary pegs but the heavy marble monuments were unearthed and destroyed. The Common Council dutifully covered Randel's additional costs for repeated surveys and replaced pegs and monuments.

Randel persevered, with a large staff that included his younger brother William as one of several assistant surveyors and some three

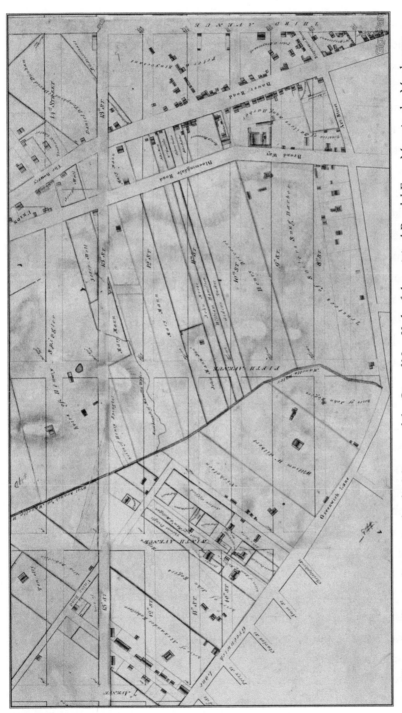

This image, from a digitization by the Museum of the City of New York of the original Randel Farm Maps in the Manhattan Borough President's Office, illustrates how the Manhattan grid was far from a plan for a virgin land. Here at the central southern edge of the grid, as elsewhere on the island, existing property lines far outnumber and diverge from the lines of streets and avenues that will replace them.

dozen others. He also spent thousands of his own dollars designing instruments with metals that did not change size in varying
temperatures, allowing for very precise measurements. "After all
the monuments and bolts were set in their proper places," he wrote
(again in the third person) many years later, "the whole work was
tested by him, at his own cost, with another instrument, invented by
him for the purpose—and re-transiting and re-measuring the same
from monument to monument, so as to prevent the *possibility of
error*; and, of course no error has, ever been found in any part of the
whole work." As Simeon DeWitt, an unimpeachable judge on such
matters, attested in 1823, Randel's work "was done with an accuracy
not exceeded, I am confident, by any work of the kind in America."

In 1821, Randel completed his maps, which provided the necessary working plans for the physical implementation of the grid plan.
By then, the physical opposition to his efforts in the field was history
and the beginnings of several avenues were laid, but the first philosophical opposition had been published. The Commissioners were
"men . . . who would have cut down the seven hills of Rome," wrote
an anonymous pamphleteer in 1818. "We live under a tyranny, with
respect to the rights of property, which . . . no monarch in Europe
would dare to exercise . . . it is a tyranny of the worst kind; for it is
under the sanction of laws which shield those who exercise it from
being called to legal account. It is time for all who are interested to
arouse, and to unite themselves for the maintenance and preservation of their rights."

The call to arms, "A Plain Statement, addressed to the Proprietors of Real Estate, in the City and County of New-York," signed
by "A Landholder," ran to sixty printed pages. As the identity of the
pamphleteer quickly became known—it wasn't hard to figure out—
it also became clear that he did not write from a position of selfless
civic-mindedness. The author, it turned out, was patrician scholar
Clement Clarke Moore, whose Chelsea estate was under attack by
the grid.

The image that tells this book's stories, as described in the Introduction. In this circa 1883 photograph looking south from the roof of a new mansion on Fourth (soon Park) Avenue at 94th Street, we see both the hard, new rectilinear world (on the horizontal and vertical planes in street and building forms) and the resistance to it (in the ephemeral footpaths through the dirt of the empty but soon filled lot). Magic city, mystic paths. (*Museum of the City of New York*)

So many Aaron Burr (1756–1836) activities end in ambiguity, including his role in the street planning of New York. He figures prominently in the fortunes of Joseph Mangin and Joseph Browne, for whom (along with Casimir Goerck) no image exists. This 1802 portrait gives a sense of what they had to deal with. (*New-York Historical Society*)

Gouverneur Morris (1752–1816), in his May 1810 wedding portrait, just after he was named to run the important commission that would consume his final years: the one to create New York State's Erie Canal, not plan New York City's future streets. (*Frick Art Reference Library*)

Simeon DeWitt (1756–1834; here in 1804) was a prolific surveyor and town planner for sixty years but the record of his actual work on the 1807 Manhattan street commission is relatively thin. (*Zimmerli Art Museum, Rutgers University*)

John Rutherfurd (1760–1840), content New Jersey landsman and indifferent 1807 commissioner. (*Zimmerli Art Museum, Rutgers University*)

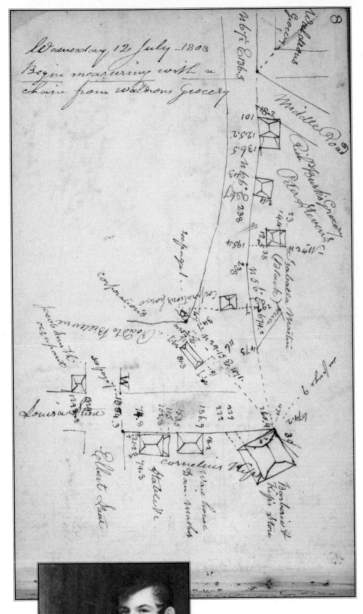

This page from one of Randel's field books records the beginnings of his surveys for the 1807 Commissioners. The area is today's Park Avenue South around 28th Street. Note the confused date: July 12, 1808, was a Tuesday, not a Wednesday. (*New-York Historical Society*)

The only identified image of John Randel Jr. (1787–1865), from a catalogue photograph of an undated, unattributed painting auctioned in 1980 and since unaccounted for. An appropriate state of affairs perhaps for the rigorous young Manhattan mapper and eventual obscurity. (*Sotheby's*)

The village of Manhattanville in 1834. The fence through the middle ground approximates the path of today's western end of 125th Street. City replaced country village long before the end of the century.

Fifth Avenue in 1847, looking south through as-yet ungridded countryside to the Croton Distributing Reservoir at 42nd Street. The Colored Orphan Asylum (at the future 44th Street) was burned down during Civil War draft riots; the reservoir was replaced in the 1890s by what is now the main branch of New York Public Library in the heart of Midtown Manhattan. (*Museum of the City of New York*)

In this lithograph from the 1859 *Valentine's Manual*, the gridded city approaches from the south, leveling the earth on its way, as Central Park rises up to confront it. (The small below-grade buildings in the center ground block the future intersection of 5th Avenue and 59th Street, now Central Park South.)

Pioneering landscape architect Frederick Law Olmsted (1822–1903; here in 1893). His decidedly naturalistic Central Park co-design ameliorated the rigidity of the grid.

Andrew Haswell Green (1820–1903; here in 1895) did his best to restrain the grid within its boundaries (with parks) and beyond (with a more naturalistic street layout above 155th Street). (*Museum of the City of New York*)

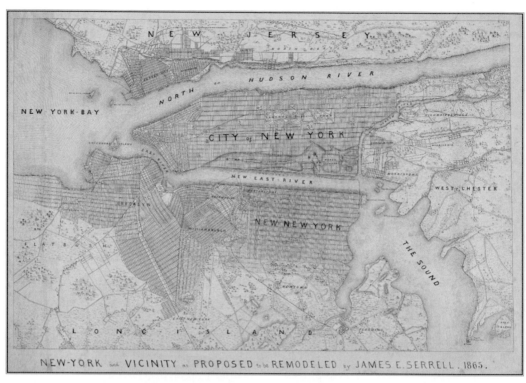

NEW-YORK and VICINITY as PROPOSED to be REMODELED by JAMES E. SERRELL. 1865.

James E. Serrell (1820–1892; here in 1876) was the first among a handful of men to propose enlarging Manhattan by filling in the East River, though his street plan of more unbroken grid was substantially less radical than the idea generally. (*New York Public Library*)

VIEW IN SIXTH AVENUE, BETWEEN 55TH & 57TH STS LOOKING WEST.

In this lithograph from the 1868 *Valentine's Manual*, Sixth Avenue is in transition from country to city: the hills have been reduced to squatter-topped outcrops; the corporate "filing-cabinet architecture" of the modern avenue is less than a century away.

In the same year, on Third Avenue at 46th Street, in a startling oil by Alessandro Mario titled "Give Us This Day Our Daily Bread," the chaos of city-building is well under way. (*New-York Historical Society*)

VIEW FROM SCHOOL HOUSE IN 42ND STREET BETWEEN 2ND & 3RD AVS LOOKING NORTH.

Another piece of changing Manhattan depicted in the 1868 *Valentine's Manual*: so-called Dutch Hill for the German immigrant squatters who will be displaced when the landscape has been flattened and the streets are fully laid.

The Brennan farmhouse, where Edgar Allan Poe wrote "The Raven" in 1844, photographed in 1879, after West 84th Street was cut through, taking the farm's hill and much of its surroundings with it. (*New-York Historical Society*)

Above, the hollow along 86th Street looking west from Eighth Avenue in 1880, as depicted in *Harper's New Monthly Magazine*, is a study in contrasts: farm fields that will be filled to support rows of lot-line dwellings, the first of which intervenes between the fields and the Ninth Avenue railway, opened through the area a year earlier. Below, from the same issue, an unnamed street where the remnants of the disappearing natural landscape for a time towered over the beginnings of grid-shaped housing.

A quick transition on West 70th Street, as depicted in *Harper's Weekly*. Above, the newly graded block between Eighth and Ninth Avenues, with ubiquitous short-lived squatter dwellings, in 1882. Below, the same block in 1896, when the avenues had been renamed Central Park West and Columbus, and the paved streets and sidewalks, street lamps, fire hydrants, and solid walls of lot-line buildings suggest an urban permanence that in reality was barely adolescent.

Alexander Hamilton's home, the Grange, on his 32-acre Manhattan estate, was completed in 1802. Above, in 1889, in its original location east of Tenth (Amsterdam) Avenue before the laying of 143rd Street. Below, after its move that year to 141st Street, stripped of its lands and grandeur, a decayed victim of the grid and its unnatural urban forms. In 2008, as a National Historic Landmark, Hamilton Grange was moved a few hundred feet to its current, comfortable, and happy location in St. Nicholas Park, the oldest building to get out of the grid's way and survive. (*Library of Congress*)

A notorious Hell's Kitchen tenement in 1890, featured in Jacob Riis's *How the Other Half Lives*, on 40th Street between Ninth and Tenth Avenues, with the last of a rocky outcrop dubbed Sebastopol (it was excavated into oblivion a few years later). The block, in a web of Lincoln Tunnel access ramps behind the Port Authority Bus Terminal, is not substantially more charming today.

In this circa 1890 view north from the roof of the Dakota apartments (opened 1884), between Central Park West and Columbus Avenue, the American Museum of Natural History (opened 1877) dominates Manhattan Square (77th to 81st Streets), one of the few 1811 Commissioners' Plan open space survivors because it was officially appended to Central Park in 1874. (*New-York Historical Society*)

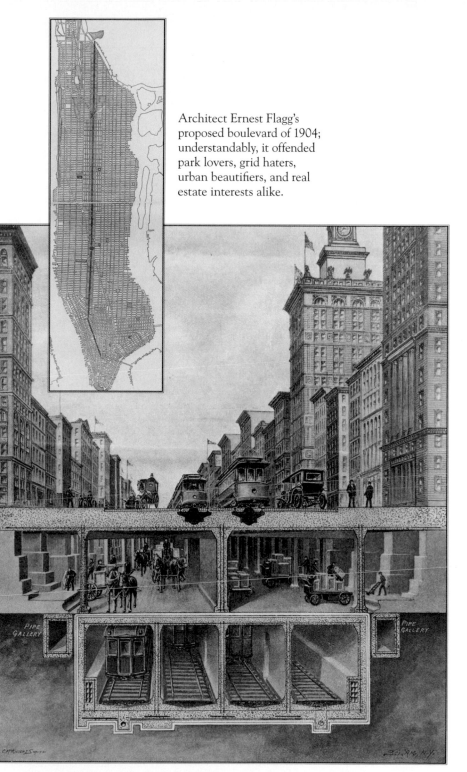

Architect Ernest Flagg's proposed boulevard of 1904; understandably, it offended park lovers, grid haters, urban beautifiers, and real estate interests alike.

A proposal for double-decked streets in the already congested street grid was front-page news in *Scientific American* in 1907; over the next quarter-century, as many as six-layer streets were proposed, linear fantasies that would only have compounded congestion as have their vertical cousins, increasingly taller buildings.

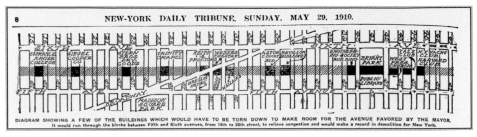

DIAGRAM SHOWING A FEW OF THE BUILDINGS WHICH WOULD HAVE TO BE TORN DOWN TO MAKE ROOM FOR THE AVENUE FAVORED BY THE MAYOR.
It would run through the blocks between Fifth and Sixth avenues, from 14th to 59th street, to relieve congestion and would make a record in demolition for New York.

In the spring of 1910, Mayor William Gaynor proposed a new avenue between Fifth and Sixth, from 14th Street to Central Park. That summer, Gaynor was shot, staggering him and his plan, and the many significant buildings in his avenue's way were spared.

A month before Gaynor was shot, real estate lawyer Wilber C. Goodale proposed this extraordinary roadway slashing through the grid from the Queensboro Bridge to Pennsylvania Station. Shown here, in the *New York Tribune*, to the intersection with Fifth Avenue at 51st Street, it would have continued south between Fifth and Sixth for ten blocks before turning diagonally through Broadway to the station. Goodale promoted variations of the idea (nonviolently) for several years before giving up.

MR. THOMSON'S PROPOSED PLAN

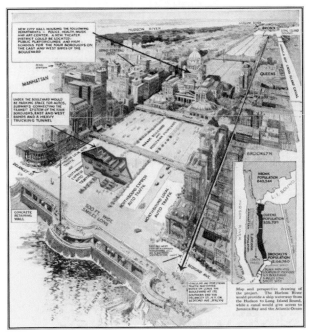

In this 1913 iteration, top left, of his many years of proposals to reshape the city (five-boro Greater New York after 1898), civil engineer T. Kennard Thomson (1864–1952), top right, substantially expanded James Serrell's original East River filling idea. Dapper traffic engineer John A. Harriss (1875–1938), bottom right, also had ideas for the East River, promoted in *Popular Science* in 1924, left: a 3,000-acre civic showplace that might have decongested the Manhattan grid by adding numerous north-south routes.

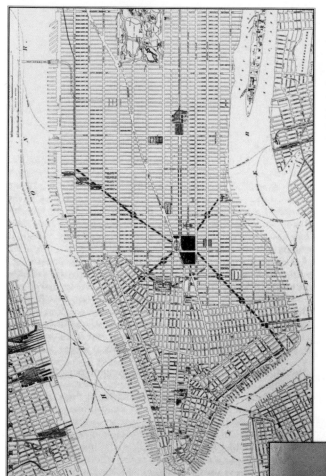

Architect Julius Harder's 1898 plan to introduce radials centered on Union Square. The modest proposal disappeared as surely as the paths in the dirt uptown.

Ludwig Hilberseimer's 1944 proposed redesign of the streets of congested Manhattan (and beyond), where "the central problem is not merely a technical but basically a structural one." A central belt of express and local highways would "attempt to ruralize the stony wastes of the city." Hilberseimer and other thinkers displaced from decivilized Europe imagined gradual implementation of their plans, but it's hard to imagine such radical restructuring without prior devastation.

Moore is mostly remembered now as the author of "A Visit from St. Nicholas," the now classic bit of whimsy originally written at Christmas 1822 for his children. In 1818, he was more concerned with Ninth Avenue, which was soon to be laid through the middle of his family's old estate, on high ground from the Fitzroy Road down to the Hudson, from the grid's 19th to 24th Streets. On the east, the grid's Eighth Avenue had begun replacing the winding Fitzroy Road in 1816. On the west, landfill would soon create Tenth Avenue from the river. "Our public authorities seem unwilling to depart from their levelling propensities," Moore wrote, "but proceed to cut up and tear down the face of the earth without the least remorse, and, apparently, with no higher notions of beauty and elegance than straight lines and flat surfaces placed at angles with the horizon, just sufficient to suffer the mud and water to creep quietly down their declivities."

Though he threatened legal action, Moore recognized that the legal basis for the grid plan was ironclad, and he ultimately would find greater and likelier satisfaction in joining the land value bonanza than fighting it. He kept the estate intact for many years despite the streets running through it but finally, in 1835, widowed and approaching sixty, he began subdividing Chelsea at great profit for his heirs into the neighborhood that retains the name. Moore remained in the estate house, between 22nd and 23rd Streets, west of Ninth Avenue, put a stone wall around it, and added a floor. But in February 1849, the ancient trees on the estate house grounds started coming down, to the horror of the old guard. "*There*, at least, is the original soil of Manhattan island; there stand the trees which were fanned by the free winds that swept over the bosom of the Hudson two hundred years ago," observed *The Knickerbocker* magazine, literary home of Irving, Cooper, and Longfellow, among many others.

With commendable spirit, the worthy proprietor declined the de-"grading" system which has brought the thoroughfares of

New-York to a dead level [and] built a massive stone wall to protect the home of his fathers and his "native soil." But what is he
now doing? It is a still morning; not a breath of air is abroad; but
as we live, there goes one of those old ancestral trees; and we
hear the sound of the fall thereof, "like the sound of the fall of
a mighty oak in the stillness of the woods." Eloquent author of
"Christmas" . . . tell those "hack"-men to disperse, go away, clear
out, and "get along!" Our malison on them!

Eloquent curses or not, the trees came down and eventually the
estate house itself. After the bluff overlooking the river had been
turned into Tenth Avenue, "it was thought advisable," Moore tren-
chantly noted, "if not absolutely necessary to dig down the whole
place, and throw it into the river."

Other landowners faced with streets laid through their acres
and anterooms were less literary and more litigious. Long legal battles were waged by many propertied Manhattanites, all to increasingly inevitable conclusions. In dozens of cases that began in the
1810s, some continuing for decades, all the litigants learned that
the grid map was not just a physical plan of right angles and street
dimensions but also a legal instrument that conveyed rights and
obligations.

Two questions that arose soon after the Commissioners handed
in their plan in 1811 and while Randel was beginning work on the
maps for its practical application were how streets should be opened
and paid for and how owners should be compensated for land
claimed by streets. These issues were often at the heart of landowner
disputes with the city. Landholders eventually realized that their
land was no longer uniquely theirs but pieces of a uniform plan ruled
by simple economics.

The 1807 law addressed the issue only generally. The city would
both determine damages to owners whose property was in the way
of streets and assess those owners for the benefits of street access to

the property, with both valuations appealable to the state supreme court. This might have been workable enough if the 1807 Commissioners had come up with a plan of relatively few streets. But they didn't, and before many streets could be opened, a substantial revision was necessary. By November 1811, the Common Council was developing its approach to the state legislature. In April 1813, the legislature replaced the original single clause with a comprehensive ten-page replacement that would guide street-making for the next half century.

In brief, when the city sought the opening of a street mandated by the 1811 plan, or property owners requested the city to do it, the state supreme court appointed a trio of "commissioners of appraisal and estimate" to determine both the value of the land to be taken from the landowner and the benefit of the new street to the landowner. These commissioners, who generally were local surveyors familiar with the territory and its residents or owners, could assign up to a third of the expected cost of opening the street to the city; the rest would come from the difference between benefit and damage to the landowners. The court reviewed the findings, either asking for revision or confirming them as "binding and conclusive."

This is what so galled many landowners, that streets were not public works to be built at the city's expense and the individual, as Moore put it, was "to become a capitalist for the public." But, of course, the city at the time had relatively little revenue to build public works on its own, although it would soon get richer from increasing real estate and other taxes. The legislature raised the city's share of street opening costs to 50 percent in 1869, when the city had developed into a complex (and during the Tweed era, massively corrupt) financial organism. It was another century before the local assessment regime was finally replaced by indirect general taxation.

And, of course, landowners who opposed the process wondered at the commissioners' "spirit of divination" in determining benefit and damage. But the complainers for the most part were the hereditary owners like Moore who saw the grid dividing their land. Land speculators for the most part were more willing to accept a substantial assessment in the short term for the long-term benefit of increased access and value.

But "opening" was just the first step in creating an actual city street. Opening meant that a desired street, or portion of one, had been legally enabled and the expected costs determined. Then the complicated part started: collecting the assessments from the property owners, who, as the months and even years passed, changed and often multiplied along increasingly desirable or speculative streets. Only after the money was collected was the street physically opened or "worked" and "regulated": cleared, excavated or filled, leveled, and paved. With the new Croton water supply in 1842 came the first major underground infrastructure—water pipes and sewers—that complicated street-making and maintaining.

Among the many aggravations even for compliant property owners who accepted the locations of streets was the level of those streets. While the grid plan was clear about where streets would be located *geographically*, it was silent on where they would be *topographically*. The street Commission was created and given executive power because everyone understood that the Common Council was not up to such assignments, yet when the Commission passed out of existence having provided only for street locations, it fell to the Council to determine street elevations. And, in typical fashion, after deciding at one meeting how high or low a street should be, the Council might decide at a subsequent meeting a different elevation. Landowners looking to build were left anxious about whether their street entrance would actually be at the street level.

Over time, the numerous appeals of assessments to the state supreme court—nearly all unsuccessful, especially those claiming the entire process was an unconstitutional taking of property— resulted in a body of decisions that mark the beginning of modern administrative law. Likewise, the volumes of assessment registers and associated documents formed the beginnings of the modern city's extensive archives. The city's modern bureaucracy traces back to the opening of the city's public water supply in 1842. The creation of the Street Department, appointed by the mayor, and acting independently of the Common Council, came along in 1849, adding substantially to the city's expanding bureaucracy.

In the meantime, the Common Council, empowered by state law, rigorously administered the city's street plan. When John Jacob Astor, already accumulating the real estate that would make his fortune, complained in late 1818 about assessments for avenues bordering his properties and threatened to take the matter to state court, the Council offered him no relief and he backed off. In early January 1819, Astor and other landowners threatened to seek legislative appointment of new commissioners to modify the plans for streets not yet opened. A Council committee countered with an aggression entirely new in the history of its street management. "The evils which would grow out of a measure that shall take from the Corporation the power of completing the plans for the permanent regulation of the Streets and Avenues on which so much time and money have been already expended and which are in some instances carried into effect, are incalculable." The seven-man committee featured plain-speaking Stephen Allen, an impoverished orphan who'd grown rich as a sailmaker before devoting himself to public service and who barely tolerated speculators like Astor. In 1832, as part of a major revision of the city government, Allen would become the city's first popularly elected mayor. Allen's committee suggested that the Council communicate immediately with the legislature to counteract Astor's gambit, and openly questioned Astor and friends' motives: "Were it not for the known intelligence and respectability of the gentlemen concerned [the committee] should be ready to attribute them to something more than public good or general utility." Again, Astor backed down. It was a remarkable moment. For generations, the government of the city had deferred to its landowners on the issue of streets. Now, the government talked down to them.

Of course, John Jacob Astor was a different sort of landowner. He was a German immigrant who owned land by buying it. Previous generations of owners to whom the government deferred were mostly hereditary landsmen. New York was a changing city in the 1810s. New rules applied. But they applied now to all landowners. In 1828, Peter Lorillard, of the thriving snuff and tobacco family established in the city in the 1760s, was incensed that the city was taking some of his property to extend Cedar Street from William to Pearl Streets, that is, far south of the purview of the 1807 street law and subsequent amendments. "These Laws were intended to apply to the improving of the *Grounds* in the outer part of the City & N York Island—but the laws have been made use of by Speculators to the cutting up Blocks of Improved property in the Lower part of the City," Lorillard wrote to Daniel Webster, the country's leading constitutional lawyer. The appraisal process, Lorillard claimed, had been corrupted as well. The state supreme court wasn't really making judicial nominations of appraisal commissioners; in practice, the Common Council street committee was selecting them and passing the names on to the court, which duly appointed them. "The manner in which the Commissioners have been named by the Common Council & appointed by the Sup[reme] Court has become so obnoxious & the effects of the appraisements of Damage & Benefit so obnoxious & ruinous to hundreds of persons here" that Lorillard was seeking Webster's services to test the constitutionality of the entire street law regime, up to the U.S. Supreme Court if possible. "I contend that my property is sacred & ought not to be taken from me except for Public Necessity—this is the point I shall contend at any reasonable expense." Lorillard, who owned 7,000 acres of New York state and could afford any expense, also questioned the constitutionality of the appraisal process: "Because owners of Land *cannot compel* witnesses to appear before the Commissioners or the Sup

Court to state the value of the property," the commissioners judged "solely, entirely & arbitrarily." Only a twelve-member jury "before whom Evidence can be lawfully brought" could make constitutional decisions on the taking (or not) of private property. Webster did not take the case and apparently didn't even respond, presumably aware that it would be a losing effort because, regardless of the appraisal issues, eminent domain was a well-established government right in the rest of America and the Western world, if only recently in Manhattan. Lorillard pressed on until his case finally burned out in state court in 1839. In the meantime, Cedar Street made its way from William to Pearl through Lorillard's property, as hundreds of other streets made their legal way through private land further up-island.

While the bitterest litigations dragged on with similar results into the 1840s, the grid settled on the land. In 1818, when Clement Clarke Moore objected, little grid had been built. By the mid-1820s, the city's expanding population practically forced streets to be built. After only small gains from 1810 to 1816, 23,000 people became new New Yorkers from 1816 to 1820, and another 40,000 in the next five years. Over 165,000 people lived on Manhattan in 1825, a near tripling in twenty-five years that would itself more than triple in the next twenty-five years. The grid would make places to put them.

CHAPTER 10

THE GRID THAT ATE MANHATTAN

The early planners succeeded . . . in putting their city in a strait-jacket from which it has not escaped, from which perhaps it can never escape.

—Lewis Mumford, "The Plan of New York," 1932

IN 1807, THE street-making law that birthed the grid of 1811 specifically excluded the village of Greenwich. By 1825, the gridded city was closing in: "Greenwich is now no longer a country village. Such has been the growth of our city that the building of one block more will completely connect the two places; and in three years' time, at the rate buildings have been erected the last season, Greenwich will be known only as a part of the city, and the suburbs will be beyond it." From 1825, Greenwich was no longer an independent village but the new Ninth Ward of the city. That year, a record 3,000 buildings were under construction across the city.

By 1830, at least small portions of every street up to 23rd had been opened; openings above that were widely scattered. Still, relatively few of the openings had matured into worked street segments and barely any had been paved. Third and Eighth Avenues had been ordered opened for their entire lengths back in the 1810s but only portions had been turned into avenue-wide dirt roads by 1830; paving with macadam had then just begun on short stretches of Third Avenue. Ninth Avenue was opened northward in smaller increments but was entirely finished but for paving through 28th Street by 1830, much to Clement Clarke Moore's initial chagrin but quicker profit than if Ninth had come along later. By 1830, all of the Commissioners' avenues had gotten their starts but none so easily as Ninth. First Avenue, for example, had been ordered opened up to 25th Street in 1813 but by 1829 it was less a thoroughfare than an unpaved target of opportunity. "It has become dangerous and almost impassable for carriages, owing to the large pits and gulleys, which have been occasioned by unlicensed dirt carmen digging up the earth in the middle of the road, and carting it away, to fill in the sunken grounds in that neighborhood." The man in charge of filling those sunken grounds (the swampy regions of Cedar Creek, which emptied into an East River inlet at 18th Street) "does not consider it his business to enquire where the dirt comes from." A good citizen who ordered one of the pilferers to desist "was threatened to be knocked down with the rung of a cart for his interference." It is perhaps gratifying to know that street crime of various sorts is nothing new.

Despite such troubles, as the grid began to take shape it became evident to some people that for all the grid's many hundreds of intended rectilinear blocks, there were going to be too few of them. That is, there were too few avenues intersecting the many dozens of streets. The city was expanding lengthwise and the grid as planned was short on routes in that direction. The resulting deficit of building blocks was becoming most apparent in two of the three broadest expanses, the 920 feet between Third and Fourth Avenues and Fourth and Fifth Avenues, the corridor, as it happened, of the most desirable early up-island development. Thus, Lexington and Madison Avenues, in large part due to Samuel B. Ruggles.

Ruggles was born in 1800 in Connecticut, where his English forebears had flourished since New Amsterdam was a one-street town. Raised wealthy in Poughkeepsie, he was graduated from Yale at age fourteen and read law with his father until he could be admitted to the bar at twenty-one, when he relocated almost immediately to New York City, a suitable match for his aspirations. Long, lean, and attractive—flowing hair, blue eyes, sensuous mouth—Ruggles was happily married within the year to Mary Rosalie Rathbone, the daughter of a Connecticut Yankee turned leading city merchant. Mary in short order birthed three children, while Samuel thrived at law but quickly switched to land speculation, using his wife's inheritance money. During 1831, he purchased in nearly two dozen transactions an assemblage of lots that had mostly been the Gramercy Seat farm of James Duane, the city's first postwar mayor. Ruggles's purchases were centered between Third and Fourth Avenues, and 19th and 23rd Streets, which the city had recently ordered opened. Third Avenue had been opened back in 1812 and paved with macadam through the area in the late 1820s; Fourth Avenue from 16th to 28th would be opened in 1833. By the end of 1831, Ruggles had laid out plans for a private park between 20th and 21st, to be owned by the purchasers of his lots surrounding it.

It was Ruggles's idea to increase access to his development by having the city build a seventy-five-foot-wide north-south avenue from 14th up to 30th Street, excepting the block of the park. Ruggles would give up three of his twenty-five-foot lots on 20th Street and three more on 21st for the avenue. The city would get a tax-paying neighborhood that Ruggles would create from a fairly hopeless bit of real estate. Ruggles's plan looked good on paper but not on the ground. A creek, the original Dutch "Crommessie" from which "Gramercy" derived, wound through one side of the property in a deep gulley surrounded by swamp; the other side was high hill. Ruggles eventually spent $180,000 dumping a million cartloads of hill into the valley, burying the creek and filling the bogs. As the process evolved over several years, the city went to the state for permission to add an avenue to the 1811 plan, and Ruggles got naming rights: Irving Place, for his friend Washington Irving, below the park, and

Lexington Avenue, for the first Revolutionary battle, heading north. By 1838, the city was authorized to continue Lexington to 66th Street; by 1870, all the way to the Harlem River.

While formulating his park plans, Ruggles and other area landowners promoted efforts to turn the Commissioners' marginal Union Place into something of symmetry and grandeur. In 1831, it was officially designated a park, and in 1832, it was landscaped and formally renamed Union Square. Within the next decade it was a centerpiece of the expanding city.

As soon as the beginnings of Lexington Avenue were established, Ruggles extended his influence west, convincing the city that a similar avenue was needed to split the distance between Fourth and Fifth Avenues. Here was more logic than service to Ruggles's real estate interests. The eastern side of the Parade had already been cut, exposing its land to development, especially northward from the old intersection of Broadway and the Post Road. In 1833, when the state, at the city's request, allowed the extension of Lexington beyond 30th Street, it also allowed the creation of another as yet unnamed seventy-five-foot-wide avenue between Fourth and Fifth from 23rd Street to 42nd. It was another decade before actual laying of the new avenue began, giving Ruggles the opportunity to suggest naming it for late president James Madison, who had died in 1836. Madison Avenue, like Lexington, grew north to the Harlem River during the remainder of the century, stepsiblings of all their older linear relatives.

Lexington and Madison are evidence of a significant failure of the 1811 grid plan. As the Common Council wrote to the state legislature in 1838 in seeking to extend the two avenues, the space between the Commissioners' avenues east of Fifth was just too big: "Those blocks are each nine hundred and twenty feet in length, which has been found to be too great a distance for public convenience." We know that the Commissioners had conveniently opted for their three sets of 920-foot blocks because Goerck had already established two of them. Lexington and Madison are also examples of how the idea of the grid had become firmly established by the early 1830s. Though very few streets had actually been laid in the regions that would accept Lexington and Madison, no one attempted to make the area more accessible with diagonal roads.

Fifth Avenue, the first few blocks of which were opened to 13th Street in 1824 and to 21st in 1828, staked a claim to primacy among the avenues in 1829. A state law sought by the city proclaimed the complete elimination of the Parade, the 240 acres of ceremonial ground envisioned in the 1811 plan. Spread between Third and Seventh Avenues and 23rd and 34th Streets on paper only, the Parade by 1814 already had been reduced conceptually by an avenue on each side and three blocks on top. Now, with actual streets and habitation crowding at its reduced borders, the Parade surrendered to the grid, which marched in neat lines through what must have seemed its rightful domain, like an empire annexing a duchy. The map of Manhattan was amended to continue streets across, and Fifth Avenue through, the Parade as if it never existed, which it did in map alone, and the Parade's grounds, but for seven-acre Madison Square, which emerged ten years later from the Parade's dust, reverted to private property and marketable lots of Common Lands. In fact, abandoning the Parade avoided the city's expensive repurchase of sold Common Lands lots. By 1837, Fifth Avenue had been opened, though ungraded and unpaved, to 42nd Street. In a few years, the landmark Distributing Reservoir of the Croton water supply would rise at that intersection on the high ground of Murray Hill, a place of suburban attraction. By then, Fifth Avenue, running continuously from Washington Square north, had become the avenue of choice for the richest New Yorkers, planting increasingly extravagant mansions up to 23rd Street by midcentury, though paving remained a future improvement. "Fifth Avenue is very muddy above Eighteenth Street," ten-year-old Kate Havens told her diary in August 1849. On a walk up the avenue from her house on 9th Street to a friend's country seat at 37th Street "it was so muddy I ruined my new cloth gaiter boots."

Meanwhile, something different was happening on the west side of the island. While Lexington and Madison were further confirmations of the rectilinear grid on the east, Bloomingdale Road was resisting its fate. The Commissioners had retained Broadway and a bit of Bloomingdale only up to 23rd Street, where their Parade was to begin. Bloomingdale was to disappear beyond it. But the Parade shrank into Madison Square, and Bloomingdale and Broadway, with many landowners along the route, were gradually added to the city plan: in 1838 to 43rd Street, in 1847 to 71st, in 1851 to 86th, and in the 1860s (as Kingsbridge) off the island to 228th on the mainland. Until then, the road below 59th had been transformed from Bloomingdale Road to Broadway, and to 108th briefly as the Boulevard, with hopes of European-style widening and landscaping that never materialized as the grid closed around it. Not until the emergence of five-borough Greater New York in 1898 did the old native path and new grid anomaly go by the name Broadway from Manhattan's toe to tip.

In time, the anomaly became a paradigm, the graceful if slender backbone of the rigid city, creating precious irregularities and opportunities at the acute and obtuse junctions with half a dozen rectilinear avenues. Broadway gives us Madison Square and the Flatiron Building; Herald Square, Greeley Square, and Macy's; Times Square and the Great White Way; Columbus Circle and the Time Warner Center; Lincoln Square and Lincoln Center; and the snappy bowtie at 72nd: a cornucopia of urban embellishment despised by the city's grid makers. "Broadway," observed architect Julius Harder in 1898, when the grid was practically complete, "is a pathetic evidence of the economy and convenience that might have been general." "In straight New York, Broadway runs riot," wrote a sophisticated European visitor in 1902, a singular thrill in the otherwise "abominable rectangular plan." "Every one of these corners is more or less a challenge to the ingenuity of the architect," observed the architecture critic Montgomery Schuyler in 1911. "The obtuse or the acute angle not only offers, but in some sort imposes, an architectural opportunity." By then, the New York architect had few such opportunities.

Bloomingdale Road survives as Broadway, but back on the east side of Manhattan the Post Road went without much of a fight. Bloomingdale linked a string of settlements and had relatively few inconvenient bends. The Post Road had been laid out on a much more irregular course a hundred years earlier for a commercial purpose (mail delivery); it and the land it passed through lacked the natural beauty of Bloomingdale and landowners along its route had less of an attachment to it, especially as the linear routes of the grid's eastern avenues appeared.

In 1839, the Common Council resolved to close the Post Road from its starting point at 23rd Street up to 31st. This much was expected, as it ran through the Commissioners' would-be Parade, officially abandoned to the grid ten years earlier. Nothing happened, though, for five years, when the Council again ordered that stretch of road closed, this time with specific provisions: the owners of land on either side were to get quit-claim deeds to their adjoining pieces of the roadbed. Here was the most profound of the relatively rare instances in those grid-building days of land turning from street to private property instead of the reverse. In 1848, the road was ordered closed up to 42nd Street under the same arrangement. Four years later, it was closed to 66th Street, where the course of the road entered the northeastern section of the Common Lands. With its lower portions closed by the mid-1850s, the road ceased to be used and landowners gradually closed segments of roadway that crossed through their property with no objections. Thanks to the Post Road's turn to the west just above the Common Lands and the creation of Central Park in the 1850s, a bit of the road's original path survives as the park's East Drive from 90th Street to the park's northeast corner.

For a long while, the Common Lands remained remote and undesirable, and though the city was eager to sell or lease what it could, it was also willing to part with some of it cheaply for good causes. In 1827, an acre of Common Lands lot 59 (to become the block between Fourth and Fifth Avenues and 49th and 50th Streets) was sold for a dollar to the Institute for the Instruction of the Deaf and Dumb. The institute flourished there, then reaped a windfall thirty years later when it sold its land to Columbia College. In 1840, in the midst of the deep depression following the Panic of 1837, two dozen then practically worthless lots on the west side of Fifth Avenue between 54th and 55th (a portion of what had been Common Lands lot 73) went for a dollar to the Anglo-American Free Church of St. George the Martyr. No souls were saved there until the undeveloped property was transferred to the organizers of St. Luke's Hospital eleven years later; in 1893, in advance of its removal to its current location at Amsterdam and 114th, the hospital sold its hallowed freehold for $2.4 million. (McKim, Mead & White's University Club has graced the southern corner since 1899.) The dollar days returned in 1846, with the city's deed to the Roman Catholic Church for an orphan asylum on the block between 51st and 52nd from the east side of Fifth to what was just becoming Madison Avenue (the western half of former Common Lands lot 65). When the asylum abandoned Manhattan for the Bronx a half century later, the land was sold at extraordinary profit to the Vanderbilt family and others. Mansions built on land that had once sheltered orphans survive today as retail outlets for Cartier and Versace. The transition of Common Lands lots from the least to the most desirable Manhattan real estate is probably the greatest irony of the grid plan.

Ironic also is the Commissioners' worry that extending their plan above 155th Street would lead to speculation when it was the checkerboard grid itself that invited and rewarded speculation. The best of many examples is Astor. After starting his American business life in the fur trade, he dabbled in Common Lands lots around the time the Commissioners' Plan was announced but devoted himself exclusively to real estate by 1834. He bought voraciously, especially distressed properties during the Panic of 1837 and ensuing depression, when mostly new and speculative owners couldn't meet mortgage payments or needed cash. "Could I begin life again, knowing what I now know, and had money to invest, I would buy every foot of land on the Island of Manhattan," Astor supposedly said just before he went to his heavenly reward in 1848.

Astor is the most extreme example of the rewards for calculated speculation on Manhattan's game board. Some gained wealth almost by accident, like John M. Bixby.

Born in Fairfield, Connecticut, and raised "in the backwoods of New York," Bixby came to the city around 1827 as "a raw and struggling young lawyer." As he later told it, he did not flourish. "It looked as if I should starve at the law, so I was looking for work outside of it." One day, another lawyer in the office where Bixby rented a desk had to close an estate that included some farmland on former Common Lands at what was becoming the north side of 39th Street between Fifth Avenue and Broadway. The lawyer offered the farm to Bixby at the appraised price of $200, which was $200 more than Bixby had. No matter, said the lawyer, who happily took Bixby's note for the total, assuring him the land would soon grow in value. "I felt very nervous about giving my note for such a large amount, and once offered to sell the farm back to him for the note. But after two or three renewals of the note New York had grown so fast northward that I was able to sell a small part of the farm for more than enough to pay the note and interest and taxes." Indeed. By 1860, he had sold more parcels for $1.5 million and retained a portion he valued at about $7 million—"all made out of nothing, by giving a note for $200, almost against my will, and when I was practically not worth a dollar."

The story was first told publicly in 1906, thirty years after Bixby's death, in a letter to *The Sun* by Kinahan Cornwallis, the former owner-editor of the *Knickerbocker Magazine* and a friend of Bixby who had told him the story forty years earlier. It might pass as just another possibly apocryphal tale of Manhattan real estate but the story continues, with significant judicial intervention, all the way into the 1950s. Bixby and his much younger wife, Mary Poe, a Southerner and Edgar Allan relation who died at twenty-nine, had two children. The son died unmarried in 1900. The daughter, Grace, after her father's death married Russian-descended, Austrian-born, English resident Count Casimir Ignace Mankowski and quickly had two sons; the difficult birth of the second apparently caused issues resulting in Grace's institutionalization. In 1947, Bixby's only living direct descendant and heir, his grandson Count Robert Conrad Mankowski of Los Angeles, died, having stipulated in his will that just under $1.5 million of his estate go to his mother's relatives down to the seventh degree next of kin. By 1955, some 600 possible heirs had been winnowed to twenty-five mostly elderly recipients, from a longtime Georgia poorhouse resident to an Italian countess and descendants of Pocahontas and Poe. By then, all the Bixby property on 39th Street was long gone. Among the notable buildings that once graced the former $200 farm was the Union League Club on a long lease at the northeast corner with Fifth Avenue. The subject of a lengthy design competition among the country's top architects, the imposing Queen Anne–styled clubhouse was among the city's grandest buildings for half a century until the club moved out to a new building nearby in 1931. A year later the empty building burned to the ground, as outdated buildings have long tended to do in New York, especially at its many valuable corners, which due to their numbers and sameness tend toward permanent competition.

The pace of transitions like that begun on a Common Lands farm in the late 1820s accelerated rapidly. In January 1835, ex-mayor and dedicated diarist Philip Hone was offered seven lots on Second Avenue near St. Mark's Place (8th Street) for $35,000. "This I declined," he wrote in April, "for I could not imagine then, nor can I now, that they were worth so much money." In fact, they were quickly sold for $38,000, "and the speculators say they are a bargain." Hone, pushing fifty-five, was like a middle-aged modern wondering at the stratospheric rise of Google and Facebook stock. That summer, Hone was further stunned at the auction of land consisting of an old estate near newly opened 24th Street at Second Avenue and a large country seat at Bloomingdale near what would become 101st Street and West End Avenue. Hone, who had made his fortune in the auction business, estimated the two pieces, which together went for over $688,000, would have brought less than $40,000 fifteen years earlier.

The greater part of this sale was the Bloomingdale tract. A region of flowering hills and dales called "Bloemendael" by the Dutch, Bloomingdale was first referred to as a residential place in the late 1600s. Country living was spurred in 1703 with the opening of Bloomingdale Road from the suburbs of the city to the village forming at today's 114th Street. (After the Revolution, the road was extended to meet Kingsbridge Road at today's 147th Street; modern Broadway largely follows the route of the old road.) The country village center grew to twenty or so homes before it was smothered in the grid's rigid embrace in the decades after the Civil War.

The Bloomingdale property that sold in 1835 had a long history, an illustrative tale of the changes abroad in the land. It starts in 1668, just after the English takeover of Manhattan, with a vast grant of land to Isaak Bedloo from new governor Richard Nicolls. Bedloo was a wealthy New Amsterdam merchant who, along with 250 other commercially minded burghers, had compelled Peter Stuyvesant to surrender peacefully to the English in 1664. Pledging loyalty to the Crown and anglicizing his name, Isaac Bedlow was rewarded with government appointments and land. Alas, he died intestate a few years later—his new name was soon corrupted to Bedloe, the name carried by an island of his until 1956 when it was renamed Liberty for its iron lady—and subdivisions followed. Around 1749, a 115-acre portion came into the ownership of a Dutch family, the van Beverhouts, who relocated from St. Thomas in the Virgin Islands. Johannes van Beverhout promptly built a large stone house, fifty by forty-four feet, featuring a three-story colonnaded portico, thirty rooms, "Sash-Windows, Beaufets, Closets, and in all other Respects completely finished, with Cellars under the whole House." Johannes had little time to enjoy his handsome new home; he died just two years later. His widow put the estate up for sale in 1752. "The Farm is pleasantly situated either for a Gentleman or a Farmer, having delightful Prospects both up and down the River"; besides the house were "a Farm or Outhouse, and Kitchen, of Stone and Brick; a large Barn new shingl'd, two Gardens, one of near two Acres of Land, inclos'd with neat Pales and Board-Fence." Prominent merchant Humphrey Jones bought the farm (so to speak) that became known as the Homestead. His son Nicholas inherited; in 1780, he offered the estate for sale, with some urgency and less accuracy: "To be sold a Farm at Bloomingdale, about 200 acres more or less, seven miles from the city, [with] a large strong stone built house . . . conditions for the sale will be made easy to a purchaser." One imagines a potential buyer impressed with the house but skeptically walking the acreage that was more or less half of Jones's estimate. Not that a buyer would have had free range: the farm was in the midst of a seven-year occupation by British and Hessian troops who were not so gentle to the Homestead. Not surprisingly, it didn't sell. After the war, Jones apparently suffered reverses, possibly related to the occupation, that compelled sale of the estate for £2300 ($5,750) by the sheriff to satisfy judgments. Several conveyances over the next twenty-five years brought the property into the hands of William Rogers for $29,900. When he died in 1818, it passed to his wife Ann; the Homestead was transformed into the Ann Rogers House. It was her death in 1833 that prompted the 1835 sale that so stunned Philip Hone, a 2,300 percent increase in value in twenty-four years. The purchaser, Frederick Weber, lived in the house for a number of years with his two children and a new, much younger wife (the children's mother had died).

During their residence, the Webers adorned the property with a unique driveway from Bloomingdale Road: a raised stone causeway lined with abundant fruit trees that came to be known as Cherry Lane. Around 1843, Weber and family moved into the city, renting out the house and grounds that soon afterwards were operated as the Abbey Hotel, a highly patronized genteel resort an increasingly short drive from the city limits.

After such a long history, the end came fast. In 1859, the house was struck by lightning and burned to the ground. It was over a hundred years old. The sudden destruction of the handsome land-mark ironically earned it a more respectable fate than most of the many other country seats scattered around the island. Rather than a sad decline while city progressively claimed woods, hillsides, grounds, yards, porches, and houses themselves over a few gener-ations, the Homestead turned Ann Rogers House turned Abbey Hotel disappeared in a few spectacular hours, leaving memories of grandeur only. Before the year was out, the entire property was sold and reduced to building lots for speculative purchase. By the time 101st Street and Eleventh (soon West End) Avenue were opened in the 1870s, few had any idea a great old house had been there just a decade or so earlier. There was no pathetic demolition, no mourning at the loss of natural or architectural beauty, no regret about the rectilinear march of progress. Fire makes quick work of sentiment and the grid easily obliterates memory.

The grid wasn't a bonanza just for land developers and specu-lators. It was a vast strip mine of easy tax pickings. Before the grid, the city earned essential revenue from selling or leasing its Com-mon Lands holdings. With the grid, the city got out of the busi-ness of land ownership and into the role of taxing land owned by its citizens. In 1830, the city collected some $200,000 in property taxes; seven years later, $1.1 million. In 1807, the assessed value of real estate in New York was $25 million; by 1825, it had doubled; by 1835, it had nearly tripled again, to $142 million; by 1887, it had increased nearly ten times to $1.3 billion. By then, 80 percent of the city's annual budget came from real estate taxes.

Facilitating the movement up-island was the advent in the 1830s of a transportation mode that the 1807 Commissioners did not anticipate: railroads, which used the grid's straight avenues for their convenient right of way. To the thinking of Lewis Mumford, "the plan of 1811 became technologically obsolete [when] railroad transportation reduced the need for numerous cross-streets from waterfront to waterfront." In any case, streets and avenues that had been designed exclusively for animal labor and wheeled vehicles for at most a few persons were very quickly the contested and soon congested battleground of mass transportation.

The first American railroad tracks were laid in Philadelphia in 1809, a time when steam engines were developing into practical machines. A few months after the Commissioners were appointed, Robert Fulton inaugurated steamboat travel on the Hudson. When the Commissioners announced their plan four years later, there was a steamboat on the Mississippi. Rail and steam were first paired in 1825 in Hoboken.

The first rail cars, operated by the newly incorporated New York and Harlem Railroad, moved on Manhattan in November 1832, from Union Square up Fourth Avenue to 23rd Street. Like the initial response to many transformative new technologies, opinion was not entirely favorable: "Remonstrances against running the Harlem Railroad through the principal streets of the city are circulating among the citizens," Philip Hone told his diary two months later. "Public opinion is decidedly opposed to this innovation upon the rights of the citizens," he added in April. Opinion may have been opposed but riders were not. By 1837, cars were running along rails up Fourth Avenue to a station at 125th Street. It should be noted that the motive force initially was horses. Within a few years, steam engines had replaced horses above 32nd Street, below which the noisy, sooty, and occasionally explosive technology was banned in 1845 (until 1876).

In the 1850s, railroads opened on Second, Third, Sixth, Eighth, and Ninth Avenues, all with the more traditional and less intrusive and dangerous power of horses. By 1860, an array of horse railway companies counted a hundred thousand passenger trips a day up and down the island, in crowded cars notorious for foul air and pickpockets: "People are packed into them like sardines in a box, with perspiration for oil. The seats being more than filled, the passengers are placed in rows, down the middle, where they hang on by the straps, like smoked hams in a corner grocery." Nevertheless, by 1866, ridership had tripled. An option, at twice the fare, was the omnibus, a horse-drawn carriage seating twenty that debuted in the 1830s. Without the benefit of the quick, smooth ride on rails and plagued with profane drivers, the omnibus was "a perfect Bedlam on wheels" by the 1860s: "Modern martyrdom may be succinctly defined as riding in a New York omnibus." Soon, mass transportation moved aboveground to the machine-powered elevated railroads and, at the opening of the 1900s, belowground to subways, with a not always appreciable improvement in the commuting experience.

Still, it took many decades for this process to play out and the evolution was not continuous, with the development of mass transportation and the creation of new streets increasingly further north. Indeed, just after the birth of rail travel in New York in the 1830s, the creation of new streets came to a temporary halt.

The first issue was the Common Lands above 42nd Street. In December 1831, 42nd was opened from Third Avenue to Bloomingdale Road, the stretch through the Common Lands of the old Steuben Street. No other street in the Common Lands further north would be opened for another five years. The problem was the Commissioners' wide 57th, 72nd, and 79th Streets.

The problem generally with the Common Lands versus the Commissioners' Plan was that Common Lands owners and lessees behaved as though their properties were 260 feet north to south because few if any of the prescribed sixty-foot streets across the north end of every lot in Goerck's 1796 plan were ever laid. Now, under the 1811 plan that, without expressly saying so, put those streets back on the map, lots were nearly 25 percent smaller than they had been leased for or bought.

It took a few years for the problems to be fully comprehended. In July 1823, the city gave a ten-year lease, at $82.50 a year per lot, to David Wagstaff for Common Lands lots 142, 146, and 150, on the west side of the former Middle Road, renamed, though not yet opened, as Fifth Avenue. According to the 1811 plan, 78th, 80th, and 82nd Streets when they were opened, presumably not before the expiration of the lease, would pass through the middle or thereabouts of each lot. Wagstaff was the outright owner of substantial property elsewhere in the Common Lands and further west, but in September he petitioned the Council for a rent reduction on lot 150 "in consequence of a part having been taken for a public road." It's not exactly clear what road Wagstaff was talking about—82nd Street just west of Fifth wasn't opened before Central Park claimed it in the 1850s—but by the following April he was seeking to purchase the other two lots, even though streets were planned to run through them as well. The Council, clearly uncertain how to resolve such issues, decided "that under existing circumstances it would be inexpedient to dispose of the Common land Lots."

Soon, this became a policy. In 1828, the Council decided that it was "unadvisable at this time to dispose of any Common land Lots" and halted all pending and future sales. In May 1830, the Council decided it couldn't renew a lease on lot 203, east of Third Avenue around 77th Street, which by the 1811 plan was to run through lot 203. "As a general rule," reported the finance committee, "the Board should refuse to grant applications of that kind." A month later, the Council was uniformly refusing to extend the terms of unexpired leases and letting expired leases lapse.

It was an interesting conundrum. Everywhere else on the island, the Commissioners' Plan took precedence over private property lines. On the city's own land, the 1811 plan, which wordlessly had appropriated Goerck's 1796 plan, was a slave to it but a restless one, using its boundaries generally but with small though distinct modifications that made trouble for all parties. In this, the grid Commissioners were like the son who borrows the family car and brings it home with a slapdash paint job and no explanation.

Something had to be done. By 1836, no streets had been opened in the Common Lands, nor had there been any land sales, and there were just a scattering of new leases. In a very few instances, the city was able to make swaps with owners and lessees that partially cleared the way for future streets. In February 1836, the city ordered opened every street from 22nd to 42nd, most from river to river, all at least partially through the southern wedge of irregular Common Lands lots. In the next two months, it ordered opened most of the streets from 116th to 130th, as well as bits of others on either side of the main columns of Common Lands. After toying with the notion that the Council's Finance Committee could settle cases ad hoc with arbitrators, the city finally went to the state, which passed a law in May 1836 allowing the governor to appoint the familiar adjudicator—a three-man commission—that would make "final and conclusive" decisions on cases submitted to them about what land was to be exchanged and what money the city owed or was owed.

Settlements quickly ensued, and in the first four months of 1837 43rd through 57th Streets were opened river to river, 83rd through 85th from Third to Fifth, 87th from Fourth to Eighth, and 88th from Third to Eighth. Finally, a bulk of the Commons Lands would be opened to receive the grid. Portions of sixteen other streets and avenues were ordered opened by the end of April, followed by . . . none.

In May, the Panic of 1837, prompted by a collapse in canal stocks and other influences, broke in the city and quickly spread around the country into the first prolonged national depression. The only street opening for the rest of 1837 was the westernmost block of 59th Street in July. No streets were opened in 1838; in 1839, only bits of 15th, 16th, 17th, and 21st along the East River; then nothing through 1843, when city and nation began to emerge from the six-year depression. Still, for the rest of the 1840s, there were no up-island cross-street openings. Instead, there was major activity on major routes. In 1844, the widening of Houston Street began, and beginning the following year, the widening of Bloomingdale Road from 25th to 45th at an estimated cost of nearly $100,000, a major stage in its transition from a country road for which the Commissioners had no tolerance into modern Broadway. Madison Square, at what was once the southern tip of the Common Lands, was ordered opened in 1847 at an estimated cost of $75,000. In 1848, the only activity was Broadway being widened from 21st to 25th Streets— with the creation of Madison Square, this completed the disappearance of the Commissioners' Parade—and the extension of Fourth Avenue from 28th to 38th Streets. The only opening in 1849 was Lexington Avenue, extended from 31st to 42nd Streets.

None of this is to say that there was not furious activity going on related to streets. In fact, while the Panic put an end to new street openings, it also gave rise to popular outrage at the assessment process for streets already ordered open. The Panic, which ruined many fortunes and impoverished many workers, played havoc with street assessments. "A contract made to pay a dollar three years ago," reported a sympathetic Council select committee on postponing the forced sale of properties for unpaid assessments, "is essentially unjust, so far as the debtor is concerned, as he is compelled to pay his debt in a currency that is nearly twice as valuable." That was in April 1838. Collections were suspended for four months but, as the shock of the Panic turned into the new routine of a lengthy depression, rarely after.

It was natural for landowners to complain about assessments and to claim that the assessors were in league with the Council's street committee. But the problem was less often with the assessors— professional surveyors whose judicial appointment and review arguably insulated them from corruption—than with the city's administration, which was initially limited and honestly overwhelmed with the massive street expansion it had begun but eventually bloated and substantially corrupted. By 1839, for example, it was especially risky to be a nonresident lot owner. You might find your property had been auctioned to pay assessments of which you had never been notified because there was not yet a formal notification process other than newspaper notices that were easily missed. Or your paid assessment might never have been recorded. There was no central repository of assessment information: a Council committee's proposal for a register's office was rejected in 1838. In 1844, the Street Committee was required to create and maintain a block and lot map, but this was far from a guarantee of accurate financial recordkeeping.

By mid-1840, outraged citizens had formed the Anti-Assessment Committee and the following March began publishing the *New York Municipal Gazette*, which in various forms through the 1840s detailed the abuses, and occasional victories, of city landowners, the often lengthy period between street opening assessment collection and actual expenditure of the money to work the street into existence, and various other insults to "civil liberty" exercised by the "mere municipal corporation." "There are but few citizens, and very few, who are opposed to improvements," asserted the *Gazette* in its first issue, "but there are vast numbers, in fact nine tenths of this community, who are wholly opposed to the present system of making improvements, and to the enormous and most glaring abuses which have been practised in these proceedings."

In all its detailed reportage and righteous indignation, the *Gazette* and other contemporary critics of the street situation never got at the root cause of the problems. The vastness of the power given to the 1807 Commissioners, especially in relation to the powerlessness of the city government until then, resulted in an island-wide plan that the city government, best suited to a medium-sized town, was entirely inadequate to handle. Had an incremental plan, such as Mangin's, taken full effect, the city and its government might have grown more organically with each other. Instead, the small city government was staggered by the administrative demands of its immense street plan for thirty years or so, and was quickly replaced at midcentury with a government of many executive departments that soon became infamous worldwide for civic corruption.

A major charter revision in 1830, the first in a century, severed the mayor (and the recorder) from the Common Council, reconstituting it as a bicameral legislative body of separate boards of aldermen and assistants. The mayor gained veto and other limited executive powers (and from 1834 on was popularly elected), but the Council was given the power to organize and appoint permanent executive departments to replace the Council's traditional committees created on an ad hoc basis and manned by the Council's own members. In principle, this was a sensible effort to start creating administrative bureaucracy in a city that increasingly needed some. In practice, it asked the Council to cede its own authority in the management of the city to the newly independent mayor. Understandably, the Council chose not to exercise its dubious privilege. Thus, in large part, the street assessment mess of the 1840s: a daunting enlargement of governmental responsibility still handled by committees of annually elected legislators.

In this sense, the slowdown in new street opening in the 1830s due first to the Common Lands property boundary discrepancies and then to the long effects of the 1837 Panic was ironically the best thing that could have happened in a city without the bureaucracy to handle much more new street business. But, clearly, this was not healthy in the long term. And whether healthy or not in a democratic society with representative government, it was inevitable that the New York City mayor, just like executive branch heads in states and the nation, would gradually accrete the unelected bureaucracies necessary to responsibly serve increasingly larger and complex constituencies. That those bureaucracies, not directly answerable to the electorate, invited corruption was also inevitable.

In 1849, a major revision by the state legislature to the venerable Montgomerie Charter of 1731 effectively transferred superior
government power from the Council to the mayor. The Council was stripped of all executive authority, which it had effectively
maintained through its specialized committees. Now, among nine
new executive departments created to take over traditional committee roles, the Street Department was put in charge of, among
other things like wharves, wells, and sunken lots, the "opening, regulating and paving streets." Its chief officer would be a new type
of street commissioner, not appointed by the Council but popularly
elected, like all new department heads, every three years. The Street
Department would have two bureaus, one in charge of wharves, the
other for the collection of assessments, run by a Collector of Assessments and an unspecified number of Deputy Collectors. None of
these positions were elected, nor were similar positions in any of the
sixteen new bureaux (as the charter revision spelled it). Any New
Yorker howling today at city bureaucracy can celebrate its birthday
every April 2 with sackcloth, but back in 1849 no birth was more
welcomed by exasperated lot owners, large and small, and New
Yorkers generally. The popular vote two weeks later on the charter revision, required of all charter amendments then and now, was
19,339 to 1,478. That such dramatic changes in the city's government were approved by such a margin suggests how popular and
necessary they were.

As a leading historian of the city's financial affairs noted half a
century later, the charter revision of 1849 was "destined to work a
revolution in city affairs." It did just that. Five years later, Fernando
Wood was elected mayor, Tammany Hall's first claim on the office
that it would control for nearly a century. Wood may not have been
the *most* corrupt New York mayor but he was the first. For generations before Wood, the city's mayors were generally self-made
wealthy merchants retired from business and devoting their virtu-
ous senior years to public service. There were certainly political and
personal differences for all those years but never the accusation of

corruption, or at least a sustainable accusation. The political and governmental world was just too small for it to take seed and flourish. By the 1850s, the necessary expansion of government provided room and opportunity.

An easier matter during the pause in street openings was bringing order to house numbering. Official numbering ostensibly had been around since 1793 with odd numbers on the north side of streets and even on the south, but the irregular directions of the city's colonial streets and a high rate of household noncompliance made for a fairly unreliable system. With the advent of the orderly 1811 plan, house numbering initially was to be continuous from west to east starting at 13th Street (below that the irregularities of Greenwich intervened). As streets and buildings on them started appearing, trouble arose because numbers were assigned not by lot but by building, requiring the renumbering of existing houses every time a new one appeared. Changes "are often made without notice to the occupier of a dwelling," the *Evening Post* complained in 1839, "so that he who goes to bed at No. 50 in his street, may wake up the next morning at No. 100." As an interim fix, the Common Council decreed that address changes could happen only once a year, just prior to May 1, the long-established date of most lease expirations that produced its own city-wide "moving day" anarchy for generations (pending rent increases announced February 1 launched the search for cheaper lodging, culminating in the crazed migrations three months later). By the early 1840s, the wiser system of splitting addresses east and west at Fifth Avenue was in place, with the final refinement in 1861 of one hundred house numbers per original 1811 block (house numbering in blocks west of Central Park was adjusted to start at 1 instead of 301 in 1886). No such unified numerical order has ever been brought to the city's avenues.

After generations of annual alphabetical city directories by various (and occasionally competing) publishers, the city's first comprehensive directory by street and house number appeared. *Doggett's*

New York City Street Directory for 1851 included 85,000 names by address up to 25th Street, then the northern boundary of dense habitation. John Doggett had published high-quality, well-regarded alphabetical directories, loaded with almanac-worthy information, for a decade. Evidently, he believed New York by 1851 was a city knowable by the numbers. He never found out for sure because he died early the following year; no one issued an 1852 street directory. The last city directory by name was published in 1933–34, when one's address had become secondary to one's telephone number. The telephone book, as it turned out, had a considerably shorter run, made irrelevant by mobile telephony, the Internet, and digitization, which allows anyone to make whatever sort of directory they want.

The slowdown in new street openings above 42nd Street in the 1830s intensified the working, grading, and finishing of new streets below. Approaching midcentury, the grid had been thickly settled well into the 20s, especially throughout the west side and along the avenues of the east. The work of filling in the blanks went on, astounding even veteran observers of other cities at "the millions already so freely expended in blasting rocks, in removing immense hills, in reducing to a regular grade so vast an extent of rugged surface as would already conveniently locate thrice the present inhabitants of the city." By midcentury, the gridding of Manhattan would seem to some like an assault without end.

CHAPTER 11

THE CITY GRIDDED

Our perpetual dead flat, and streets cutting each other at right angles, are certainly the last things in the world consistent with beauty.

—Walt Whitman, *Sunday Dispatch*, 1849

The time will come when New York will be built-up, when all the grading and filling will be done, when the picturesquely varied rock formations of the island will have been converted into the foundations for rows of monotonous straight streets, and piles of erect, angular buildings.

—Frederick Law Olmsted, 1858

IN CROWDED WILLIAM Street on Saturday, May 12, 1849, a seeming acquaintance approached Thomas MacDonald. After a few moments' conversation, as MacDonald was trying to recall the apparent fellow gentleman's name, he asked, "Have you confidence in me to trust me with your watch until to-morrow?" The request seemed reasonable enough to McDonald, distracted by embarrassment, as he handed over his gold lever pocket watch, a very considerable $110 value. The next day, the man did not return the watch as promised to MacDonald's home. Nor did McDonald see him again until July 7, when, two months wiser, he caught sight of the man on Liberty Street and hailed a police officer, who hauled off the man, after a bit of a struggle, to jail at the city's infamous Tombs. There a judge recognized him as habitual offender William Thompson, "a graduate of the college at Sing Sing," the state prison up the Hudson. Unsuccessful in his prior schemes, in the spring of 1849 Thompson had devised a new criminal personality: the "confidence man," as the penny press giddily dubbed him. Though he met with no greater success as a confidence man than in previous illicit pursuits, Thompson was the avatar of a new criminal class in New York; by the 1860s, an estimated one in ten of the city's professional criminals were confidence men, preying on the watches, jewelry, cash, and credulity of their fellow New Yorkers. There has been no shortage of con men since.

Thompson and his disciples were enabled by a city that was becoming dense and anonymous, rich and poor, a breeding ground for fowlers and marks. The scandal-mongering *Herald*, which gave Thompson's swindler persona its enduring name, saw a city awash in all sorts of "confidence men." Some were Thompsons who worked particular streets and wound up in small rooms with iron bars. Others, the "possessors of suddenly acquired wealth," worked along the same streets but lived in massive new "evidences of a lavish and almost profligate expenditure." These

> *palazzos*, with all their costly furniture, and all their luxurious means of living, and all their splendid equipages, have been the product of the same genius in their proprietors, which has made the "Confidence Man" immortal and a prisoner at "the Tombs." His genius has been employed on a small scale in Broadway. Theirs has been employed in Wall street. . . . Long life to the real "Confidence Man!"—the "Confidence Man" of Wall street— the "Confidence Man" of the palace up town—the "Confidence

Man" who battens and fattens on the plunder coming from the poor man and the man of moderate means!

The "up town" palazzos were not the charming country estates of old Manhattan; they were the piles heaped on rectilinear lots along new city streets and avenues. By midcentury, New York was adding a lot of up to its town and Mannahatta was losing its natural beauty, a process that for the first time engaged artistic sensitivities. "I have been roaming far and wide over this island of Mannahatta," Edgar Allan Poe informed the readers of the *Columbia Spy*, the Pennsylvania newspaper to which he sent a series of "Doings of Gotham" letters in May and June 1844. On the east face of the island he found "some of the most picturesque sites for villas" where none would be built and old mansions

> are suffered to remain unrepaired, and present a melancholy spectacle of decrepitude. In fact, these magnificent places are *doomed*. The spirit of Improvement has withered them with its acrid breath. Streets are already "mapped" through them, and they are no longer suburban residences, but 'townlots.' In some thirty years every noble cliff will be a pier, and the whole island will be densely desecrated by buildings of brick, with portentous *facades* of brown-stone.

Poe was living then with his family in a rented room of a farmhouse on Bloomingdale Road at what would soon be 84th Street. He wrote "The Raven" there, a suitable place for brooding. "I could not look on the magnificent cliffs, and stately trees, which at every moment met my view, without a sigh for their inevitable doom—inevitable and swift. In twenty years, or thirty at farthest, we shall see here nothing more romantic than shipping, warehouses, and wharves."

In November 1849, Walt Whitman, then transitioning from young editor in Brooklyn to poet of America, walked "the

172 = City on a Grid

battlements" of the Croton Distributing Reservoir on Murray Hill, where city was just beginning to reach country: "The elevated and stony grounds about here will cost their owners dearly to get them graded and paved. . . . I always think it a pity that greater favor is not given to the natural hills and slopes of the ground on the upper part of Manhattan Island. Our perpetual dead flat, and streets cutting each other at right angles, are certainly the last things in the world consistent with beauty of situation."

With a bit more edge, William A. Duer, former longtime Columbia College president, lamented "the levelling system . . . which has since reduced the superficial aspect of the city to an equality corresponding with the political condition of its inhabitants. In this process, not only that variety and undulation of surface, which contributed both to its health and beauty were destroyed but the 'scythe of equality moved over the' Island." Duer was equating the leveling of Manhattan's estate hills with Marat's call for the leveling of Parisian society by swifter means a few generations earlier.

Duer was making a point. Cutting down the island's hills was not just a topographic leveling; it was a social leveling, too. The hills had been occupied by country estates with a view. As the hills went, so went vantage and advantage. The filling of valleys with the rock and soil of the hills literally leveled the social playing field: the hills of the landed repurposed to raise the soggy valleys of squatters, the new flat land passing to an expanding middle class. The grid effected a displacement of the people with land by the people with dollars, uprooting hereditary lands and replanting them as a vast field of real estate in tidy rows, a cultural crop exchange from landsmen to dollar farmers.

PAST THE TURN into midcentury, the grid was approaching the environs of what are now known as the east and west sides. "How this city marches northward!" observed George Templeton Strong, New York's second greatest diarist, in October 1850, noting "the luxuri-ent *rank* growth of this year. Streets are springing up, whole strata of sandstone have transferred themselves from their ancient resting-places to look down on bustling thoroughfares for long years to come." As the husband of Samuel Ruggles's daughter Ellen, Strong embraced the grid, from the bracing mayhem of excavations to the promise of a vast and orderly city.

One aspect of the new order—the twenty-five-by-one-hundred-foot lot—many people today assume was a part of the 1811 plan, but it wasn't. "The plan of 1807 was an effort to reduce everything to an uniform system of 25x100 lots," wrote engineer George S. Greene in an 1875 Parks Department report, and the mistaken insinuation persists. The Commissioners had nothing to say about how or if their 1,600 or so blocks were to be subdivided. But soon enough a cer-tain logic prevailed that replicated the grid in each one of its blocks. The hundred-foot depth of a lot was easy: two of them per every 200-foot-long block, with no space left over or mandated for back alleys. The twenty-five-foot width, on the other hand, had nothing to do with the grid per se, though it produced them ad nauseam. The twenty-five-foot lot goes back as far the 1640s on Manhattan because eighteen feet of sawn tree with a minimum two-by-twelve-inch cross-section was about the maximum that animal labor and hand machinery could manage. Set one end of the timber joist six inches deep in a foot-thick brick exterior wall and the other six inches deep in an interior load-bearing wall for a seventeen-foot inte-rior space, with a shorter joist on the other side spanning a three-foot hallway and three-foot staircase, and there's your twenty-five-foot lot. Of course, the main interior space could be smaller than seventeen feet, but rarely was it larger. By the late 1800s, three-quarters of the city's nearly 100,000 buildings were twenty to twenty-five feet wide.

This future was well under way by the late 1850s, as city rap-idly claimed more space. By 1858, Manhattan was solidly built up

This map published in 1852 by Matthew Dripps, over seven feet long and shown here in portion, depicts Manhattan up to 50th Street with unprecedented accuracy and detail, down to the division of blocks into built lots. It shows how 8th and 9th Avenues were the first routes of substantial up-island development.

to 36th Street on the east and 50th on west. "The time will come when New York will be built-up, when all the grading and filling will be done, when the picturesquely varied rock formations of the island will have been converted into the foundations for rows of monotonous straight streets, and piles of erect, angular buildings. There will be no suggestion left of its present varied surface, with the single exception of the few acres contained in the Park."

The writer is Frederick Law Olmsted, reporting in May 1858 to the commission that had selected him and Calvert Vaux as the winners of the design competition to create Central Park. The park relieved the grid; Olmsted reviled it. "There seems to be good authority for the story that the system of 1807 was hit upon by the chance occurrence of a mason's sieve near the map of the ground to be laid out. It was taken up and placed upon the map, and the question being asked 'what do you want better than that?' no one was able to answer. This may not be the whole story of the plan, but the result is the same as if it were." There is, of course, no good authority for Olmsted's facetious tale, though it is sometimes repeated as authoritative based on Olmsted's superlative reputation. But he was a relentless and eloquent detractor of the grid: "The great disadvantage under which New-York labors is one growing out of the senseless manner in which its streets have been laid out. No city is more unfortunately planned with reference to metropolitan attractiveness." The rigid regularity denied opportunities for nobility and grace: "If a building site is wanted, whether with a view to a church or a blast furnace, an opera house or a toy shop, there is, of intention, no better a place in one of these blocks than in another." Since Olmsted's time, there have been some modifications that have allowed large developments, such as Lincoln Center, but these "super-blocks" are just that: super-sized blocks that are still rectilinear blocks, like super-sized soft drinks that deliver more, not better. "There are numerous structures, both public and private, in London and Paris, and most other large towns of Europe, which could not be built in New York, for want of a site of suitable extent and proportions. . . . Such distinctive advantage of position as Rome gives St. Peter's, Paris the Madeleine, London St. Paul's, New York, under her system, gives to nothing."

The city determined to build Central Park in 1851, when every one of the 1807 Commissioners' open spaces to the south had been sacrificed to the grid in whole or large part as marketable real estate. As solid city approached 42nd Street, it became apparent to some that the city was building itself an urban prison. "There was no place within the city limits," wrote pioneering American art critic Clarence Cook in his book on Central Park,

> in which it was pleasant to walk, or ride, or drive, or stroll; no place for skating, no water in which it was safe to row; no field for base-ball or cricket; no pleasant garden where one could sit and chat with a friend, or watch his children play, or, over a cup or tea or coffee, listen to the music of a good band. Theatres, concerts, and lectures were the only amusements within reach of the mass of the people: the side-walks, the balconies, the back-yards, the only substitutes for the Hyde Park or Tuileries of the Old World, or the ancient freedom and rural beauty of Young New York.

The park deposited into one large rectangle the various public components of urban life that the grid excluded. The park is gridded Manhattan's salvation: its organic, pastoral, antiurban urban center.

What sealed the design competition win for Olmsted and Vaux was their sublimation of anything like a linear Manhattan street, in particular their reduction of the four transverse roads—the competition minimum—to subterranean status.

Much of the park between Fifth and Eighth Avenues, from 59th to 110th Streets (initially 106th Street), was laid where Common Lands lots used to be or still were; about half of the park constituted Common Lands acreage the city still owned or had to buy back.

When the park was first proposed to the people in 1851, the estimated cost of land purchases was just $1.4 million. A Common Council special committee arrived at this seemingly low number—$1,800 per acre, or $10,000 per block, in what "is now, and probably will ever be, the metropolis of America [and] already one of the first cities of the world"—because the park area was so undesirable. "All the lands within its limits are among the most uneven and rocky on the island [with] very numerous abrupt and rocky elevations, intersected constantly by ravines and gentle valleys, through which run several small streams of living water." Therefore, the land was "almost entirely useless for building purposes," but very well suited for a park. In fact, the purchase price (driven by expensive repurchases of Common Lands lots) rose so substantially through the early 1850s that the Common Council voted in March 1855 to shrink the park plan, eliminating the area south of 72nd Street and four hundred feet on the sides. In a move that forever weighs against his later corruptions, newly elected mayor Wood vetoed the Council measure. The city eventually spent $5 million purchasing the park's land, a third of it ultimately recovered in assessments on proximate land.

At 843 acres, Central Park represents a bit over 6 percent of Manhattan's land area; that is, Manhattan equals sixteen Central Parks. By one count in the 1870s, the park removed just under 12,000 twenty-five-by-one-hundred lots from the real estate market.

While the park is revered as a place of off-street recreation (and re-creation because it was entirely designed and almost entirely unnatural nature), its marvelous sinuosities all happen internally within a rigid rectangular border. The park is not a conqueror of the grid but its prisoner, the exercise yard in a rectilinear penitentiary. As Le Corbusier observed in 1935, perhaps channeling the park-reducing Council of 1855, "Central Park is too large and it is a hole in the midst of buildings. It is a lesson. You go through Central Park as if you were in a no man's land. The verdure, and especially the space, of Central Park should be distributed and multiplied throughout Manhattan." Neither the grid nor New Yorkers generally would allow that.

At about the time democratic New York was making rectangular space for its park, monarchal Paris was undergoing citywide redesign. "Despotic governments are generally bad governments, but when one hears of the marvels Napoleon has accomplished in Paris, in the way of street improvements, it makes us wish that he, or some one like him, could be made Emperor of New York for about ten years. What a superb city we could have if re-planned and re-built aright!" So ruminated the editor of the influential *Real Estate Record and Builders' Guide* in 1868. He probably was not aware that Napoleon III had visited New York three decades earlier, when he was just young Louis-Napoleon, nephew of the late emperor and in exile after an ill-conceived coup attempt against Bourbon king Louis-Philippe in October 1836.

During his sojourn in New York in the spring of 1837, Louis was quietly celebrated in discrete circles but fairly depressed, solitary, and often brooding. The prince is "a person who never looks you in the face," observed Knickerbocker poet Fitz-Greene Halleck, who dined with him, "and who always drops his eye if an individual, in turning suddenly, detects him looking at you." The poet thought the royal dull but Louis observed closely, taking notes. When a fellow hotel guest, previously noted for his limited wardrobe ("*un pauvre diable qui n'avait pas de chemise*") appeared one evening with stunning news of a successful land speculation—an entire town to be built and with all the necessary contracts in place—Louis marveled at the spirit of Americans: "masters of the world because they are masters of themselves." The gloomy prince brightened: "On that day I made a solemn promise to myself: on my return to Paris—for I never doubted I would return—I would rebuild the capital of capitals, which I am going to do, God allowing."

The Paris cherished by tourists and travelers, poets and players—the Beaux Arts buildings with their green tile mansard roofs and ornate balconies, the boulevards, plazas, and parks—is younger by a half century than grid-planned Manhattan. It is the triumphal "Second Empire" Paris envisioned by Napoleon III and ruthlessly executed by Baron Georges-Eugène Haussmann. With the unassuming title Prefect of the Seine, Haussmann dispatched dirty, dense, diseased, medieval Paris. The boulevards are glorious but those roofs and balconies are no less of an accident: they were mandates imposed by Haussmann on any developer who dared to build.

"We have no Emperor here to rebuild New York as Paris was rebuilt and beautified," lamented the *Real Estate Record*. A century and a half later one has not yet materialized here, for better or worse. Some might argue that during his thirty-year reign in the mid-1900s Robert Moses—visionary master builder or despotic and misguided champion of the automobile, depending on your point of view— had Haussmann's effect and Napoleon III's power in New York. But Moses's greatest public works triumphs (or tragedies) were the webs of highways and bridges around, not in, Manhattan. By triumphing cars and trucks over rail transportation for people and freight, Moses in the end intensified gridded Manhattan's congestion, quite the opposite of what his icon Haussmann achieved a century earlier in Paris.

Unlike Moses, who *read* about his favorite "brawny Alsatian," Olmsted actually went to Paris to study Haussmann's boulevards but, as a landscape architect not urban planner, he was never was in a position to change Manhattan's grid. Indeed, Olmsted had to admit in 1876 that by then the grid he despised had won.

> The objections at first hotly urged against this plan (chiefly by property holders whose lands it would divide inconveniently, whose lawns and gardens it would destroy and whose houses it would leave in awkward positions), have long since been generally forgotten, and so far as streets have been opened and houses built upon them, the system has apparently met all

popular requirements. Habits and customs accommodated to it have become fixed upon the people of the city. Property divisions have been generally adjusted to it, and innumerable transfers and pledges of real estate have been made under it with a degree of ease and simplicity probably without parallel.

Between 1870 and 1875, the number of New Yorkers living above 14th Street finally surpassed the number below. In 1870, the population below peaked at just under half a million; over the next five years, it dropped for the first time, by nearly 20,000. In the same period, the population living entirely on what was or would be gridded Manhattan soared by nearly 65,000, to 511,000. By 1880, nearly two-thirds of the grid's streets up to 96th had been laid, though most were still empty of buildings. Of an estimated 90,000 building lots from 14th to 155th Streets, nearly 40,000 remained undeveloped in 1875; by 1887, 30,000 above 59th Street were still vacant.

The process of street-laying eradicated the island's natural contours, creating grotesques, ghosts, and other hangers-on. Excavations for large buildings became Brueghelian scenes of protoindustrial chaos. An excavation at 46th Street and Third Avenue in 1868, depicted by a contemporary artist, was a mud-covered hell of water hoses and pumps, fire pits, carts overloaded with explosives and rubble, straining work animals, and half-naked labor gangs. Elsewhere, country houses originally set on hills with scenic views became phantoms on jagged precipices, the remnants of the hills that had been blasted for avenues. In 1861, as seen on the cover of this book, a once elegant mansion's front porch collapses over the canyon of newly laid Second Avenue (at newly laid 42nd Street) thirty feet below. At the time the lithograph was made, the wooded ridge once viewed from the parlor windows had become a four-story brick apartment building, the first in a row that will materialize as soon as more hill disappears. Over on what was becoming Manhattan's West Side, the large Brennan farmhouse, where Poe had lived and lamented the advent of the grid three decades earlier, was newly isolated in 1879 on the remains of a rugged rise and severed from its fields by Broadway and 84th Street: a wooden vestige of country life in a land that soon would be dominated by brick, stone, and asphalt.

By 1870, the city's dense habitation had crept north into the 50s. Land that had been remote just a generation earlier was the target of extraordinary speculation. An auction sale in 1868 of a former estate that was being turned into two urbanizing blocks—57th to 59th Streets, between Sixth and Seventh—was a spectacle attended by 2,000. In what may then have been the largest sale of a single unimproved property, the first lot, at the southwest corner of 59th and Sixth, went for $36,000, and the remainder in sales totaling nearly $1.5 million. By 1887, the total assessed value of city real estate was over $1.2 billion. That year, of the millions in real estate taxes, the largest noncorporate payer was the estate of John Jacob Astor, at nearly a quarter million dollars.

In 1869, the grid spawned its logical stepchild, the first "apartment building," beginning the transition for comfortable New Yorkers from private houses to shared housing, from living on the land to living above it. It was as if an invisible hand grasped the buildings of a block and squeezed them upward, leaving lots of empty space on the block for more upward thrusting. The Manhattan apartment building was the natural outgrowth of the Manhattan grid, which encouraged dense population that had nowhere to live but up. The pioneer builder in 1869 of what were initially called "French houses" or "French flats" was, fittingly, Rutherfurd Stuyvesant, the great-grandson of John Rutherfurd, who had been legally compelled at age six to reverse his birth name to claim his maternal Stuyvesant family inheritance. The Stuyvesant, at 142 East 18th Street, designed by Paris-educated architect Richard Morris Hunt, was an instant hit (it survived for nearly a century) and many similar buildings followed. Fifteen years later, the Dakota, far up the West Side, seemed a speculation only to the unknowing: it was fully rented before it opened.

Lagging behind developments in the construction of buildings on the grid was progress in finishing the streets that fronted them. The Stuyvesant went up on an unevenly cobbled street; the Dakota rose where Eighth Avenue did not yet intersect with 72nd Street. As noted earlier, many years might elapse between when a section of avenue or street was "opened" and when it resembled anything like an urban road: cleared, leveled, graded, and paved. "To Fifty-ninth Street this afternoon" went fastidious George Templeton Strong on October 22, 1867, "traversing for the first time the newly opened section of Madison Avenue between Fortieth Street" and the new campus of Columbia College ten blocks north. The "opened" streets were "a rough and ragged tract, as yet, and hardly a thoroughfare, rich in mudholes, goats, pigs, geese, and stramonium. Here and there Irish shanties 'come out' (like smallpox pustules), each composed of a dozen rotten boards and a piece of stove-pipe for a chimney." A paved, permanent neighborhood was a remote aspiration.

Manhattan's first paved street was cobbled in 1658 and, not surprisingly, took the name Stone Street; the work in those simpler times was happily paid for by assessment on every house along the street. Cobbles ruled the streets for generations after, until the developing grid turned Manhattan into a laboratory of paving technology, starting with experiments in the 1830s with macadam, woodblocks, and other surfaces, with mixed results. At midcentury, most streets were still paved with round cobbles that were cheap but easily broken, rough, unsanitary—"form[ing] receptacles for vegetable matter that is constantly decomposing, and filling the air with a miasm which is very injurious to health"—and noisy to the touch of shoed horses and iron wheels. But there was great hope for "Russ pavement," recently invented and introduced in several streets by Horace P. Russ, who was not yet thirty. "Though expensive, it is most durable," wrote an 1850 admirer, "and will doubtless prove in the end the cheapest that could be used." It featured a surface of rectangular granite blocks about a foot on each side, laid diagonally across the street on a foundation of removable concrete sections that allowed access to water and sewer pipes below. "There can be no doubt that this pavement will, in a few years, supersede all others in the great thoroughfares of the city."

In fact, in a few years, Russ pavement was history. Despite very favorable terms offered by Russ to pave all the city's streets—one-third paid by the city (just twice the cost of troublesome cobbles), two-third by property owners—the admittedly durable pavement was proving incurably slippery, causing injuries to horses and their thrown riders.

Belgian trap block followed. Also cut granite but less slippery than Russ pavement, rectangular Belgian block was larger than cobbles, with fewer crevices between stones. By 1876, half of the city's 300 miles of paved streets (including streets below the grid) were paved with Belgian block, eighty-six miles still with cobbles, and the remainder with an assortment of wood, concrete, and macadam. But the cost of Belgian block had started to rise dramatically and a more economical permanent solution was still needed. It arrived in the 1880s with asphalt. First demonstrated in front of a downtown hotel in 1881, asphalt was next laid on ten blocks of Madison Avenue and finally in 1890 officially adopted as the city's pavement. In the fall of 1897, a long stretch of Fifth Avenue was laid with asphalt, making it "at once the delight of the bicyclist and the parade ground of the pleasure driver, and, in fact, of everyone who can command a hansom." Not everyone was sold—asphalt was cheap, smooth, and easily cleaned, but frequently in need of repair. "There are some days when I will not undertake to drive my horses up Fifth avenue," complained a livery stable owner less than three years after the avenue was paved. "The din of wheels on the rough pavement no longer torments the ear so cruelly," sniffed William Dean Howells, "but there is still the sharp clatter of the horses' shoes everywhere; and their pulverized manure, which forms so great a part of the city's dust, and is constantly taken into people's stomachs and lungs, seems to blow more freely about on the asphalt than on the old-fashioned pavements." But he and everyone else got used to it. By 1938, all of Manhattan's 500 miles of streets were paved, nearly all of them with asphalt. Today, only a bit of a private alley on East 26th Street survives as the single vestige of unpaved Manhattan.

The onetime village of Greenwich is now *the* Village of the city—the long-gridded East Village is a 1960s invention of artists and real estate brokers—but through the 1800s many more villages were strung along the west side of the island, linked like charms in the chain of rural Bloomingdale Road. Greenwich, though closest to the city at the southern tip of the island, had a long history and substantial population that largely kept the grid from its doors, but the grid doomed the rest. Settlements like Harsenville (now the Lincoln Center area), Striker's Bay (80s to upper 90s), Bloomingdale Village (90s to 112th), Manhattanville (112th to 140th), Carmansville (140th to 158th), and smaller communities simply disappeared under the grid's relentless march. On the east side, no pre-grid village had the substance of Greenwich. The Dutch farming village of Nieuw Haarlem initially rivaled the commercial Dutch outpost to the south and retained its autonomy for over two centuries until the grid and elevated railroads finally straightened its cockeyed streets, leaving only the state of mind that is Harlem in rectilinear New York.

Most of the villages along the Hudson were formed as natural expansions of country settlement in the years just prior to the advent of the 1811 grid plan. Jacob Harsen, for example, inherited in the 1750s a portion of an original Dutch land grant and built a homestead on a hill overlooking the Hudson west of Bloomingdale Road and just south of what would become 71st Street. In 1803, the Harsens began developing a village, with a road that by 1811 ran roughly along the future 71st Street from the Hudson through Bloomingdale Road to the Common Land's West Road. Harsen's descendants starting selling off their various properties as gridded city lots in the 1860s. Similarly, Gerrit Striker (or Stryker), the great-grandson of a prosperous New Amsterdam magistrate, in 1764 bought a fifty-acre portion from a larger estate and built a country house he dubbed Striker's Bay, overlooking a cove at what became 96th Street. A settlement developed around the property; starting in the 1830s, his descendants leased out the house, which operated as a resort hotel for several decades until the grid made urban lots of the farm.

Manhattanville was unique among the pre-grid villages in several ways. It was the only settlement founded by a non–New Yorker, Philadelphia-born Jacob Schieffelin, and expressly as a speculative development, instead of as a natural outgrowth of long family presence. Schieffelin was a Loyalist during the Revolution, did exile's time in Canada, and reinvented himself in 1794 in New York in his Quaker in-laws' wholesale drug business. The following year, Schieffelin began making speculative land purchases far up-island along the Hudson at what was called Harlem Cove, the mouth of a hill-ringed valley centered on what would become 130th Street. With two brothers-in-law, Schieffelin hired Adolphus Loss (Charles's brother) to lay out a grid for a village, incorporated in 1806, with streets named for various family partners plus the broad central Manhattan Street giving the village its name. This was the new village that inspired the confidence of Gouverneur Morris, passing through in January 1807, that the whole island would soon be developed. Indeed, by that summer, "Manhattan Ville" was already a "flourishing little town," with a wharf, school, public buildings, and the first private residences. The village continued to flourish (as did the Schieffelin drug company, which later transitioned to wines and spirits and was bought by Moët & Chandon in 1981), but it eventually had to come to terms with Morris's grid. Rotated to the east even more than the Kips Bay grid down-island, most of Manhattanville's streets have disappeared, except for its main drag, which survives as the curiously angled western end of 125th Street (as does another original Manhattanville street as the western end of 126th).

Even though Randel's 1811 map dispatched all of Manhattanville, the city soon realized that Manhattan Street had to stay: as part of its arrangements with Schieffelin, the Common Council had agreed early in 1807 to lay the road itself, paying a contractor $600 to do so that summer. In 1808, the Council had decided that no matter what its newly appointed street commission decided, distant Manhattan Street in a private land development was actually a city street that "ought not to be rejected or altered." In 1849, the western end of the Commissioners' 125th Street was officially discontinued on its rectilinear path and Manhattan Street became western 125th.

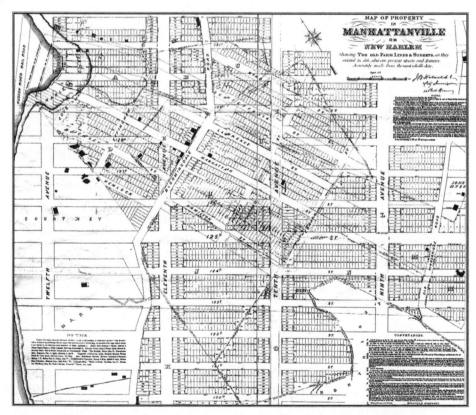

This 1878 map, drawn by city surveyor John Bute Holmes, depicts how the grid conflicted with the pre-grid Manhattanville development, the central street of which had already been officially redesignated as the angled western end of 125th Street.

The vestige of Manhattanville was a rare victory for the Bloomingdale villages over the advancing grid. Eighth Avenue was opened in 1816 from Greenwich to the Harlem River. Tenth Avenue was opened beyond 155th Street to Kingsbridge Road in 1836. In 1855 Ninth Avenue was opened to 125th Street. The cross streets mostly followed afterwards, for example, 75th, 76th, and 77th Streets in the 1860s, by which time it was clear that the rural villages of western Manhattan would disappear into the gridded city.

Still, in 1865, much of the west side remained relatively undeveloped. From 50th to 86th Streets, Eighth Avenue was entirely paved, but Ninth Avenue was paved only to 54th Street, graded only to 63rd Street, and intermittently graded above. Tenth Avenue was graded only to 74th Street. Eleventh Avenue, ordered opened to 144th Street in 1854, was a decade later graded only to 59th Street with no development above. Pavement, where it existed, was a mix of cobble and block. There were rail tracks on all the avenues below 59th Street, but only on Eighth above. Broadway was graded to 70th Street, paved with block until 59th, and macadamized to 70th. Most of the streets below 59th were open and graded but not paved. Above 59th, only 86th was entirely opened, a rough country road in its western portions, unpaved but curbed and guttered, with a sidewalk between Tenth and Eighth Avenues. Roughly 16,000 residents lived predominantly in basic two-story wood structures but fully a third were squatters living in shanties. Only 630 or so families lived in 147 brick structures, most of them four-story buildings, built on grid lots.

From 86th Street north only a few streets had been laid. "The general aspects of the country present still some of its natural scenery," reported the district's sanitary inspector. "A few streets have been cut through the hills, and a few of the avenues partly traverse the length of this portion of the Island." Bloomingdale Road was still the main thoroughfare, a macadamized country road sixty feet wide without sidewalks or gutters. The avenues existed mostly in name alone, except for Eighth Avenue, which was newly passable for horse cars to 125th Street. A handful of streets existed as ungraded dirt roads. Only 129th Street was paved, with gutters, curbs, and flagged sidewalks. Of 819 anticipated city blocks in this area, only 369 existed even partially in shape.

The relatively slow spread of the grid on the west side of the island—the more level east side was developing much more quickly—provided an unexpected opportunity to keep the grid at bay permanently. The chief actor was Andrew Haswell Green, who despised the grid as much as Olmsted did, though Olmsted despised Green nearly as much.

Green (1820–1903) was a career civic leader and planner, an incorruptible person in a city ruled for a time by the Tweed ring. Trained as a lawyer by fellow lifelong bachelor Samuel J. Tilden, Green ran the Board of Education in his thirties. His emergency service as city comptroller led to Tweed's downfall and imprisonment. As an executor of Tilden's contested will, Green secured the trust that enabled the creation of the New York Public Library. In his seventies, he presided over the 1898 consolidation of the city and its neighboring municipalities into the five-borough Greater New York that he had first envisioned thirty years earlier as president and comptroller of the commission that built Central Park.[*]

After his life's work was mostly done, Green died tragically in November 1903. On a Friday the thirteenth, he was shot five times with a heavy revolver in the vestibule of his Park Avenue brownstone by a furnace tender who had been stalking him for a week. "He deserved it," Cornelius Williams declared. "He forced me to do it!" Williams had mistaken the white-bearded Father of Greater New York for another white-bearded octogenarian gentleman who had become the benefactor of sorts of an "abandoned woman" whom Williams fancied. The murder was a sensation across the

---

[*] Green also had a connection to Aaron Burr: uncle Timothy Green, a Burr friend and business associate, was conducting Burr's adored daughter Theodosia from Charleston to New York in January 1813 when their ship was lost at sea.

United States and in Europe, with elements of classic tragedy: the intended and actual victims were wealthy and white; the killer and the love interest were poor and black. Green among all the players was entirely innocent and dead (Williams was committed).

It was Green who oversaw the construction of Central Park, often with a frugality that infuriated designer Olmsted. "Not a cent is got from under his paw that is not wet with his blood & sweat," Olmsted complained in 1861. Green's thrift, Olmsted grumbled to Vaux three years later, was "a systematic small tyranny, measured exactly to the limit of my endurance." Still, the men were united against the tyranny of the grid.

As a result of popular resistance to the grid on the west side, the Central Park commission won state approval in 1867 to see what improvements might be made above 59th Street. In the run-up, Green had made his opinions clear. The 1807 Commissioners, he wrote in late 1865, "in making a plan for the island, appear to have done no more than to indicate on paper (for they did no actual work on the ground) the lines of certain avenues, streets and squares; and it is not too much to say, that they carried to an extreme, a system perhaps well enough adapted to the tolerably level ground of the lower part of the city." And, he knew, the system was not even theirs: "They found something similar to it already existing in the neighborhood of the Seventh Ward"—Goerck's Common Lands plan—"and they fixed it upon irregular and precipitous portions of the island, to which it was not at all adapted." Green went so far as to recall favorably the partial plan of Mangin in 1803. But the 1807 Commissioners "failed to discriminate between those localities where their plan was fit, and those to which its features are destructive, both in point of expense and of convenience." Green noted that since 1814, some three dozen laws had passed modifying "almost every one of the features of the plan"—we've covered the major ones, like the shrinking of the Parade and other open spaces and the extending of Broadway—"excepting that of the rectangular system" itself. Manhattan west of Central Park and continuing north was particularly unsuited to the 1811 grid plan. "The plan of this part of the city . . . is simply the extension over an irregular, rocky, and sometimes precipitous surface, of a rectangular system of ways, which, however well devised it may be for a more regular and less uneven surface, is obviously illy adapted to considerable portions of the territory in question, as well on account of considerations of economy as of convenience."

Green intended to do something about that. If he were planning the west side in the 1860, "the rectangular plan would not be exclusively adopted," saving the vast expenditures experienced elsewhere in the city on excavations and street grading. Instead, the natural heights and valleys would have been preserved, with diagonal streets running along the valleys and providing drainage as the many natural watercourses did.

Unfortunately, it was mostly too late. Even though little of the grid had been laid, "the lines of property already largely conform to it." The hundreds of blocks existed on paper, the city had purchased much of the land for their streets, and many thousands of future lots had owners. So Green did what he could, mostly where the most prohibitive topography had daunted planners and speculators. He created Morningside Park from a long rock ridge and, taking greater liberties, fashioned Riverside Park along the rugged Hudson River shoreline. Olmsted and Vaux planned the details of both.

Green acted just in time. By 1880, the west side was catching up to the east side in development. "If you stand in the hollow at the corner of Eighty-sixth Street and Eighth Avenue, you will see a long reach of garden, with a weathered old cottage near the middle, and if you do not raise your eyes, it will seem to you that you are in Ireland," observed *Harper's Weekly* that fall. "But the actual locality is recalled to you by the elevated trains buzzing to and fro on Ninth Avenue; and through the thread-like trestle-work you can see, still farther away, an abandoned mansion, with an aristocratic cupola blinking in the sunshine."

This detail of a remarkable six-foot-long map of Manhattan, drafted by William Taylor and published by Galt & Hoy in 1879, shows how, in the quarter-century since the Dripps map, the eastern side of the grid has filled dramatically, the western side lags, and Central Park, with its serpentine shapes, forms a physical and conceptual barrier between them. (*Library of Congress*)

After securing approval for revisions of the upper western portion of the grid, Green had a go at the portion of Manhattan that the 1807 Commissioners had decided was improbable to be settled "for centuries to come." It took less than half a century for the land above 155th Street to attract the attention of planners. Green wasn't the first.

In their remarks, the 1807 Commissioners explained, thinly, that "to have gone further might have furnished materials to the pernicious spirit of speculation." They had no qualms with such spirit all over gridded Manhattan. Their other morsel of explanation for the hands-off approach to northern Manhattan rings truer: "They have in this respect been governed by the shape of the ground." The bulk of old Mannahatta was hardly flat: the names Rose Hill, Murray Hill, Carnegie Hill, Lenox Hill, Sugar Hill, Morningside Heights, and Hamilton Heights are grounded in reality, not realty. But the northernmost miles of Manhattan were and are a relative palisade, the eastern wall of the deep canyon that the diluvial violence of the most recent glacial recession turned into the slender tidal estuary we call the lower Hudson River. The Commissioners wisely, and perhaps not entirely disingenuously, concluded that their flatlander's grid was ill suited to upper Manhattan. Or, as suggested earlier, they simply ran out of time to explore a more organic plan that might have worked for the entire island.

In 1851, the Common Council directed the street commissioner to present a plan for upper Manhattan. But no money was allocated to the effort and nothing happened. In 1860, a state law empowered a seven-man commission specifically to plan something different from the grid to the south: it would be "impracticable, and ruinous to land owners, and injurious to the interests of the city, to grade and lay out streets and avenues north of One Hundred and Fifty-fifth street . . . upon the present plan of the city, at right angles, and in blocks of uniform size, on account of the elevated, irregular, and rocky formation of that district." Olmsted and Vaux were hired as landscape architects to the commission.

There were high hopes that this commission would do for uppermost Manhattan what the commission of a half century earlier had failed to do for the bulk of the island. "Instead of perpetrating the stupid vandalism of reducing these elevated and beautiful grounds to the grade level, and intersecting them with avenues and streets," the *New York Herald* editorialized, "the idea now is not to interfere with the natural beauties of the location." The *Herald* was "delighted to learn" that these commissioners were "manifesting so much good sense and refined taste" with plans for curving roads and boulevards. "In a few years New York will be able to point a Parisian to a Champs Elysée and Boulevards more exquisite than his own."

Alas, nonresident speculators and railway interests worked the hands and minds of certain of the commissioners. The commission's 1863 report played "the march of progress" tune and, disregarding their legal mandate, called for leveling and a grid to seamlessly extend the first one. The public was outraged, newspapers took up the cause, and within two years the state abolished the 1860 commission and awarded planning power to the Central Park commission run by Green.

"The surface of this territory is exceedingly varied, irregular and picturesque; it includes the monotonous level of the salt marsh, and the rolling pasture, and rises at times to a high degree of craggy wildness," observed Green. The area had a population of a few thousand, mostly in villas and farms scattered through the rugged, natural landscape. The bulk of the roughly 1,800 acres was owned by just 250 people and was subdivided into plots of various sizes, from twenty-five-foot lots to extensive tracts. Isaac Dyckman owned the single largest tract, an estate of some 400 acres. The area was readily accessible from the south by only two routes: the old Kingsbridge Road, which led all the way north to Spuyten Duyvil Creek, originally crossed in 1693 by the first bridge connecting Manhattan with what is now the Bronx mainland; and Tenth Avenue, a premature extension of the grid to the area of what became 190th Street.

Green conducted what amounted to an environmental impact study, a century before anyone had conceived of an EIS. He studied upper Manhattan's weather and air, food and water supplies, sanitation, even the vocations of its residents. In 1868, he announced a plan that called for some rectilinear grid in the flat valleys but other streets and avenues plus parks that followed the contours of the land: Manhattan above 155th Street as organic as its development below 155th Street was not, with segments of curving or angled streets up to 220th mingled with the hills, valleys, cliffs, and forest left much as nature made them. As a matter of urban planning history, Green's curving streets mark their "first appearance in an official plan of an American city."

"It is the only portion of Manhattan Island," Green wrote proudly in 1901, "where any trace of its pristine beauty remains undesecrated and unrased [sic] by the leveling march of so-called 'public improvements.'" Had a lunatic not mistook him two years later for the imagined rival of an imaginary lover, Green might have forestalled the denser development that ultimately took hold of the area by the 1930s. But the forested parks, ancient rocks, and curving streets distinguish today's upper Manhattan and contrast sharply with the rest. If the 1807 Commissioners had put some more thought into it, much of the island might have looked like Green's bit of Manhattan. Green's Manhattan is the sort of city that Joseph Mangin had in mind before anyone else was thinking of New York as a place that needed a plan.

Curiously, though, Green reversed the error of the Commissioners he despised. They planned too few avenues; he planned too few streets. Green anticipated that predominant movement in northern Manhattan would be the same as further south, that is, north-south. In fact, in that narrow portion of the island, the predominate movement is east-west: "a series of lateral avenues would have served the region better." Further proof that any plan is just that: an educated guess at best about what the future holds.

CHAPTER 12

THE CITY UNBEAUTIFUL

The exasperating idiots who ruined New York . . .

—*Real Estate Record and Builders' Guide*, 1883

From the moment a New Yorker is confronted with almost any large city of Europe, it is impossible for him to pretend to himself that his own city is anything other than an unscrupulous real-estate speculation.

—Edmund Wilson, *Europe Without Baedeker*, 1947

A S MUCH AS Morris, DeWitt, Rutherfurd, and Randel may have intended to create a cityscape of uniformity and equality, their streets are not the equals of their avenues. The fewness of the avenues makes them superior; the multitude of the streets makes them common. In the congress of Manhattan, the avenues each have exceptional authority; the streets have power only in their numbers.

As enough new streets and avenues appeared on Manhattan's open plate, patterns emerged, especially for distant observers. "If you suppose that the skeleton of a sole had a number of cross-bones parallel to the back-bone," wrote an essayist in London's *MacMillan's Magazine* in 1862, "you will have an exact idea of the plan of New York. The back-bone is the Broadway; the parallel cross-bones are the Avenues; and the bones at right angles to the back-bone are the Streets, numbered consecutively from the sole's mouth." Manhattan's materializing grid helped Europeans understand how the youthful United States, free and chaotic (and in 1862 at war with itself), might become a proper orderly place.

All these bones stuck in the gullet of Clinton Sweet. Sweet, the publisher of the *Real Estate Record and Builders' Guide*, considered the Commissioners and their surveyor "the exasperating idiots who ruined New York." The streets should have been avenues and the avenues streets, Sweet insisted; that is, there should have been relatively many north-south routes and relatively fewer east-west routes. At the very least, the streets should have been 150 feet apart, not 200, making for building lots a much more reasonable seventy-five feet deep. Sweet, writing in 1883 when the grid had successfully swept north, realized that "these things are past praying for." (He eventually put a revolver bullet through his head, demoralized about matters weightier than the grid.)

Sweet was hardly alone in his thoughts. New York's grid plan treated it as a commercial city "with its chief movements from river to river," observed Samuel McElroy, the man planning Brooklyn's streets in 1874, "but experience has not confirmed this theory, and the system of blocks is reversed from what it should be, for up and down town travel." McElroy was then a respected civil engineer involved in many aspects of Brooklyn's development. He cast a sideways glance across the river at the already "crowded avenues" of New York: "As the streets lie across the lines of movement, there is great inconvenience from the limited number of channels, and from the continued interruption of those which do exist, at short intervals, by the street crossings."

The Brooklyn street planner was a fan of many parallel lines if they were in the correct direction but also saw ample "want of forethought" in the lack of diagonals: "In the earlier days of city life, lines may be considered radical in size or direction, which prove, in time, wise preventatives to legislation and costly rearrangement."

Oddly, some years before Clinton Sweet's unfortunate demise, Samuel McElroy himself had a dark denouement. His death of a sudden heart ailment in 1899 exposed a Gothic private life. Maliciously pronounced insane in his will, his quite sane second wife refused to leave their house for his funeral for fear of being locked out by his children; thus ensconced, she revealed to a reporter that "my husband was not very strict about some things." She produced a passel of lovers' letters that proved the bad-hearted McElroy a congenital lothario. A few years later, his namesake engineer son was electrocuted by a trolley car. Any linkage between Manhattan grid criticism and notorious death is an illusion, one hopes.

Sweet and McElroy publically identified two major issues with the grid: the lack of diagonals and the reversed primacy of lateral and lineal routes. The grid Commissioners of course had expressly disdained radials, while their adoption of Goerck's Common Lands plan restricted them to 200-foot blocks. But these issues continued to trouble New Yorkers for generations.

"If our remote ancestors failed to realize, through no especial fault of theirs, the enormous growth and traffic of American cities, it is our duty and our profit to correct these blunders as rapidly as we can. The rectangular formation of streets is well enough for a beginning," wrote a contributor to the *Engineering News*, the country's most important engineering journal, in 1891, but "as the city grows in area the gridiron plan more and more fails to meet the requirements of rapid traffic, and the want of diagonal streets is more keenly felt." Walkers also were inconvenienced: "The citizen must always go around the two sides of a triangle in passing between points diagonally opposite." As we know from those footpaths in the dirt of the empty lot up on Carnegie Hill, walkers take any diagonal opportunity they can get. And, of course, diagonals have importance beyond the merely utilitarian: "They relieve the city from the dull monotony of the rectangular street formation and give abundant opportunity for civic adornment, which latter is almost as important."

Coming at the birth of the City Beautiful movement in the rapidly urbanizing United States, the comments in the *Engineering News* would be echoed by many others, such as architect Julius Harder at the end of the decade. "It is truly remarkable that the men who are responsible for the 'gridiron' plan," Harder wrote, "completely omitted the diagonal system of primary avenues." Harder, who had worked on the 1893 Chicago World's Fair, which many hoped would be the avatar of improved urban design, believed that diagonal avenues would not just relieve the rigid grid and open vistas but also were essential to harmonizing the city's transportation and commercial networks. Broadway, narrow and congested along its middle course, "should have become, by reason of its position in the peculiar geography of Manhattan Island, our most magnificent and impressive street . . . as the only one diagonal to the rectangular system [but] is a pathetic evidence of the economy and convenience that might have been general." The essential part of Harder's proposal was an "x" of diagonal roads centered on Union Square, from 34th Street and Tenth Avenue to South Street just below the Williamsburg Bridge (under construction), and from Bellevue Hospital at 27th and First to Christopher Street in Greenwich Village, with numerous traffic circles along each route. These locations were calculated not just for traffic flow but also to introduce aesthetic vistas into a city that had none. Harder also diagrammed how three-block segments of existing grid between avenues could be modified to increase the number of corners, shorten the distance between them, and provide street-accessible interior courts for deliveries. "Civic pride and interest in municipal affairs will in time evolve a logical city plan," Harder wrote hopefully as the nineteenth century drew its last gasp.

Proposals for diagonals did not die with the century, nor did Sweet and McElroy's sense that the grid got the street to avenue ratio wrong. "Even on the score of utility," wrote New York historian Thomas Janvier in 1894, "the Commissioners fell into one grave

error, for which . . . there was absolutely no excuse . . . their provision of longitudinal streets was one-third less to the square mile
than was their provision of latitudinal streets. The city has not yet
expanded to the point where the inconvenience arising from this
blunder has become sufficiently marked to attract attention. It will
begin to be felt very soon." With the development of railways, subways, midtown commercial piers, and automobiles, and dense settlement of the entire island, the shortage of avenues was very quickly
felt. "It is now easy to appreciate," appreciated Arthur Pound thirty
years later, "that the Manhattan of the present would be better
served if the number of north-and-south avenues had been doubled,
and the number of cross streets cut in half, since north-and-south
traffic is now the more demanding." Pound was an economist, editor
(*Atlantic Monthly*), poet, popular historian (many novels and non-
fiction works), and the New York State Historian and state archives
director. He was generally a fan of the grid and its makers—"the
Commissioners probably could not have worked out a better plan for
all purposes"—but saw its failings, especially "in the eyes of modern
city planners coping with traffic conditions which the Commission
could not have foreseen."

Radical as they were, the defining plans of 1800s Manhattan—
the street grid of 1811 and Central Park of the 1850s—were also
conservative projects: one outfitted the island permanently with a
checked suit, the other tucked in an attractive pocket rectangle. By
contrast, a plan of the 1860s was the most radical idea yet proposed
for Manhattan and reverberated in varying and even greater forms
for generations. While the grid was fit to the island, and the park
to the grid, the 1860s proposal was out of bounds. It proposed to
increase Manhattan's size by some 2,500 acres, or 20 percent of the
existing island, three times the size of Central Park.

The idea man was James E. Serrell. He came to New York as
an eleven-year-old in 1831, when his parents emigrated from London with their large family. Educated in greatest part by his surveyor

father, Serrell early on impressed local engineers and inventors like Samuel F. B. Morse, who in 1843 endorsed Serrell's substitute for service pipe made of health-impairing lead to bring newly available Croton water into homes from city mains.

Two years later, Serrell was named a city surveyor, making him at twenty-five among the youngest ever to hold the position (older brother John was twenty-six on his appointment in 1841; Joseph Mangin was thirty-one when he was named in 1796). Serrell very actively retained the position until his death in 1892, when he was the oldest city surveyor. By then, he "had probably surveyed more property on Manhattan Island than any other person" and was "identified with all the large street gradings and water supply operations in this city during the last forty years." While not a nationally important civil and military engineer like younger brother Edward, Serrell was a force in public, private, and institutional surveying on Manhattan. His client list was long and distinguished, including prominent landowners like Cornelius Vanderbilt and Henry Brevoort; businesses and institutions like Trinity Church, Roosevelt Hospital, the New York Stock Exchange; and many of the city's railroads and banks. His most important public survey work included the Central Park Reservoir, the difficult grading of Second Avenue, the widening of Broadway from 34th to 59th Streets, and public hospitals and other facilities on the city's East River islands. Among his early mainland projects was the layout in 1848 of Tarrytown's Sleepy Hollow Cemetery, now a national historic landmark, where Serrell, his wife, and many relatives, along with Andrew Carnegie, Walter Chrysler, IBM's Thomas Watson, and legend-maker Washington Irving are buried.

Serrell was a handsome man, with an open, intelligent face, friendly smile, deep-set expressive eyes, and a prematurely thinning head of hair balanced in his younger years by a thick handlebar moustache and eventually by a bushy, graying beard. He had the look throughout his life of a man justifiably comfortable with himself and the world. He was well and happily married, with several children (though his namesake died at twenty-seven of unrecorded causes), and homes for many years in the West 50s between Eighth and Ninth Avenues, a modest but proper neighborhood for the period.

Unlike certain surveyors, such as John Randel, who were lost outside the exactitude of their professional work and trapped within it, Serrell was a man of many interests. He was captain of the engineer corps of the local state militia regiment and wrote a military engineers drill book in 1861, when such things mattered. He was active in the National Anti-Monopoly League, which took aim at railroad, telegraph, coal, and oil companies in the early 1880s, when these things mattered.

Serrell knew his workplace. During his first year as a city surveyor, he redrew Goerck's Common Lands map, Mangin's abandoned plan, and the complete 1821 Manhattan atlas of John Randel (who was still kicking around). As one of the city's busiest surveyors, Serrell was hired to put dozens of Manhattan country estates to the grid. It's safe to say that for many decades, few knew the island better. He also knew its place in the local geography. Among his many passions was improving the movement of people and commerce to, from, and around Manhattan. In 1857, he joined a lengthening list of people seeking a permanent link between Manhattan and Brooklyn, to minimize the increasing reliance on weather and time-dependent ferries. He proposed an "East River Tunnel," of masonry and cement and copper-lined, at either of two locations, roughly in line with where the Manhattan and Williamsburg Bridges would be built over the river a half century later, suspension then having advanced more quickly than subaqueous technology. The Holland Tunnel, the city's first and the world's longest, linking Manhattan and Jersey City, didn't come along until the 1920s. Though much publicized, Serrell didn't dwell on his premature tunnel idea.

For many years, though, he did ponder a solution to a different navigational issue: the treacherous Hell Gate, where the East and

Harlem Rivers met at Randall's and Ward's Islands with generations of shipwrecking turbulence. Serrell was hardly the first to think about taming Hell Gate.

By the 1850s, the confusion of currents, winds, and rocks grounded a thousand ships a year and scuttled or seriously damaged nearly two dozen, despite the efforts of pilots. Though Hell Gate affected interstate commerce, Congress wasn't showing much interest, so a transplanted French engineer, Benjamin Maillefert, with local mercantile backing, started blasting away at some of the rocks and reefs in 1850. After partial success, the effort ended two years later when Maillefert accidently blew up his nearby supply boat instead of an intended rock, killing or injuring all five men involved. Maillefert himself was blown from his boat into the air, landing in the river "severely injured and burnt, and . . . very near being drowned" before he was rescued. The catastrophe was a national story but the only blame assigned by a coroner's jury was to a Hell Gate pilot who passed by in his boat, loudly refusing to save anyone: "They ought to have been blown to hell long ago!" The pilots' profits flowed from Hell Gate hazards. Maillefert survived, was found faultless (we live in different, or perhaps similar, times), recovered, and became a celebrated military and commercial demolition expert and educator.

In the meantime, Hell Gate continued to attract vulnerable ships and ingenious men intent on taming it. In 1865, when American attentions were returning from war to commerce, Serrell made his move. He was as motivated as ever about local commerce around Manhattan and also about something new: the recent loss of dozens of buildable Manhattan blocks to Central Park. His fantastic idea was a greater Manhattan.

Serrell laid out his vision in a detailed map, augmented over four years with essays, public lectures, and much newspaper coverage. The map graphically transforms Manhattan from the familiar, seductively slender island into a nondescript mass, like youth bloated with age by sedentary habits. Specifically, Serrell proposed landfilling the East River from 125th Street to 14th Street, extending Manhattan east beyond the natural shorelines of Queens and Brooklyn to a new East River. At a uniform width of 3,600 feet (greater than the distance between Third and Seventh Avenues), the new linear river would be roughly triple the average width of the existing river. In re-creating the navigational route between the upper and lower portions of the natural river, the new river would essentially broaden and straighten the strait (like the Harlem River, the East River is really a tidal strait) for five and a half miles. Gone would be Hell Gate, rocks, reefs, and other navigational river hazards, all converted to manmade land of a greater Manhattan.

And yet, as the grid and Central Park were conservative radical projects, Serrell's idea, while radical in size and shape, was profoundly conservative in detail: the street plan for the 2,500 acres of new Manhattan land "would be the same arrangement" as the existing Manhattan grid. Up in his mainland grave, Gouverneur Morris had a warm feeling: Serrell was a man after Morris's heart and design. Over half a century after Morris's grid for an island ruled by animal transportation, railroad age Serrell was for laying out an expanded Manhattan just as Morris and company had. No circles, ovals, stars, radials, curvilinears, or other beautifying embellishments. And no open spaces or parks to balance the added recreational burden on Central Park, which with many more east-lying avenues would no longer be central. This is what makes Serrell's image of Manhattan seem like bloating: in addition to all the Commissioners' rectilinear blocks, Serrell would simply have added hundreds more, unbroken and unrelieved by parks or other urban splendor.

By 1869, Serrell had promoted his plan to the city, the state, and even Congress as a matter of interstate commerce. But he gained few adherents. The *Herald*, which published his memorial to the state legislature in 1867, four days later mocked it: "Now, if Mr. Serrell has enough time, money and science to carry out successfully all his plans, we shall suggest that he also engage the services of the famous astronomer in Dr. Johnson's tale of Rasselas, and change our detestable climate. . . . Perhaps Mr. Serrell will postpone the realization of his stupendous plan for remodelling New York until the astronomer shall have arrived from Abyssinia."

In its day, Serrell's idea seemed mad to many. But, regardless of its unoriginal street plan, the enlargement of Manhattan was at least technologically plausible, had some urban historical precedent—Serrell pointed all the way back to the landfilling for St. Petersburg, done a century and a half earlier albeit under orders of a czar—and its effects would have been profound.

Was Serrell's greater Manhattan any crazier than the Commissioners' gridded Manhattan? The grid seems normal, even "great" to some, because it happened, we've had it for two centuries, it seems impervious to substantial changing, and many, even most, of us generally like it. That's our grid and we're sticking to it. Regardless of whether adding more unbroken rectilinear grid lacked imagination or justification, we could just have easily gotten used to the greater Manhattan Serrell had in mind, much as we might have gotten used to another now obscure local "fantasy," Mangin's 1803 plan.

Serrell abandoned local waterway rearrangements to future generations but kept a wary eye on schemes elsewhere, particularly a strongly advocated French plan of the 1870s to flood the Sahara Desert into a vast inland sea. "If such a project should be started," Serrell warned, "and not under the complete control of those in charge of the work, the earth could, and no doubt would be thrown off its present balance, and . . . might cause the 'end of the world.'" Fortunately, the chief promoter died, Suez Canal builder Ferdinand de Lesseps cooled his ardent support, and all parties, pro and con, were spared any embarrassment (though Jules Verne eventually turned the idea into *Invasion of the Sea*, his final science fiction novel). Nobody thought seriously again about making sea of the Sahara, but Serrell's East River ideas and more would be back.

In the meantime, gridded Manhattan filled up. "It can only be a few years, at most, before all the empty spaces will be occupied," observed William Dean Howells in 1896, "and the town, such as it is, and such as it seems to have been ever since the colonial period, will have anchored itself fast in the rock that underlies the larger half of it and imparted its peculiar effect to every street an effect of arrogant untidiness, of superficial and formal gentility, of immediate neglect and overuse." As New Yorkers contemplated the extension of streets over their entire island, the nation itself reached a similar milestone: the closing of the continental frontier. As Manhattan ran out of northward island, the pioneer centuries of "Westward ho!" bucked up at another coast. The sea-to-shining-sea nation was finally born; it would, after some soul searching, seek other frontiers. Similarly, in 1898, New York would leap its Manhattan boundaries to claim portions of its proximate islands and mainland as Greater New York.

By the close of the 1800s, nearly all of Manhattan's planned streets had appeared physically, two-thirds of them paved. The island was densely populated as far as 168th Street, with nearly 100,000 buildings. By the 1920s, Manhattan was almost entirely built over. "At every turn," wrote Montgomery Schuyler, casting his eye over the repetitive sameness of it all, "when one is looking backwards through the architectural history of New York, he finds fresh occasion to execrate the authors of the street system of 1807." Schuyler was particularly appalled at the deep lot of one hundred feet that the Commissioners' 200-foot blocks ordained, creating endless rows of narrow buildings. "The deep lot was one of the dire inventions of those unconscious vandals."

One unconscious result of the 1811 plan that Schuyler didn't consider was its inhospitality to play spaces. New York had no municipal playgrounds through the 1800s, though arguably for much of the century there had been enough open space for informal play at a time when play in organized spaces was not yet a concept.

By the 1890s, though, open space on Manhattan was disappearing, the concept of the playground was emerging, and the Manhattan grid plan, with little park space and no interstitial spaces, offered few evident spots for siting them. "In the original plan of the city of New York the children seem to have been forgotten," charged a special committee on city parks in 1897. The committee, dominated by urban reformer Jacob Riis, acknowledged that all the unoccupied land that had been available in the earlier parts of the century excused "this oversight" but in recent decades children had been left with "no other opportunity for play but such as can be found in the streets." Twentieth-century New Yorkers grew up on stickball, stoopball, boxball, hopscotch, and ring-a-levio in the streets and sidewalks, but those and other games thrived there because there weren't other places to play. This developing situation horrified the 1897 committee: "The streets themselves have been largely occupied by car tracks and new servitudes, so that it is dangerous as well as obstructive to traffic for the children to use them for games of any kind, without incurring the interference of the police. A sense of hostility between the children and the guardians of public order is thus engendered, leading to the growth of a criminal class and to the education of citizens who become enemies of law and order." This seems extreme now, especially to postmoderns lamenting the loss of Spaldeen-based street life to thumb-driven indoor electronics, but the street as play space was bound to be confrontational. "Many complaints are received daily of boys annoying pedestrians, storekeepers, and tenants by their continually playing baseball in some part of most every street," a sympathetic uptown precinct captain reported to the committee. "The damage is not slight; arrests are frequent—much more frequent than when they had open lots to play in. These lots are now built upon, and for every new house there are more boys and less chance for them to play." The committee could get away with "the failure to provide for the reasonable recreation of the people, and especially for playgrounds for the rising generation, has been the most efficient cause of the growth of crime and pauperism in our midst." Again, it seems hyperbolic now, but the fervent recommendations of the 1897 committee, soon backed by the new Playground Association of America (founded in 1906; now the National Recreation and Park Association) led the city to start creating playgrounds and small parks wherever empty lots and vacant spaces could be had. It wasn't so easy making playgrounds in existing parks, especially Central Park, whose advocates, protesting a 1910 proposal for a North Meadow playground, noted "the antagonism between a park and a playground. . . . A park is for the whole community, not for any one class; and to thus divert any part of it to the exclusive use of one class is wrong and wasteful."

By 1915, young New Yorkers had the option at least of seventy playgrounds, most of them interlopers in grid territory. Carmansville Playground, for example, was born in 1912 on a half acre of what had been a village developed from farmland by Richard Carman in the 1840s. Long after Carman's heirs parted with all of their land, including this parcel, it became urban along Tenth Avenue between 151st and 152nd Streets. The Parks Department acquired a tiny portion—0.142 acres—by condemnation in 1906 and another—0.431 acres—by transfer in 1911 from the Bureau of Water Supply, whose Croton Aqueducts of 1842 and 1893 crisscrossed underneath. In the 1960s, Carmansville's basketball courts became famous as the Battlegrounds of future NBA stars.

While some playgrounds did appear in the naturalistic settings of existing parks—over the objections of starchy administrators who dreaded boisterous child clusters in manmade pastorality—most playgrounds were grid-located and, like Central Park itself, creatures of their defining borders: play space in rigid rectangles.

But the battle for control of the streets accelerated—literally—in the 1920s as more and faster automobiles appeared. It took much of the century to nudge children from their asphalt play spaces, and the car made all-out war on pedestrians who dared to enter the street space. The term *jaywalker*—a "jay" being a rustic who didn't know the ways of the city—appeared in the 1910s in American cities and especially in New York, where the police commissioner in 1915 pinned the stigmatizing label on any midblock crosser and threatened arrest. This roused the *New York Times*, outraged at the term—"a truly shocking name and highly opprobrious"—but supportive of the practice: "Vehicular currents are more confused and confusing at the intersections of the streets than midway between them." At the time, practically all Manhattan streets were two-way, so the logic of "jay-walking" is even stronger on today's one-way streets, though the city's policing authorities have never quite grasped it.

Regardless, the future was clear. The common-law tradition— all users had an equal right to the highway and a duty not to injure other users—was dead, and the traditional motive force, the relatively slow-moving horse, was disappearing, dramatically, in the late 1910s. Now the car was king, especially in gridded Manhattan where the long linear streets were better-suited to machines than living things. "The automobilist has absorbed the pedestrian's ancient right to cross the street at the intersection," wrote an aggrieved Manhattan walker in 1925. "The pedestrian must cross the street where and as best he can. He is no better off at the intersection than as a jaywalker, because the motorist of these days does not recognize the right of the pedestrian to cross the street at any point."

WHEN IS A street grid complete? The northern boundary of the 1811 grid, 155th Street, was laid from river to river in 1837 but it was a dirt road—albeit a straight and wide one—through a rural landscape. In 1837, the nearest actual street to 155th was 125th, also laid out that year, as were 86th, 57th, and 42nd, with no grid connecting them, like siblings separated at birth. It could be said that the gridded place that is Manhattan was "complete" in 1898 when "New York City" became more than just Manhattan, and Manhattan became just one of the five boroughs of Greater New York. By then, 57th Street on either side of Fifth Avenue was shedding a generation of grand mansions for commercial houses: luxury commerce—jewelers, furriers, and such—but "trade" nonetheless. The wealthy headed north by west and (mostly) east, the hoi polloi in their wake. But still, in 1898, Manhattan above 155th Street remained mostly a curiosity.

Upper Manhattan would develop differently from the island's gridded bulk, which attracted much greater attention and dismay, in particular from native son Henry James. Born and raised in genteel comfort on Washington Square in 1843, James spent much of his youth and twenty of his middle years abroad. When he returned to the U.S. for a few of the first years of the twentieth century, he was fairly appalled at the decadence of the continental nation and the citified island of his birth. In the city's "impertinent cross-streets," the closeted erotic old bachelor spied despoliation incarnate:

> New York pays . . . the penalty of her primal topographic curse, her old inconceivably bourgeois scheme of composition and distribution, the uncorrected labor of minds with no imagination of the future and blind before the opportunity given them by their two magnificent water-fronts. This original sin of the longitudinal avenues perpetually, yet meanly intersected, and of the organized sacrifice of the indicated alternative, the great perspectives from East to West, might still have earned forgiveness by some occasional departure from its pettifogging consistency. But, thanks to this consistence, the city is, of all great cities, the least endowed with any blest item of stately square or goodly garden, with any happy accident or surprise, any fortunate nook or casual corner, any deviation, in fine, into the liberal or charming. That way, however, for the regenerate filial mind, madness may be said to lie—the way of imagining what might have been and putting it all together in the light of what so helplessly is.

A pillar of so-called American letters, James nonetheless returned to the squares, gardens, and liberal charms of London and died there a British citizen. But he had happened back to New York just as more dedicated urban thinkers were focusing renewed attention on the city's "original sin."

"The commissioners, after choosing the abominable rectangular plan," observed Jean Schopfer in 1902, "had not even sufficient intelligence to foresee that certain districts of the city would be centers of luxury." Manhattan has no boulevard, making New York unique among world cities. It should have been apparent to the Commissioners, "whose names ought to be execucrated [sic] by every inhabitant of New York," that Fifth Avenue, central to their grid and naturally likely to become the locus of luxury, should have been laid two to three times the width of its parallel friends. But the Commissioners "did nothing of the kind, and now Fifth Avenue is a narrow, treeless, congested avenue, the like of which would not be tolerated by a provincial town at any price." Fifth's accidental role as the eastern boundary of Central Park provided a couple of miles of uptown relief, in the manner of an eventually treed promenade, but it is hardly a boulevard.

Schopfer could be dismissed as a European dilettante—yes, he was a French tennis champion before he put his good education to work in criticism and other serious writing—but he was lamenting as a visitor what had been gnawing at locals for decades.

"What a difference there would now be in the attractiveness, and consequently in the wealth of the city," wrote Olmsted back in 1876, "if twenty-five years ago, when it was quite practicable, Fifth avenue from Madison Square to the Central Park, had been laid out fifty feet wider than it is, with slightly better grades, a pad for riding horses, broad sidewalks and an avenue of trees."

Finally, after all the complaining about the city's boulevard deficiency, someone, and a native New Yorker at that, actually proposed building one. Ernest Flagg was already an important architect locally—the Scribner Building, St. Luke's Hospital—and nationally—Corcoran Gallery of Art, U.S. Naval Academy. He was already designing the Singer Building, the world's tallest then and one of the city's most beautiful ever when it was completed on lower Broadway in 1908. With its slender, graceful setback tower rising thirty-five stories from the twelve-story lot-line base Flagg had designed a decade earlier, the Singer Building was the apotheosis of Flagg's growing horror at city streets darkened by skyscrapers piled increasingly higher on their lot lines. If there were fewer "huge masses [that] rear their heads like monuments to greed" and more Singers, "we should soon have a city of towers instead of a city of dismal ravines." Flagg remains an enduring hero of livable city advocates; his strenuous arguments for setbacks and density limits would be enshrined in the city's first zoning law in 1916.

In 1904, grid detractors with boulevard envy thought they had a hero of their own when Flagg proposed, in the influential *Scribner's Magazine*, "to break the bond imposed on the city by the adoption of the unfortunate plan of 1807 [sic]." Like others before and after him, Flagg pointed his compass at the Commissioners' basic error. "So little did the makers of the plan foresee the enormous pressure which would be brought upon the longitudinal means of transit when the city should be built up, by the daily ebb and flow of the vast population for which lots were provided, that only one avenue running north and south was laid out in a given distance to four tranverse [sic] streets." Like Olmsted and Schopfer, Flagg found all of those few avenues lacking. "New York ought to have . . . an avenue like the Champs-Élysées of Paris, Unter den Linden of Berlin, or the Ring Strasse of Vienna, but more ample than any of them; for here, of all places, owing to the shape of the island, there is the most need of such a thing." Like none so authoritatively before or after him, Flagg proposed such a thing: a boulevard a thousand feet wide, lined with trees, paths, and plantings around a roadway of 160 feet.

Flagg's boulevard would occupy all of the space between Sixth and Seventh Avenues, from Christopher Street in what had become the neighborhood of Greenwich Village all the way to the Harlem

River, ten miles distant, which is to say, straight through the central axis of the city . . . and the center of Central Park. At this, Park lovers gasped. And then he lost the grid foes. On either side of the boulevard between 59th and 110th Streets, the remaining park itself would disappear, reclaimed by street grid, albeit less dense than on the unfortunate 1811 plan. Flagg envisioned large blocks on the opposite axis, formed by two new avenues between Fifth and Sixth, and Seventh and Eighth, crossed from Fifth to Eighth by eight blocks a mile instead of the existing grid's twenty. It was a strange bargain, adding a grand boulevard to a gridded city that had none but subtracting substantially from the relentless grid's great and singular relief.

Flagg's proposal might have induced fatal apoplexy in otherwise boulevard-envious Olmsted, but he had died at age ninety-one twelve months earlier. Perhaps Flagg had observed the courtesy of a year's mourning before proposing to reduce Olmsted's park to a strip mall. Fortunately (most would say) it was not only by then too late to claim so much real estate between Sixth and Seventh above and below the park for the boulevard—even, as Flagg proposed, systematically over fifty years in exchange for other park lands—but it was also unconscionable to violate the by then sacrosanct park to any degree.

While the *Scribner's* ink was still damp, the *Times* started howling, in an editorial titled "To Destroy Central Park," at Flagg's "laying violent hands upon the most valued of our municipal possessions." Indeed, "Central Park [is] the one thing of beauty in which the community agrees in taking pride and delight." Perhaps if there had been more than one thing of beauty, the reaction would have more tempered, but the park is all that the grid allowed.

Flagg's extraordinary idea did not get off the drawing board, but it alternately haunted and animated New Yorkers for years. The proposal "was written by a man who has one of the highest reputations in New York as an architect. That such a man could seriously consider such a scheme an improvement . . . is certainly

most astounding." Robert Wheelwright, a young Harvard-educated
founding editor of *Landscape Architecture* magazine, could not even
bring himself to use Flagg's name in 1910, six years after his apostasy.
It was the worst in half a century of "attacks upon Central Park" but
the inspiration for many subsequent and continuing "schemes for
cutting up and for building over the Park."

In fact, numerous plans were afoot to put more city in the park,
which one "excellent if somewhat eccentric citizen" considered
"an irredeemable disfigurement of the city: an ugly, inappropriate
square of wilderness slapped down in the middle of the city, cutting off the East Side from the West Side, and about as picturesque
as a cabbage patch." Because that citizen was Robert B. Roosevelt,
whose nephew Teddy was president, people listened and his ideas
were widely discussed and enthusiastically supported by influential
men like Andrew Carnegie. Roosevelt detailed numerous proposals to introduce diagonals and other boulevards to "break up the
rectilinear enormity of the Park" in its southern regions. Most significantly, he suggested widening Fifth Avenue into a broad boulevard by claiming a suitably sized strip of the park. By 1918, when the
Times presented an illustrated retrospective of a score of recent park
"improvement" plans, it labeled Roosevelt's as "the most visionary
scheme of all," but mistakenly conflated it with Flagg's boulevard.

It wasn't coincidence that Flagg, Roosevelt, and others were
giving Central Park a hard look. Their proposals came amidst the
workings of the City Improvement Commission, which also went by
the names City Beautiful Commission and Municipal Improvement
Commission. The wavering identity gives a hint of the hopeful commission's ultimate ineffectuality.

In December 1903, the Board of Aldermen had empowered
lame-duck mayor Seth Low, a political and civic reformer, to name
a commission charged with creating a comprehensive development
plan for the new five-borough city. The commission featured an
array of leading businessmen (no women), bureaucrats, engineers,

and architects, none of whom was particularly distinguished as a civic improver per se. They flattered themselves with mildly pejorative allusions to their planning forefathers. "In the report of the earlier Commission, appointed in the first years of the last century to formulate a plan for laying out the streets in the City of New York, it was stated almost by way of apology that it might excite the merriment of many that the Commission had contemplated streets as far north as 155th Street."

The three 1807 Commissioners had indeed suggested in their remarks that some would find "merriment" in the vastness of their grid, but their plan stands. In 1907 the many-peopled City Improvement Commission finally announced a "comprehensive plan" that no one much bothered to comprehend. Among other things, it proposed a parkway from the Queensboro Bridge to Fifth Avenue and possibly on to the Hudson, and a diagonal extension of Madison Avenue either to Fourth Avenue at the northeast corner of Union Square Park or to Broadway at 12th Street, creating a triangular extension of the park.

Unlike the plan of the 1807 Commissioners, which was enforceable by law, the 1907 planning report had no authority. "There is not the slightest reason to suppose that hereafter, when the City of New York is obliged to deal with some of the serious problems arising from its inconvenient lay-out, the recommendations of the City Improvement Commission will carry with them any more authority than that, say, of an editorial article in a daily journal." This from Herbert Croly, editor of the influential (then and now) *Architectural Record*.

Croly, a Harvard-educated and devoted progressive (and later founder of the *New Republic*), was all for modernizing the city's "inconvenient" grid but recognized there was little to be done. "What New York particularly needs is diagonal thoroughfares cutting through the heart of Manhattan Island and relieving such centers of congestion as Herald Square, Fifth Avenue and Twenty-third Street and the like." Unlike Julius Harder a few years earlier, though,

Croly had little hope for diagonals: "No matter how useful they would be [they] are wholly impracticable, because it is in the neighborhood of these congested centers that land is so valuable and the number of skyscrapers so considerable. No clear-headed municipal administration would dare to accept the responsibility of adopting and beginning the realization of a plan which, in the course of its fulfilment, might easily double the municipal debt, and effect an enormous increase in the tax rate."

Croly understood how and why the international City Beautiful movement never found a place in the streets of Manhattan. Its failure here was probably preordained.

A few years earlier, in 1900, the *New York Herald* asked five smart people "How Can New York Be Made the City Beautiful?" The lengthy interview was conducted in a four-in-hand drag during a day's drive up, down, and across Manhattan, and published at two-page length on the last Sunday of April. The four local interviewees—the president and landscape architect of the Board of Park Commissioners, a livery company owner, and the architect and sculptor Charles R. Lamb—all said essentially that making New York more beautiful was a good idea and during the drive pointed to and discussed some ways it might be done. The fifth traveler, Danish-born Niels Gron, wondered at the question.

"Before I came to this country," said Gron,

and in all the time I have been here, it never has occurred to me to think of New York as being beautiful. Therefore all this talk of beautifying New York seems strange to me. If we were discussing Bismarck I might ask five hundred questions about him before I should think of asking whether he was beautiful. The five hundred and first might be, "Was he beautiful?" So it is with New York. We expect of her power and magnificence, but not beauty. If a European came over here and found that New York was beautiful in the same way as the European cities he knew he would be very much disappointed. I do not see how you can make New York beautiful in that way with the laws and the democratic spirit that you have here. The kind of beauty that makes Paris charming can only exist where private rights and personal liberty are or have been trampled on. Only where the mob rules, or where kings rule, so that there is at one time absolutely no respect for the property of the rich and at another time for the rights of the poor can the beauties of Paris be realized.

A bit about Gron, who is perhaps the most curious character to have deep insight about New York, a place where he was socially prominent but never resident. Born with a couple of days left in 1867, he came to the U.S. as a boy, graduated from Harvard in 1894, and over the ensuing decades, spent all over the U.S. and Europe, played enough roles to drive a biographer (if he had one) mad. In 1896, as a Republican National Committee official, he gathered Scandinavian-American votes for William McKinley, putting Gron in line to be named foreign minister to Greece (which he knew well). Instead, Gron opted to become a strategic player for Denmark in rejecting an intrigue-riddled treaty to sell the Danish West Indies to the U.S. (at the behest of Standard Oil) for $2 million in 1900; the U.S. eventually got its Virgin Islands for $26 million in 1917, as a wartime hedge against possible German expansion. Gron then made use of his various international contacts to help preserve Danish neutrality during World War I, the start of which propelled an idea that increasingly dominated his final years. "Potentia" was Gron's visionary quest to develop an international trademark for useful commercial products, the fees from which would be used for disseminating scholarly scientific ideas that would "guarantee peace and order throughout the world, subdue Bolshevism, and bring about a reign of good will." Like world peace, Potentia attracted much attention and few adherents, leaving Gron frustrated and broke. For a time the debonair Dane was known as the "handsomest man in Europe," a reputation enhanced by his 1912 whirlwind marriage to "society sculptress" and gay widow Madeline Masters, sister of poet Edgar Lee Masters. Gron's reputation went out the window in a spectacular divorce and lost battle for child custody in 1922. Two years later, the increasingly eccentric, isolated, and reportedly alcoholic Dane went out the window himself, back in Copenhagen, "during a fit of nervous depression."

And yet, as a rising star in April 1900 on a carriage tour, Gron somehow got the essence of the gridded city: "We expect of her power and magnificence, but not beauty."

The conversation turned to the idea of connecting Manhattan's parks by converting portions of certain streets into "park roadways." "How about restricting traffic on Fifth Avenue?" asked the *Herald* reporter. "Well, that could be done," offered John De Wolf, landscape architect. "There is not a city in the world that has not some restricted street or avenue," added George Clausen, president of the Board of Park Commissioners, suggesting that Fifth could be turned over to the Parks Department: "I believe that if we were to take one street at a time and keep on adding to the system [of park roadways] the problem [of traffic] would solve itself in time." "You could not restrict traffic on Broadway," said the reporter. "What the public want they can have if they will only make up their minds collectively," said Charles Lamb; they "can bring about the restriction of Broadway or any other street if they determined upon it." Indeed, a century later, traffic on portions of Broadway and other streets has been restricted without public riot. Gron provided a contemporary example. "On the principal thoroughfare in Copenhagen—the street where all the shops are—driving is not allowed at all for certain hours of the day. There is not a single dwelling house along the street; it is filled with stores. Everybody goes shopping there, and during the hours when it is restricted it becomes a grand promenade." But Gron issued a universal caution: "It is a difficult matter for the public to get their ideas crystallized." Whether or not New Yorkers could crystallize their ideas as well Copenhageners, Gron questioned whether any city should have a grand boulevard: "Is it not a mistake to build magnificent avenues in a city? Wherever one finds magnificent avenues he is likely also to find great slums. It tends to classify, to develop one part of the city at the expense of the rest, and to make the city vain of certain parts."

Gron probably didn't know how New York had come to be a city with a uniform grid of rectilinear streets and avenues and no boulevards. He probably didn't know that the grid's imposition was not entirely friendly to "private rights and personal liberty," that three men with unilateral power had imposed their vision of how virtually the entire island was to take shape.

Was Gron's belief in New York's "power and magnificence but not beauty," his failure to ever "think of New York as being beautiful," an unconscious result of the intentional exclusion of beauty by the Commissioners in 1811 that was practically complete in 1900? In other words, which came first: New York's power or its grid? That is, was there something inherently powerful about the overgrown town at the southern tip of Manhattan in the earliest 1800s that the grid harnessed, or was the grid itself spontaneous combustion? If Aaron Burr and Joseph Browne had not short-circuited Joseph Mangin's more beautiful, less powerful plan in 1803 and had the 1811 grid plan not replaced it, would Manhattan have grown into the magnificent, powerful, unbeautiful place that Gron perceived in 1900 and many others have before and since?

"Let the new cities of the United States profit by New York's experience," advised Jean Schopfer in 1902, "and take care not to follow her example." By then, though, the ship of urban American beauty had pretty much sailed: rectilinear cities had sprouted from coast to coast and everywhere in between, following the old rectangular lead out of Washington, though none so densely and unrelievedly as Manhattan.

Yet, even with the failure of the City Improvement Commission in 1907 and other modifying plans back to James Serrell in the 1860s, New Yorkers concerned about their dense, congested, unbeautiful city continued to propose relief.

If not for James J. Gallagher, Manhattan might now have a broad boulevard relieving the vastness between Fifth and Sixth Avenues. Lexington had divided the 920 feet between Third and Fourth, Madison had done the same between Fourth and Fifth. Those prescient splits were made in the 1830s, when grid-building was just beginning and the land was available. In 1910, when the grid was built and the city's street congestion was already infamous, Mayor William Jay Gaynor proposed a new avenue running from 14th Street to Central Park. Gaynor, a respected reformist judge newly elected mayor as a Tammany progressive, intended to do something about the congesting effects of the last swath of 920-foot survivors in the city's century-old street plan, clogging the middle ground like fossilized dinosaurs where smaller, quicker, and more options were wanted. The proposal was splashed across page one of the Sunday *New York Times Magazine* on May 29, with artwork and a diagram. Among many quoted supporters was J. Clarence Davies, a major developer of the Bronx (and important collector of historical New York images): "That more northerly and southerly avenues are a necessity anybody who travels daily north and south on Fifth Avenue or parallel avenues must admit." Davies understood that construction needn't be immediate: "It should be extended over a long period of years, so that the present property owners should not be too heavily assessed or taxed and the future generations made to pay the expense." Indeed, Davies favored "a broad scheme of street improvements . . . if New York City is to become what it is entitled to, the London or Paris of the American Continent."

The idea of substantial change achieved gradually was not new. In 1829, the original green cities designer, John Claudius Loudon, proposed remaking London into alternating belts of parkland and urban grid (with radial streets), like a dartboard with St. Paul's for a bull's-eye surrounded by mile-wide rings of city and half-mile rings of country. Loudon, a prolific architect and landscape gardener, recognized that his radical plan could not be accomplished quickly "unless in consequence of accident or revolution." Absent such blessing (and even London's Great Fire of 1666 had proved inadequate motivation for substantial redesign), the ring plan could be accomplished with time. If the government were to determine the boundaries of future zones, require that buildings in designated park zones not be repaired after a specified year, compensate those owners with city-owned property of equal value in urban belts, and establish a planning office to manage everything, London could be gradually rebuilt within a century or two without "the slightest injustice or inconvenience."

Loudon's sweeping vision for London advanced no further than a notion. Gaynor's comparatively modest reform for New York failed more dramatically. The mayor spent two months heavily promoting the plan, which remained headline news until he became news himself. "You took my bread and butter away; now I've got you!" shouted James Gallagher on the deck of a Europe-bound steamer docked at Hoboken as he shot Gaynor in the throat at close range with a revolver. Gallagher was not one of many outraged property owners whose buildings were in the way of Gaynor's avenue; he was a recently fired city dockworker who unreasonably blamed his misfortune on Gaynor, yet another would-be grid tamperer meeting with violence. Incredibly, the mayor survived (Gallagher was committed), but without its chief promoter pumping life into it, his controversial artery died. Gaynor survived for three relatively healthy but increasingly irascible years, until the bullet congesting his neck artery moved and killed him. No one since has made the idea of an avenue between Fifth and Sixth seem more doable.

Another 1910 plan, for a diagonal road linking the new Pennsylvania Station and the recent Queensboro Bridge, also died, amidst threats from owners of Midtown properties in its path. A hundred years after its creation, the grid, it seems, could not be violated.

After the rising tide from the mid-1800s about the wrongness of the rightedness of the grid, the new century brought an endless stream of ideas about how to ameliorate its congestive, numbing effects. Most of these ideas worked within the grid with new linear or diagonal roadways of varying size. But ideas like James Serrell's, back in the 1860s, to relieve the island's congestion by expanding the island, also flowed from creative minds, to a mostly dubious public.

At about the same time Jules Verne was in Paris writing *Invasion of the Sea*, inspired by the earlier French fancy to flood the Sahara Desert, another famous thinker was in New York reviving the old idea of filling in the East River to make a greater Manhattan.

Though Serrell ceased after the 1860s to promote the eastern expansion of Manhattan, one of the problems he had been seeking to solve—dangerous East River navigation—remained. In 1869, Benjamin Maillefert, by then a national demolition expert, had rejoined the death struggle with Hell Gate. Having killed others and nearly himself back in 1852, Maillefert's final go featured much blasting, no casualties, and, as before, marginal success. Not until the U.S. Army Corps of Engineers started precision blasting in the 1870s and 1880s (a spectacular 1885 detonation that obliterated notorious Flood Rock entertained thousands along the shore and rattled china for fifty miles) did shipping gain predictably safe passage.

Meanwhile, the other aim of Serrell's plan—to add buildable land to congesting, Central Park–ed Manhattan—lay dormant until the opening years of the next century. After anonymous contributor "Terra Firma" resuscitated the idea in the *Evening Post* and *Scientific American* in 1904 (without credit to the late Serrell), Thomas Edison gave it star quality. Edison's entry into the East River conversion conversation was first reported in New York in July 1906. Editors embraced it, from Honolulu to Anchorage and back east. "EDISON'S DARING SCHEME . . . to abolish the East River and make it dry land," ran the headline of a Raleigh, North Carolina, paper: "It is a magnificent conception and may prove the solution of

New York's present traffic perplexities." Even before the automobile was set upon the people of the grid, the perplexities of their linear prison were famous.

Closer to home, the reaction wasn't so favorable. *Indoors and Out*, a monthly "devoted to Art and Nature" with offices on Union Square (until absorbed by *House Beautiful*), agreed Edison's was "a daring scheme" but "accretion is the evil of New York," where "easy transportation . . . is the only remedy for this evil. Certainly it is not to be found by destroying a natural and superb waterway." The lecture continued: "There are many forces acting upon a great city other than the pressure for additional square feet of office room. Water commerce, light and air for workers, wholesome conditions for the inhabitants are but a few of these. To appropriate any of the water area around New York would be to repeat Nassau canyons by the score." Dated only in its reference to office towers rising along Nassau Street downtown, this warning from 1906 might be heeded in density and planning debates today.

Edison's East River ideas evaporated like so much cocktail talk. Unlike Serrell, he never made a formal proposal. But the concept of enlarging Manhattan was hardly dead, though no one had the courtesy or awareness to credit long-dead Serrell for being first. In fact, it took only five years for the next proposal, which became a two-decade campaign for all sorts of changes to Manhattan and its bordering lands and waters.

Like Manhattan add man Serrell a half century before him, T(homas) Kennard Thomson was not a native son. He was born in 1864 in Buffalo of Mayflower pedigree and Canadian influence: his father built Canadian railroads and served in Parliament. Thomson was raised and educated on the Canadian side of the border, graduated first in his class at the University of Toronto in 1886, and married Miss Mary Julia Harvey, a proper anglophone Quebecer. After establishing himself as a bridge and railway engineer in Canada and the U.S., Thomson moved his large family in 1893 to New York

City, where he opened an engineering office specializing in sky-scraper foundations and underwater caissons. His business thrived; eventually Thomson was involved in the construction of hundreds of bridges and major buildings, including the Singer, Municipal, and Mutual Life Buildings in Manhattan.

It took Thomson only a few years on the island to offer his first planning idea to the public: a four-track passenger train loop between the Hudson River waterfront and downtown Brooklyn over the Brooklyn and abuilding Williamsburg Bridges. This first proposal for interborough rapid transit was aimed at reducing sur-face congestion by eliminating transfers at bridge portals with a dozen direct connections to existing rail lines. The plan was favor-ably received but "spoiled" in the execution. By 1913, the city had spent over $10 million constructing what it called the Centre Street Loop, a four-track subway that merely ran under Centre Street and connected only the Manhattan terminuses of the Brooklyn, Man-hattan, and Williamsburg Bridges. Thomson's great east-west loop came out as merely a short north-south arc, "a bit of folly" as he saw it that actually increased congestion.

Thomson may have been disappointed with the result of his first big idea, but greater ideas and frustrations were ahead: decades of ingenious, gigantic proposals that helped fill newspapers and lecture halls (and client rolls) but went entirely unbuilt. But they are fuel for the postmodern imagination.

In 1915, he proposed, in an illustrated article in the Sunday *New York Times*, to break "the serious congestion" at Fifth Avenue and 42nd Street by lowering 42nd Street under Fifth, erecting pedes-trian bridges over the avenue, and cutting a new street from 42nd to 43rd between Fifth and Sixth to allow turns that the sinking of 42nd Street prevented. It was a relatively modest and reasonable but already unpopular proposal: "The opposition is very similar to the early objections to surgical operations, with similar benefits if the operation is performed and like disastrous results if it is not or if it is postponed too long." Even as he formally proposed it, Thomson foresaw that it would be ignored: "It is surprising how the idea of removing a small wart from the face of the city frightens New Yorkers."

But he already was airing much grander ideas. "Thomson is a large man of pleasing personality and address, and with a keen mind, used to grappling with scientific problems of great magnitude," the Brooklyn Daily Eagle informed its Sunday magazine readers on August 31, 1913, under a banner headline: "BIG PLAN TO WIPE EAST RIVER OFF THE MAP." Substantially expanding on (but not referencing) Serrell, Thomson proposed filling the entire East River, from Hell Gate at the north all the way to the southern tip of Manhattan and beyond, expanding Brooklyn west to fill most of the Upper Harbor. A new canal-like East River would run from Flushing Bay to Jamaica Bay. (Other aspects of the plan included substantial landfill in the Lower Bay and a dam across most of the narrowed passage between Brooklyn and Staten Island, ideas which seem extraordinarily prescient in a stormy, rising-sea-level world.) By filling the East River out to the eastern borders of Queens and Brooklyn with the rest of Long Island, Thomson envisioned a Pangaea of three city boroughs.

The East River filling was actually the latest addition to Thomson's harbor ideas, which he'd been promoting for a couple of years. This newest incarnation involving the expansion of Manhattan reached newspapers across the country and as far away as Tasmania. Ideas about Manhattan had (and have) that effect on editors.

Thomson pursued his plans for nearly twenty years. Regarding the new land where the river used to be, he saw a population of three million people, living on a modern design. "Think what a wonderful opportunity there would be to improve each and every detail, especially if you did not have to start rebuilding without having time to think, as is usually the case after an earthquake or a fire." Thomson offered no specifics of street organization, but he had an admirer in Thomas Edison: "Your extension of New York is bold and seems practicable, so far as engineering is concerned," Edison wrote in 1922. "It beats my old suggestion of filling up the East River." By then, the land creation methods Thomson suggested had already been employed to enlarge Governors Island in New York Harbor and were then being used to create the islands that became Miami Beach.

For much of the 1920s, Thomson had a competitor in the East River filling idea: the city's chief traffic engineer, Dr. John A. Harriss. Harriss, a photogenic millionaire with tipped mustache and trim Vandyke, is perhaps the only traffic expert to serve as a spokesmodel, for "toasted" Lucky Strike cigarettes in 1930. ("I do not smoke," he attested in nationwide newspaper ads featuring his suave visage and signature, "but . . . your use of the Ultra Violet Ray in connection with your Toasting Process . . . has opened a new era for common-sense smokers.") In an attempt to bring order to what was still two-way traffic on Fifth Avenue, Harris had developed the city's first traffic signals in the early 1920s. The signal towers became icons, but the congestion only got worse. Earlier he had offered numerous plans to relieve Midtown congestion with layers of elevated roadways. Despairing of any solutions within the confines of the existing island, Harriss, like Serrell, Edison, and Thomson before him, turned his attention east in 1924.

Harriss's idea was to dam the river at Hell Gate and the Williamsburg Bridge, drain it, and roof it over on stilts (the river would be replaced by a new channel down to the harbor through the western portions of Queens and Brooklyn, as Serrell had long ago proposed). Unlike Serrell and Thomson, who envisioned urban residence on the filled river, Harriss wanted transportation services below the deck and, above, a great boulevard of multiple lanes for express, local, and pedestrian traffic and "majestic structures" (there was no structural engineering issue: substantial buildings on stilts had already risen along Park Avenue north of Grand Central

Terminal). The centerpiece would be a grand new City Hall, augmented by an arts complex, schools, playgrounds, and more. Harriss built on his East River vision the following year by suggesting two broad boulevards running west from it across Manhattan to the Hudson River, in the vicinity of 42nd and 34th Streets. He offered few details of these but noted, like so many people before and after, that tightly gridded Manhattan's density and congestion demanded solutions: "New York has been, in a sense, a laboratory in which such problems have been worked out. We must continue to be progressive if we are to maintain this position." Harriss was perhaps fantasizing that New York was a place where congestion problems were worked out. All of his would-be decongestants quietly expired. Like celluloid monsters, the idea of a gargantuan Manhattan, born at the time of Civil War, may never die. When the island is as filled to the sky as imagination and building technology will allow, the idea may become reality.

As the bright ideas of the Roaring Twenties peaked, Thomson had a go at the idea of stacked avenues. In 1927, he suggested four levels: trucks at existing street level, express and local trains above, buses and automobiles above them, and pedestrians up in the air. The workings of the various necessary access points were not fully worked out. In early 1930, Harriss proposed a full half-dozen layers of roadways to decongest Manhattan. By then, the Depression had come and, while highways and bridges got built all around the expanding metropolitan area, utopian visions of multilevel Manhattan avenues quickly faded.

In April 1952, approaching his eighty-eighth birthday, Thomson gazed out the window of his office above 40th Street west of Fifth. "Look at that traffic crawling out there," he sighed at the jammed streets below. "I proposed the solution to that . . . thirty years ago, long before Robert Moses was heard of." Thomson was recalling his four-decker avenues and enlarged Manhattan Island. In any case, the seeds of the city's "traffic tangle" were planted many years earlier,

Thomson said, by "Gouverneur Morris, who laid out the streets at the beginning of the Nineteenth Century with too few north-and-south avenues." Two months later, Thomson collapsed in his office from the summer heat and died a week later. He had been involved in the construction of hundreds of major buildings and bridges but had failed to undo what Morris had done. All that's left of Thomson's two decades of efforts to expand Manhattan beyond its grid is his thick, carefully assembled scrapbook of pamphlets, letters, and newspaper clippings, crumbling at the edges and slowly approaching oblivion in offsite storage of the New York Public Library.

Doubling, tripling, quadrupling, or sextupling avenues were half-baked ideas. They ignored the subterranean world below the streets already laced with water, sewer, gas, electric, and subway lines, to which access would be impossibly complicated. And the stacked avenues had no practical engagement with how vehicles would enter and exit their assigned decks, how their exhaust would be ventilated, how breakdowns would be cleared, how garbage (and, in the early years, animal waste) would be removed and the streets cleaned, plowed, and repaired, and so on, to say nothing of heightened driver anxiety. It's quite enough even now to choose between George or Martha across the George Washington Bridge or the inner and outer roadways of the Williamsburg Bridge. Multiple choices in the middle of Manhattan would induce mental gridlock.

But, if they were half-baked ideas, they were still ideas and ideas prompt thought and thinking leads to better ideas. While subterranean decking would never fly now in a climate-changing world, intelligent layering of certain functions above ground is always possible. Still, the original sin of the 1807 Commissioners remains: simply too few north-south avenues. Well on now into the grid's third century, congestion is simply a fact of the grid.

If after the early addition of Madison and Lexington Avenues it became increasingly impossible for new avenues or other roadways to ease the grid's essential flaw, two of the grid's original avenues got a last laugh. Greenwich Village was pierced by the southerly extension of Seventh Avenue in the 1910s and in the 1920s by the southerly extension of Sixth Avenue. It is so like the grid to successfully resist change to itself, while spreading its reach into areas where it had once been prohibited. The buck finally stopped in the 1950s when urban activists defeated Robert Moses's fervent desire to split Washington Square with a southerly extension of Fifth Avenue. Henry James would have been gratified.

Meanwhile, Moses also struck out with his Mid-Manhattan Expressway, a six-lane elevated highway linking the Lincoln and Queens Midtown Tunnels along 30th Street. Moses dreamed it up in 1937; Governor Rockefeller finally killed it for good in 1971.

"OUT OF DOORS, in the mean monotonous streets, without architecture, without great churches or palaces, or any visible memorials of an historic past, what could New York offer to a child whose eyes had been filled with shapes of immortal beauty and immemorial significance?" Three decades after Henry James was appalled at how his city had grown, his younger lifelong friend and fellow European traveler Edith Wharton chimed in, when it seemed to her in 1934 that no substantial relief would come to "rectangular New York . . . this cramped horizontal gridiron of a town." Henry James had spied the beast in the urban jungle in 1906, during a brief repatriation with his hometown before skulking back to London. He came and left in the middle of a flurry of hopefulness about reforming Manhattan in the generation following consolidation. But the creation of Greater New York did nothing to disperse the density and congestion in Manhattan.

CHAPTER 13

BACK TO THE
RECTILINEAR FUTURE

Crosstown traffic
All you do is slow me down
And I'm tryin' to get on the other side of town

—Jimi Hendrix, "Crosstown Traffic," 1967

I found it the way I expected it to be: a kind of immense
vertical mess set upon a square horizontal order.

—Nicolas Nabokov, *Bagázh: Memoirs
of a Russian Cosmopolitan*, 1975

Iᴎ 1913, ᴛʜᴇ New York Public Library put on the most comprehensive exhibition to date of American and foreign city planning.
Hundreds of cities participated, as did the country's leading city
planners. The exhibit was organized by the city and overseen by
a committee including architects Charles R. Lamb and Cass Gil-
bert. Complementing the wide array of exhibits were featured state-
ments on city planning. "A proper city plan has a powerful influence
for good upon the mental and moral development of the people,"
offered George McAneny, Manhattan borough president and
municipal reformer. "It is the firm base for building a healthy and

happy community." Lawson Purdy, an organizer of the exhibit, long-time head of the city's tax and assessment department, and future first chairman of the Regional Plan Association, contributed this: "City planning is the laying out of such streets, public spaces and parks as will best serve the health, safety and convenience of the people, and will most facilitate the production of wealth." Health, safety and convenience: not much had changed from the message sent a century earlier by Gouverneur Morris and company. Happiness and wealth were added to the mix, but beauty still failed to make the cut.

Purdy was also a future zoning official. The same year that he helped organize the city planning exhibit that had nothing to say about urban beauty, the city took its first steps toward zoning regulation with an analysis of its building stock. The Heights of Buildings Commission, featuring top experts on housing, planning, and real estate issues, spent most of 1913 assembling data on height, area, and occupancy regulations of dozens of American and European cities. The commission's authoritative findings aren't the direct concern of this book—but for the record Manhattan had 92,749 buildings with an average height of 4.8 stories, 10 percent above six stories, and fifty-one over twenty stories, with more abuilding—but the commission's fundamental concerns *are* important to the story of the grid. "The present almost unrestricted power to build to any height, over any proportion of the lot, for any desired use and in any part of the city," the commission concluded, "has resulted in injury to real estate and business interests, and to the health, safety and general welfare of the city." Again, as it has in New York forever, and especially since the imposition of the grid, beauty was not a part of the conversation. In the report's three hundred pages, the concept of urban beauty appears rarely, but most often in connection with European laws. "In the interest of beauty," an 1871 Bavarian law allowed localities to pass and police building ordinances; the first town-planning law of any nation, enacted by Sweden in 1874, specified "beauty of arrangement" among such usual building and planning requirements as health, comfort, traffic, and fire prevention. Regarding New York, beauty is only considered an important thing in the building commission report for one stretch of one avenue—Fifth Avenue above 23rd Street. As a general consideration, beauty was a concern, curiously enough, only for two gentlemen representing the national and New York fire underwriters boards: "A reasonable limitation in the heights of buildings," they write in a statement to the commission, will reduce fire risk, enhance property values, and promote "the beauty, health and comfort of the city." In joining beauty with health and comfort, Mr. Ira H. Woolson and Mr. F. J. Stewart were striking a civic triad not much heard around New York since James Jay was ignored by the Commissioners of 1807. Likewise, the concept of civic beauty was largely ignored by the building height commissioners of 1913. Their detailed report, the brilliant genesis document of the city's now epic zoning regime, did not see beauty in their mirror of the city. It was not really their fault: they recognized that "the rectangular street and block system . . . destroy[s] many a picturesque street."

The overarching concern from 1913 until the enactment of the nation's pioneering urban zoning law of 1916 was keeping New York a city of manageable height and light. Even though in 1913 the average building height was under five stories and only fifty buildings were over twenty stories, those numbers were beginning to rise dramatically as the grid filled and people needed space to live and work. As unrestricted street development brought disorder and crowding addressed by the 1811 street grid, unregulated vertical development, embodied in massive early street-darkening skyscrapers like the Equitable and Woolworth Buildings, led to vertical zoning. The 1916 zoning resolution did to the air what the grid did to the land. The grid was a way to move up-island; zoning was a way to move up. The 1811 grid was the two-dimensional map for vast city planning; the 1916 zoning law was the three-dimensional diagram for comprehensive city building, requiring that skyscrapers set back like ziggurats as they rose higher.

"The zoning laws are the Napoleon and Haussmann of New York architecture," wrote poet Orrick Johns in 1924 during his stint as *Times* architecture critic, wondering if "the New York which will go down to posterity . . . as Luxor and the Parthenon, the Taj Mahal and the Cathedral of Rheims have come down to us can at last be previsioned." Thanks to zoning, "wherever possible the unit of construction will be the entire city block," he prophesied. But things didn't quite turn out that way. Nor this way: "Prominent architects even now contemplate the possibility of great single structures erected on a unit of two or four blocks, thus eliminating streets or turning them into tunneled arcades. . . ." As always, the future confounds the present, like the forecast blizzard that turns to drizzle, the promising wave that flattens unridden, the sidelined revolution. In fact, zoning requires and enforces stasis in the streets.

If the lack of beauty was and is the gridded city's heartache, congestion was and is its pounding headache. "The city's illness," according to the *New York Times*, "is too much traffic . . . too few places for the traffic to go. Attempts to ease the strain by involved and ingenious traffic regulations have apparently reached their limit." That was in March 1929, the morning rush hour of the automobile age. Traffic lights, one-way streets, and turn restrictions were in the offing, but "a given system of streets can hold a limited number of vehicles."

The "cure," the *Times* believed, was an astoundingly expensive array of new tunnels, bridges, and highways in and around Manhattan: a West Side Motor Highway (already authorized), an East River Drive and Connecting Highway (proposed), a Crosstown Tunnel (proposed between Weehawken and Long Island City under Manhattan), the Fort Lee Bridge (under construction and soon named for our George the First), a Tri-Borough Bridge (authorized), a 10th Street Tunnel from Queens (proposed), a Connecting Highway through Queens and Brooklyn (proposed), and a Narrows Tunnel (authorized as a rail freight tunnel but soon transmogrified by Robert Moses into the Verrazano-Narrows highway bridge).

In one form or another nearly all of these road projects, and eventually many more, would be added to the existing Holland Tunnel; Brooklyn, Manhattan, and Queensboro Bridges; and a half dozen smaller bridges linking upper Manhattan and the Bronx over the narrow Harlem River. In 1929, everyone jumped aboard the automobile on the happy highway to modern living. Within a few years, it was evident to some that something had gone wrong. "The period of the car has come; it is here with its tragic consequences: circulation in New York is hopelessly clogged," observed grid-lover Le Corbusier on his first visit to New York in 1935. Nothing was wrong with the grid—"the principle on which the streets were planned is clear, useful, simple, true, human, and excellent"—that couldn't be fixed by the replacement of clusters of congested small blocks and small buildings with superblocks of high towers. Take the people (and their cars) off the street and put them in the air with adequate mass transportation and the "vertical city," the "radiant city" emerges. It hasn't happened yet, in part because we've stopped building mass transportation.

Now we understand how the car cure became an incurable disease, congesting the grid of Manhattan and clogging the arteries of the sprawling metropolis. Was change possible?

In 1913, the building height commission was afraid of tall buildings, and the zoning laws that emerged attempted at least to temper the mad dash skyward by narrowing it in business places and restricting it in residential places. At the same time, Le Corbusier and others saw the future and it was tall and taller everywhere. He imagined, visiting New York in 1935, that the answer was changing the average Manhattan building height from four and a half stories to sixteen, thereby recovering three-quarters of built space for park space, and coincidently combating urban sprawl into Connecticut. Not surprisingly, the fifty-six residential buildings of Stuyvesant

Town and Peter Cooper Village are each fifteen stories and together house 25,000 people: a suburb in the city but, like its Central Park cousin, an antiurban development in the vast penitentiary of the grid. Stuy Town and Peter Cooper are a Corbusian vision: a working-class neighborhood of tenements and walkups reclassified as a slum to be cleared for modern middle-class living. Planned and constructed beginning in 1942, they must have flattered Le Corbusier, who spent his war years in Vichy seeking commissions from whomever was offering. New York is still channeling Le Corbusier with the proposed rezoning of eastern Midtown Manhattan into a high-rise, high-density district that seeks to add people but not mass transportation or streets.

Haussmann was empowered by an emperor fearful of rebellion that the broad boulevards discouraged, Robert Moses by cowed mayors in thrall to the automobile. The car is now branded an enemy of urban life. Should the grid that was built for hand and horse carts in the epilogue of the premachine age be adapted for modern, postautomotive transportation? Can the congestion engendered by the many streets originally servicing river-to-river movement and the too few avenues for contemporary up-and-down movement be relieved in some practical way, either by plan or necessity? Detroit's mansion-lined boulevards were grand while the Motor City made cars for the world. Today empty lots and abandoned prospects warn other cities that believe the present will never be the past.

Cities often need a disaster to provoke change. London was redesigned to some extent after its Great Fire in 1666. Brussels was remade after the French bombardment of 1695. In 1830, Yale scientist Benjamin Silliman mused on the sacking of Rome and the burning of London: "Both events have been a blessing to these cities, though regarded as calamities at the time." At a distance of millennia and centuries, respectively, Silliman could get away with discounting death and destruction for the benefit of new and improved planning. Is there anything that should or could be done with New York?

In 1661, John Evelyn proposed remedying the choking smoke of dense and dirty London with a surrounding palisade of greenery "diligently kept and supply'd, with such *Shrubs*, as yield the most fragrant and odoriferous *Flowers*, and are aptest to tinge the Aer upon every gentle emission at a great distance." London didn't get a green wreath but it did get its Great Plague four years later and its not surprisingly devastating Great Fire a year after that. Evelyn and Christopher Wren each proposed radical rebuilding plans that would soften the city's dense medieval streets with radial roads and plazas, but cautious King Charles II eventually opted for lesser improvements plus the obligatory and now landmark Great Fire monument—the towering Wren-designed Doric column near London Bridge—unwittingly commemorating the failure to do more.

"THREE HUNDRED YEARS from now," transient New Yorker Ernest Hemingway unhappily informed Gertrude and Alice in 1923, "people will come over from Europe and tour it in rubber neck wagons. Dead and deserted like Egypt. It'll be Cooks most popular tour. Wouldn't live in it for anything." That was less than a hundred years ago, so there's still time.

"I see in the distance the Empire State and Chrysler Buildings pointing vainly to the sky, and it suddenly occurs to me that New York is on the point of acquiring a history and that it already has its ruins." That was Sartre in 1946, on his second visit to New York a year after his first. The place assaulted his European sensibilities. "New York is a city for the long-sighted: you can 'focus' only at infinity. My gaze met nothing but space. It slid over blocks of identical houses, there being nothing to arrest it on its journey to the indistinctness of the horizon." The problem was the grid: "The grid pattern is New York: the streets are so alike that they have not been given names; like soldiers, they have merely been assigned a number." As he wandered, he wondered: "I looked long and fruitlessly for distinct 'neighborhoods' [but] I could only find atmospheres—gaseous masses stretching out longitudinally, with nothing to mark their beginning or their end." Over days and weeks, he began to distinguish the avenues' different atmospheres—"the staid elegance" of Park, "the cold luxury and stucco impassiveness" of Fifth, "the merry frivolity" of Sixth and Seventh, "the food fair" of Ninth, "the no man's-land" of Tenth. "Each avenue enwraps the neighboring streets into its atmosphere, but a block away you suddenly plunge into another world." Sartre loved New York—"I have learned to love it"—but "in this immense, malevolent space, in this desert of rock that brooks no vegetation" the Parisian was lost: "Amid the numerical anonymity of streets and avenues, I am simply anyone, anywhere . . . there is no valid reason to justify my presence at one spot rather than another, since one place is so like another. I am never astray, but always lost."

Sartre wrote several essays in 1945 and 1946 for French publications about his American visits. His one essay for an American magazine, the May 1946 issue of *Town and Country*, has been republished several times as "New York, Colonial City" after retranslation back into English from the first French translation. The *Town and Country* original appeared under a much different title: "Manhattan: The Great American Desert." The original seems to convey better the vast anxiety that Sartre felt in "the harshest city in the world."

Predicting the future of New York or any place is no easy thing. "As for those who have given careful study to the matter, all agree that Manhattan, in the comparative near future, will practically not be used for residential purposes at all. Everybody will live on the mainland or on Long Island, leaving Manhattan entirely for business, with a sprinkling of hotels, theatres, clubs, and the like." So thought the *New York Times* in 1907, observing the centennial of the 1807 Commissioners. Another century later, things have turned out quite differently. How things might be in 2107 is anyone's guess but could be someone's design.

The landmark 1916 zoning plan, which did nothing about streets but dealt with density by requiring buildings to set back increasingly as they grew higher, anticipated a city of fifty-five million people. The city then had five million. The less successful 1961 zoning plan, which again did nothing about the streets but gave us a floor area ratio (FAR) that traded heft for height (resulting in privately owned public plazas and tall box buildings), anticipated a city of twelve million people. The city then had eight million people; it has about the same number now. It is very hard to design the future. It is easier to understand the past.

"The future is but the obsolete in reverse," warned Nabokov in *The New Yorker* in 1952, but he was writing under the protection of (science) fiction. We have to live in the real world. "When we walk in New York, we always hope to randomize our too neatly gridded city existence," Adam Gopnik wrote recently in the same magazine. Why must we always have to hope for something else?

"The street and block system on which our cities are built is as old as recorded history and probably even older," wrote Ludwig Hilberseimer a few years before I was born. "This system functioned relatively well until the coming of the motor vehicle made it out of date and dangerous . . . we need to replace the archaic block or gridiron system with a new city element, a new settlement unit." The opposite has happened. In 2006, Paul E. Black, a computer scientist at the National Institute of Standards and Technology, enshrined the essential structure of New York's grid in his online *Dictionary of Algorithms and Data Structures*. The "Manhattan distance" is "the distance between two points measured along axes at right angles." It's an honor of sorts, though the concept of measuring length by Cartesian rather than Euclidian geometry originated a hundred years earlier in Germany as "taxicab geometry." Still, it indicates how ubiquitous New York's right angles have become. Indeed, the math heads have also nominated the vertical expansion of the rectilinear grid: "We define 'Manhattan Tower (MT) polyhedra' to be the natural generalization of 'Manhattan Skyline polygons.'" I don't in the slightest understand the computer scientists' algorithm "for unfolding the surface of any orthogonal polyhedron that falls into a particular shape class we call Manhattan Towers," but it is easy to see how the flat blocks of Manhattan streets have spawned the building blocks of orthogonal polyhedra towering above the earth. Even now, the skyline is being raised in Midtown Manhattan by a new generation of stretched rectangles in the sky. A skinny new tower on Park Avenue is nearly 1,400 feet high but just ninety-four feet square. Its short reign as the tallest residential building in the Western Hemisphere will be ended by another nearby that at just sixty feet wide will also claim the peculiar honor of thinnest tower in the world.

These emaciated giants seem like endgame polyhedra. The World Trade Center towers had height to width ratios of seven to one; the new buildings will more than double and triple that. The Twin Towers seemed extreme throughout their thirty years of existence; the new twigs almost seem not to exist at all. The Manhattan skyline used to be topped by office buildings filled with workers. The newest generation are empty condo stacks, glass-walled aeries for absent elites, that seem old and anachronistic even as they are built: the weird progeny of incestuous rectilinear generations. "Etiolated oddities," architecture critic Martin Filler has called them, the architectural equivalents of *Being There* idiot non-savant Chauncey Gardiner, "mathematically generated super-spires" that inspire a Mae West paraphrase: "Architecture has nothing to do with it." Filler doesn't mention it but these extreme buildings, like every other Manhattan building, have everything to do with the grid: free to rise as high as air rights and zoning laws allow, they remain right-angled captives of the rectilinear ground lots that hold them.

But our senses are gradually changing. Technology now allows us to build not just tall but without straight lines; curves may in due

This pioneering axonometric map, a large color fold-out in a visitors' guide prepared in advance of the 1964 World's Fair, was the work of German cartographer Hermann Bollmann. Intended to convey "the soaring beauty of the City . . . with exact accuracy to the smallest detail," the map is also a graphic illustration of the vertical extension of the grid after its horizontal plane had been filled. (*Image courtesy of Geographicus Rare Antique Maps*)

course become more cheap and more convenient than they were to the 1807 Commissioners. When that happens, the rectilinear block will be a constraint, not a cheap convenience. "There are no right angles here," says Lucas Hill, student resident in one of the dome homes plopped on the campus of the University of California, Davis, in the 1970s. "It makes you think creatively." Not everyone wants to live in a dome, but the desire to escape the prison of rigid lines is universal.

Understanding the history of Manhattan's street arrangement is necessary in contemplating its future arrangement. The grid is Manhattan's first and only master street plan. At some point and for reasons of choice or necessity, Manhattan may need another. The past should offer some insight to the future. The street grid was laid on a preindustrial island that is now a postindustrial city in a world struggling with sustainability. Sustainability has made the grid's un-green density dangerous. Satellites have made the grid's predictability irrelevant. Should the grid change? Can it? Will it? Fortunately for me, these are questions the historian doesn't have to answer.

NOTES

ABBREVIATIONS
  LOC: Library of Congress
 NYHS: New-York Historical Society
  NYT: *New York Times*
  NYH: *New York Herald*
  MCC: *Minutes of the Common Council*
  JFM: Joseph François Mangin
   GM: Gouverneur Morris
  SDW: Simeon DeWitt
   JR: John Randel Jr.

In an effort to minimize the number of notes and citations, an ellipsis after a textual reference generally indicates that the citation covers all quotations up to the next textual reference.

INTRODUCTION
   xi **"There will come a time . . . "**: Walt Whitman, *Brooklyn Daily Standard*, Jun 3, 1861.
   xi **"But in analysing history . . . "**: Ralph Waldo Emerson, *Journals of Ralph Waldo Emerson* (Boston: Houghton Mifflin Company, 1910), 4: 160.
  xiv **"Magical peoples . . . "**: L[udwig] Hilberseimer, *The New City: Principles of Planning* (Chicago: Paul Theobald, 1944), 22.
 xvii **"Like the streets . . . "**: William Dean Howells, *Impressions and Experiences* (New York: Harper and Brothers, 1896), 247.
  xix **"It's fun and it's cathartic . . . "**: Alan Pyke, "Mayor Bloomberg's False Explanation of the Mortgage Crisis," *Political Correction* (blog), Nov 1, 2011, http://politicalcorrection.org/print/blog/201111 010006; "Bloomberg blames Congress," YouTube video, posted by Azi Paybarah, Nov 1, 2011, www.youtube.com/watch?v=mPXVZONjqek.

xix **"Our perpetual dead flat . . . "**: Walt Whitman, *New York Sunday Dispatch*, Nov 25, 1849.

xix **"primal topographic curse . . . "**: Henry James, "New York Revisited," *Harper's Monthly Magazine*, 112:672 (May 1906), 900.

xix **"rectangular New York . . . "**: Edith Wharton, *A Backward Glance* (New York: D. Appleton-Century Company, 1934), 55.

xx **"We are all agreed . . . "**: Montgomery Schuyler, "The Art of City-Making," *The Architectural Record*, 12:1 (May 1902), 1.

xx **"civic folly"**: Lewis Mumford, *The Culture of Cities* (New York: Harcourt Brace & Company, 1938), 183.

xx **"blank imbecility"**: Lewis Mumford, "City Planning and the American Precedent," *The New Republic*, 39:497 (Jun 11, 1924), 79.

xx **"long monotonous streets . . . "**: Lewis Mumford, *Sticks and Stones: A Study of American Architecture and Civilization* (New York: Boni and Liveright, 1924), 68.

xx **"a street goes on and on . . . "**: Jane Jacobs, *The Death and Life of Great American Cities* (1961; New York: Modern Library, 1993), 493.

xx **"man-trap of gigantic dimensions"**: Frank Lloyd Wright, *The Disappearing City* (New York: William Farquar Payson, 1932), 22.

xx **"deadly monotony"**: Frank Lloyd Wright, *An Autobiography* (1943; Petaluma, Ca.: Pomegranate, 2005), 316.

xx **"filing-cabinet architecture"**: Igor Stravinsky, *Themes and Conclusions* (1972; Berkeley: University of California Press, 1982), 174.

xx **"if I stop . . . "**: Jean-Paul Sartre, "New York, Colonial City," *The Aftermath of War (Situations III)*. Translated by Chris Turner (New York: Seagull Books, 2008), 126, 127. This essay first appeared as "Manhattan: The Great American Desert," in *Town and Country* magazine in May 1946. It was first published in French in July 1946 as "Ville Coloniale," the title that subsequent English retranslations generally use.

xx **"mechanical dullness . . . "**: John W. Reps, *The Making of Urban America: A History of City Planning in the United States* (Princeton, NJ: Princeton University Press, 1965), 298, 299.

xx **"implacable gridiron . . . "**: Vincent Scully, *American Architecture and Urbanism* (New York: Praeger, 1969), 76.

xx **"one of the worst city plans . . . "**: Peter Marcuse, "The Grid as City Plan: New York City and Laissez-faire Planning in the Nineteenth-Century," *Planning Perspectives*, 2 (1987), 288.

xxi **"Even in 1811 . . . "**: Richard Plunz, *A History of Housing in New York City* (New York: Columbia University Press, 1990), 11.

xxi **"The map and plan . . . "**: James Kent, *The Charter of the City of New York* (New York: McSpedon & Baker, 1854), 253.

xxi "The streets are at right angles . . . ": Le Corbusier, *When the Cathedrals Were White* (1937; New York: McGraw-Hill, 1964), 47.

xxi "I insist on right-angled intersections": Le Corbusier, *The Radiant City: Elements of a Doctrine of Urbanism to Be Used as the Basis of Our Machine Age Civilization* (1933; New York: Orion Press, 1967), 123.

xxi "This is the purpose . . . ": Roland Barthes, "Buffet Finishes Off New York," in *A Barthes Reader* (New York: Hill and Wang, 1982), 160.

xxi "is the best manifestation . . . ": Hilary Ballon, ed., *The Greatest Grid: The Master Plan of Manhattan 1811–2011* (New York: Museum of the City of New York and Columbia University Press, 2012), 101.

xxi "the most courageous act . . . ": Rem Koolhaas, *Delirious New York: A Retroactive Manifesto for Manhattan* (1978; New York: Monacelli Press, 1994), 18.

xxii "a thing impossible to overpraise": Philip Lopate, *Waterfront: A Walk Around Manhattan* (New York: Anchor Books, 2005), 14.

xxii "New York is a city . . . ": Gerard Koeppel, "Digging the Urban Past: A Subterranean Panorama," *New York Observer*, Jan 21, 2002.

xxii "Unlike Rome . . . ": Michael de Certeau, *The Practice of Everyday Life* (Berkeley: University of California Press, 1984), 91, 93.

xxiii "There are some far-seeing people . . . ": Eliza Greatorex and Matilda Pratt Despard, *Old New York from the Battery to Bloomingdale* (New York: G. P. Putnam's Sons, 1875), 12.

CHAPTER 1: COME HITHER OLD GRID

1 "They were like children . . . ": Jorge Luis Borges, "The Gospel According to Mark," *The New Yorker*, Oct 23, 1971.

2 "The arrangement of private houses . . . ": Aristotle, *The Politics of Aristotle*. Translated by B[enjamin] Jowett (Oxford: Clarendon Press, 1885) 1: 226–227.

3 "We Europeans . . . ": Sartre, "New York, Colonial City," 122–23.

4 "simply grew . . . ": "Diagonal Avenues in Cities," *Engineering News and American Railway Journal*, Oct 10, 1891.

6 "the boundaries were drawn . . . ": Bill Hubbard Jr., *American Boundaries: The Nation, the States, the Rectangular Survey* (Chicago: University of Chicago Press, 2009), xi.

6 "If the older cities . . . ": Mumford, *Sticks and Stones*, 87.

7 "Theyr streets are Nasty . . . ": Wayne Andrews, "A Glance at New York in 1697: The Travel Diary of Dr. Benjamin Bullivant," *New-York Historical Society Quarterly*, 40:1 (Jan 1956), 65.

9 **"full power . . . "**: James Kent, *The Charter of the City of New York* (1836; New York: McSpedon & Baker, 1854), 15.

10 **"This was a noble provision . . . "**: Ibid., 218.

10 **"have full power . . . "**: Ibid., 100.

11 **"a grant of ample powers . . . "**: Ibid., 243.

11 **"It is a matter . . . "**: [John Hunn], *Observations on the Improvement of the City of New-York South of Grand Street* (New York: James Cheetham, 1806), 4.

CHAPTER 2: FIVE ACRES AND A RULE: THE GREAT GRID'S COMMON ORIGINS

17 **"The Surveys made by . . . "**: *Minutes of the Common Council of the City of New York 1784–1831*, 19 vols. (New York: City of New York, 1917), 5:220 (Jul 25, 1808) [hereafter, MCC].

18 **"waste, vacant, unpatented . . . "**: Kent, *Charter*, 143.

21 **"as near as may be . . . "**: MCC, 1:145 (Jun 20, 1785).

23 **"for work done . . . "**: MCC, 1:492 (Oct 6, 1789).

23 **"at the Request . . . "**: MCC, 1:494 (Oct 12, 1789).

24 **"is perfectly agreable . . . "**: MCC, 1:545 (May 14, 1790).

24 **"to value his services . . . "**: MCC, 11:76 (Apr 17, 1820).

25 **"Goerck, no doubt . . . "**: John Bute Holmes, *Map of the Common Lands from 59th to 76th Street* (New York, 1874). The quote is in the descriptive marginal notes.

26 **"were intended to be . . . "**: MCC, 5:220 (Jul 25, 1808).

27 **"The Commissioners' Plan . . . "**: New York City Landmarks Preservation Commission, *Upper East Side Historic District Extension Designation Report* (New York, 2010), 6.

28 **"A far-sighted policy . . . "**: George Ashton Black, *The History of Municipal Ownership of Land on Manhattan Island*, 2nd Ed. (New York: Columbia University, 1897), 38.

CHAPTER 3: THE CITY TO BE OR NOT TO BE?

29 **"My plan . . . "**: JFM to Common Council, Dec 17, 1798, manuscript letter, New York City Municipal Archives. The greatest single source of information about Mangin is contained in the diligent research conducted over many years by University of Iowa professor Robert L. Alexander, who died in 1998 before he could substantially publish any of his findings, beyond the Mangin entry in the *American National Biography*. I am deeply indebted to his daughter for providing full access to her father's research, which informs much of the writing about JFM in this book. This may be a good place to knock down some recent mythologizing about JFM. Since

the early 1990s, perhaps first in a February 1991 article in the journal *Progressive Architecture*, the idea has spread in some online and printed sources that JFM was black, a slave who rose to become an architect; this canard arises as conjecture from the fact of JFM's exodus to New York from Haiti.

30 **"The city of new york . . . ":** "Sketch of a project to construct Docks in the interior of the town, in New York," Feb 15, 1796, quoted in I. N. Phelps Stokes, *The Iconography of Manhattan Island, 1498–1909*, 6 vols. (1915–28; New York: Arno Press, 1967), 5:1328. The document is signed "Mangin Brothers," being JFM and his apparent relation but not brother Charles-Nicolas Mangin (1769–1821), who worked briefly with JFM in Saint-Domingue and New York before eventually returning to France in 1810.

31 **"I was born French . . . ":** JFM to Alexander Hamilton, Jan 11, 1799, *Papers of Alexander Hamilton*, mss, LOC; original in French, translated for me by Richard Sieburth, NYU professor of French and Comparative Literature, in exchange for single malt Scotch at our favorite local bar.

33 **"general and accurate . . . ":** Stokes, *Iconography*, V:1339.

33 **"wrong levels . . . ":** Ibid., 1340.

33 **"Sandy Hill Road . . . ":** Ibid., 1346.

34 **"The present sickness . . . ":** *New York Spectator*, Sep 22, 29, 1798.

35 **"to demand of me . . . ":** JFM to Common Council, Dec 17, 1798.

35 **"whenever they become . . . ":** MCC, 2:477 (Nov 5, 1799).

35 **"The Street Commissioner . . . ":** MCC, 11:151 (May 22, 1820).

35 **"we have ever since . . . ":** *The Private Journal of Aaron Burr During His Residence of Four Years in Europe*, Matthew L. Davis ed., (New York: Harper & Brothers, 1838), 1:433–434.

36 **"I was singularly surprised . . . ":** JFM to Common Council, Dec 17, 1798.

38 **"the new Map of the City":** MCC, 2:532 (Apr 10, 1799).

39 **"for the Regulating . . . ":** Ibid., 2:448 (Jun 13, 1798).

39 **"having declined to execute . . . ":** Ibid., 2:492 (Jan 7, 1799). Furman was given a $500 annual salary; the prior salary is unclear.

40 **"agreeably to the present . . . ":** Ibid., 3:46 (Oct 29, 1801).

40 **"great inconvenience is sustained . . . ":** Ibid., 3:62 (Nov 30, 1801).

42 **"No one can study . . . ":** Talbot Hamlin, *Benjamin Henry Latrobe* (New York: Oxford University Press, 1955), 187.

42 **"save one":** Ibid., 186.

42 **"a large majority of votes":** MCC, 3:133 (Oct 4, 1802).

42 **"vile heterogeneous composition . . . "**: Hamlin, *Latrobe*, 188. Latrobe, who thought his City Hall effort was "my best design," apparently confused the junior McComb with his father, who had designed New York's Brick Church back in 1767, and didn't realize Mangin was a Champenois, not a Caribbean colonial.

48 **"to examine the New Map . . . "**: MCC, 3:200 (Feb 14, 1803).

CHAPTER 4: THE CITY NOT TO BE

49 **"The Map of the City . . . "**: MCC, 3:404 (Nov 28, 1803).

50 **"disgusting"**: *Proceedings of the Corporation of New-York, on Supplying the City with Pure and Wholesome Water, with a Memoir of Joseph Browne, M. D. on the Same Subject* (New York: John Furman, 1799), 25.

51 **"upon the special . . . "**: Gideon Granger to Rufus Easton, Mar 16, 1805, in William Van Ness Bay, *Reminiscences of the Bench and Bar of Missouri* (St. Louis: F. H. Thomas and Company, 1878), 598. Granger, the U.S. Postmaster General, was informing Easton, a new judge and acting postmaster in St. Louis, of various appointed officials heading his way, including Browne and James Wilkinson.

51 **"Browne will obey . . . "**: Aaron Burr to James Wilkinson, Apr 5, 1805, in Mary-Jo Kline, ed., *Political Correspondence and Public Papers of Aaron Burr* (Princeton: Princeton University Press, 1983), 930.

51 **"his good character . . . "**: *Journals of the Continental Congress 1774–1789* (Washington: General Printing Office, 1910), 17: 679.

52 **"the sequence of events . . . "**: Kline, *Burr Political Papers*, 919–20.

52 **"General Map of the City . . . "**: MCC, 3:203–204 (Feb 14, 1803). At this session, the Council also agreed to a proposal by Browne and Comptroller Selah Strong effectively regulating the city surveyors in their work for the city. Instead of fees that historically were negotiable and generally in the surveyor's favor, they were henceforth to be paid four dollars a day for Council-ordered surveys, delivery of survey included, and four dollars per hundred feet of new street surveys, including information on adjoining lots and owners and a profile of the street, the better to make accurate assessments. In 1803, four dollars was a pretty good day rate, but it was just that: a rate that the city could control and budget, effectively bureaucratizing city surveying.

53 **"the Committee appointed . . . "**: MCC, 3:273 (Apr 25, 1803).

53 **"A Plan and Regulation . . . "**: *New York Daily Advertiser*, Jul 12, 1803. "Gorrek" and "Gorreck" were frequent phonetic misspellings of "Goerck."

53 **"extreme violence of party politics . . . ":** *Manual of the Corporation of the City of New York for 1854,* ed. David Thomas Valentine (New York, 1854), 449 [hereafter, *Valentine's Manual* for the given year].

54 **"for making the large map . . . ":** MCC, 3:390 (Nov 14, 1803).

54 **"in relation to the laying out . . . ":** Ibid., 3:393 (Nov 21, 1803).

55 **"The Map of the City . . . ":** Ibid., 3:404 (Nov 28, 1803).

56 **"This Plan . . . ":** The quote is from the pasted label on the copy of the Mangin-Goerck plan (formally titled *Plan of the City of New York, drawn from actual survey by Casimir Th. Goerck, and Joseph Fr. Mangin, city surveyors,* 1803) in the New-York Historical Society.

58 **"It happens in this . . . ":** *Report of the Committee of the Common Council Upon the Subject of New Streets* (New York: James Cheetham, 1803), [3]-4.

58 **"the maps exhibit a view . . . ":** Ibid., 7–8, 9, 10.

62 **"reputed":** *NYT,* Sep 29, 1915.

CHAPTER 5: NOW WHAT?

65 **"Individuals *even at this period* . . . ":** [Hunn], *Observations,* 4.

65 **"The evils daily experienced . . . ":** *Report of the Committee of the Common Council Upon the Subject of New Streets,* 4.

65 **"with all convenient speed . . . ":** MCC, 3:434 (Jan 3, 1804).

67 **"from time to time . . . ":** Ibid., 435.

67 **"required to insert . . . ":** Ibid., 436.

68 **"the greatest number of votes":** Ibid., 669 (Jan 14, 1805).

68 **"a rapid succession of [financial] misfortunes":** Ibid., 6:238 (Jun 18, 1810).

69 **"made use of so little coercion . . . ":** [Hunn], *Observations,* 4, 5–6.

69 **"It is highly important . . . ":** MCC, 4:127–28 (Jan 20, 1806).

70 **"commissioners to regulate . . . ":** Ibid., 133 (Feb 3, 1806).

70 **"A correct Map . . . ":** Ibid., 238 (June 30, 1806).

71 **"taken ill":** John Vaughan to Thomas Jefferson, Dec 20, 1806, in Florian Cajori, *The Chequered Career of Ferdinand Rudolph Hassler* (Boston: Christopher Publishing House, 1929), 42.

CHAPTER 6: THREE MAN ISLAND

73 **"From the respectability . . . ":** *New York Evening Post,* Jun 27, 1807.

73 **"Men of genius were needed . . . ":** Jean Schopfer, "The Plan of a City," *The Architectural Record,* 12:7 (Dec 1902), 698.

74 **"haughty, proud, overbearing . . . ":** Thomas Jones, *History of New York During the Revolutionary War* (New York: New-York Historical Society, 1879), 223.

74 **"ardently wishes to render . . . "**: *New York Evening Post*, Dec 20, 1806.

76 **"to unite regularity . . . "**: MCC, 4:353 (Feb 16, 1807).

77 **"fit and proper persons"**: Ibid., 368 (Mar 4, 1807).

77 **"to the more agreeable . . . "**: *Newark* (New Jersey) *Daily Advertiser*, Feb 24, 1840.

78 **"I can assure you . . . "**: George Washington to Thomas Jefferson, Mar 3, 1784; Jefferson to Washington, Mar 6, 1784, in George Bancroft, *History of the Formation of the Constitution of the United States of America* (New York: D. Appleton & Co., 1882) 1:346, 347.

79 **"meticulously drawn"**: Jo Margaret Mano, "History in the Mapping: Simeon DeWitt's Legacy in New York State Cartography," *Middle States Geographer*, 22 (1989), 31.

79 **"the most important map . . . "**: David Y. Allen, "How Simeon De Witt Mapped New York State," New York Map Society, 2008, http://www.academia.edu/12688958/How_Simeon_De_Witt_Mapped_New_York_State.

79 **"a noble, serious face . . . "**: *The John Bogart Letters* (New Brunswick, NJ: Rutgers College, 1914), 41.

81 **"He went through life . . . "**: M[ary] E[lizabeth] W[ilson] S[herwood], "The Homes of America: Old Morrisania," *The Art Journal*, 4 (New Series) (1878), 81.

81 **"an irreligious and profane man"**: *The Life and Correspondence of Rufus King* (New York: G. P. Putnam's Sons, 1894–1900), 1:420.

81 **"the promptitude, with which . . . "**: George Washington to GM, Jan 28, 1792, in Jared Sparks, ed., *The Writings of George Washington* (Boston: Russell, Shattuck, and Williams, 1836), 10:218.

82 **"a certain married woman . . . "**: Howard Swiggett, *The Extraordinary Mr. Morris* (Garden City, NY: Doubleday, 1952), 80. This is the first published appearance of this subsequently oft-repeated but never sourced quotation. Alas, I have joined the list of possible apocryphists.

82 **"Gouverneur's Leg . . . "**: John Jay to Robert Morris, Sep 19, 1780, in James J. Kirschke, *Gouverneur Morris: Author, Statesman, and Man of the World* (New York: St. Martin's Press, 2005), 119.

82 **"President"**: JR, Field Book 65.4, NYHS.

83 **"an act relative . . . "**: *Laws of the State of New York*, 1807, Chap. 115 (Apr 3, 1807).

87 **"the respectability and talents . . . "**: *New York Evening Post*, Jun 27, 1807.

87 **"by the Way of Haerlem Cove . . . "**: GM diary, Jan 10, 1807, Papers of Gouverneur Morris, LOC [hereafter, GM Papers].

CHAPTER 7: INTO THE WOODS

89 **"The *time* within which . . . ":** JR, "City of New York, North of Canal Street, in 1808 to 1821," *Valentine's Manual* (1864), 839. For those who may be wondering, our John Randel—variously misspelled or miswritten as Josiah or Jonathan, Randal, Randall, or Randell—is not related to two other similarly named New Yorkers. Jonathan Randell (or Randal or Randel) was a Morris friend and neighbor and onetime owner of the East River island that now bears his own misspelled name. Robert Richard Randall was a sea captain who in 1801 bequeathed his Manhattan farm near today's Washington Square to establish Sailors' Snug Harbor, a hospital for retired seamen that was later relocated to Staten Island.

89 **"Meet with DeWitt . . . ":** GM diary, Jun 29, 1807, GM Papers.

90 **"Go immediately after Breakfast . . . ":** Ibid., Jun 21, 1808.

90 **"Raw damp . . . ":** Ibid., Mar 28, 1811.

90 **"I leaved the residence . . . ":** JFM to "General," Jan 27, 1808, Record Group 94, Letters Received by the Office of the Adjutant General, 1805–1821 (microfilm M566, roll 3), National Archives.

90 **"my Health permitted . . . ":** GM to SDW, Oct 2 1807, Commercial Letterbooks, vol. 26, GM Papers.

93 **"absent three weeks . . . ":** GM diary, Sep 4, 1807, GM Papers.

93 **"and again I am disappointed":** Ibid., Oct 13, 1807.

93 **"very high Wind . . . ":** Ibid., Oct 21, 1807.

94 **"Not having the Materials . . . ":** GM to SDW, Jan 14, 1808, Private Letterbooks, vol. 19, GM Papers.

94 **"the Bridge Men . . . ":** Ibid., Feb 29, 1808.

95 **"prevented by Visitors . . . ":** Ibid., May 24, 1808.

96 **"Gridlock? Blame John Randel Jr.":** NYT, Feb 10, 2013.

96 **"Randel's matrix":** NYT, Sep 2, 2012.

97 **"I have always been . . . ":** JR, Field Book 64.10, NYHS. The quote is from a letter that appears as an undated draft in this field book, which has other entries dated 1823. It is unclear if the actual letter was sent, but the sentiment rings true.

97 **"This J.R. is so full . . . ":** Benjamin Wright to John B. Jervis, Sep 11, 1825, Jervis Papers, Jervis Public Library, Rome, NY.

97 **"a complete Hypocritical . . . ":** Ibid., Wright to Jervis, Jul 9, 1824.

97 **"shocking oppression and injustice":** Mathew Carey, *Exhibit of the Shocking Oppression and Injustice Suffered for Sixteen Months by John Randel, Jun., Esq., Contractor for the Eastern Section of the Chesapeake and Delaware Canal, from Judge Wright, Engineer in Chief, and the Majority of the Board of Directors* (Philadelphia, 1825).

98 **"I am a ruined man . . . "**: JR, *Explanatory Remarks and Estimates of the Cost and Income of the Elevated Railway, and Its Appendages, &C., For Broadway in the City of New-York* (New York: George F. Nesbitt, 1848), 14. Randel liked the "pride and boast" line so much he reused it in "City of New York," *Valentine's Manual* (1864), 848.

99 **"Friday 9th July 1808 . . . "**: JR, Field Book 68.2, NYHS.

99 **"Wednesday 12 July 1808 . . . "**: Ibid., Field Book 68.1.

100 **"Although they would answer . . . "**: Ibid., Field Book 65.4. The entry here, under a December 1816 date, is an apparent draft of a long progress report to the Common Council, with many edits, cross-outs, and inserts. A portion of this draft refers to pre-1811 surveying, providing details beyond Randel's actual surveying notes.

100 **"Exploring line run . . . "**: Ibid., Field Book 68.1 no. 2. The Kips Bay development was finally overwhelmed and eradicated by the 1811 grid in 1851, the last of the Dutch *bouwerijs* to disappear; it was sold in lots that conformed to the orientation of the 1811 grid, on its twenty-nine-degree axis. Much of the old farm today is the entrance and approaches for the Midtown Tunnel.

102 **"I was arrested by the Sheriff . . . "**: JR, "City of New York," *Valentine's Manual* (1864), 848.

102 **"encountered in our surveys . . . "**: Ibid., 850.

103 **"an estimable old woman"**: Martha Lamb, *The History of the City of New York* (New York: A.S. Barnes and Co., 1877), 3:572. This marks the first appearance of the nameless legendary vegetable hurler, nearly seventy years after the fact.

103 **"He was opposed to offsets . . . "**: Samuel Stilwell Doughty, *The Life of Samuel Stilwell* (New York: Brown & Wilson, 1877), 33.

103 **"difficulties and impediments . . . "**: MCC, 6:250 (Sep 5, 1808).

103 **"the impracticability of . . . "**: JR, "City of New York," *Valentine's Manual* (1864), 848–49.

104 **"It shall and may be lawful . . . "**: *Laws of the State of New York*, 1807, Chap. 115 (Apr 3, 1807).

105 **"being equally divided . . . "**: MCC, 5:291 (Oct 17, 1808). In the fluid, factionalized politics of the early 1800s, Clinton would be the antiwar Federalist candidate for president in 1812.

105 **"where surveys or other . . . "**: *Laws of the State of New York*, 1809, Chap. 103 (Mar 24, 1809).

109 **"for laying out the Island"**: GM diary, Jun 18, 1810, GM Papers.

109 **"Manhattan Comm[ission] . . . "**: Ibid., Nov 29, 1810.

109 **"I am directed to inform . . . "**: MCC, 6:405–406 (Dec 3, 1810).

112 **"Manhattan Comm[ission]** . . . "**: GM diary, Dec 11, 28, 1810, GM Papers.

113 **"with a view to ascertain** . . . "**: *The Historical Magazine*, 3:3 (March 1868), 166–168.

114 **"The *time* within which** . . . "**: JR, "City of New York," *Valentine's Manual* (1864), 839.

114 **"only a Plan of New York** . . . "**: JR, Field Book 65.4, NYHS.

CHAPTER 8: A GRID IS BORN

117 **"A City is to be composed** . . . "**: *Report of the Commissioners for Laying Out Streets and Roads in the City of New York*, 1811, NYPL. This is the printed title on the leather folder holding the original document in the Manuscript Division of the New York Public Library. In fact, the untitled manuscript document is not so much a formal report as a set of minimal remarks accompanying the Commissioners' map; thus, hereafter, *Remarks*.

117 **"Such plans fitted nothing** . . . "**: Lewis Mumford, *The City in History* (New York: Harcourt, Brace & Company, 1961), 422.

117 **"The street plan** . . . "**: J[ulius] F. Harder, "The City's Plan," *Municipal Affairs*, 2:1 (Mar 1898), 35.

118 **"The Commissioners of Streets** . . . "**: *Remarks*.

120 **"They even** . . . "**: Thomas A. Janvier, *In Old New York* (New York: Harper and Brothers, 1894), 58.

120 **"supposed improvements** . . . "**: *Remarks*.

124 **"his habits of intemperance"**: Philip Hone, *The Diary of Philip Hone 1828–1851*, Allan Nevins, ed. (New York: Dodd, Mead and Company, 1927), 1:426.

124 **"irregular trapezium** . . . "**: *Remarks*. Bloomingdale Square was given back to the grid in 1857, Observatory Place in 1865, Hamilton Square by 1868. Haerlem Square was closed in 1836 but was replaced with nearby Mt. Morris Square (now Marcus Garvey Park) for the simple reason that it was an impenetrable outcropping of rock that the 1811 plan had failed to recognize as such.

126 **"Right now it's only a notion** . . . "**: Woody Allen, Marshall Brickman, *Annie Hall*. Film script. http://www.dailyscript.com/scripts /annie_hall.html. The line comes at 1:12 of the film.

127 **"the width of all the streets** . . . "**: JR, "City of New York," *Valentine's Manual* (1864), 839 (italics in original).

127 **"the most northern** . . . "**: *Remarks*.

127 **"should be of *equal breadth*** . . . "**: JR, "City of New York," *Valentine's Manual* (1864), 839 (italics in original).

128 **"a quick solution . . . "**: Rebecca Shanor, *New York's Paper Streets: Proposals to Relieve the 1811 Gridiron Plan* (master's thesis, Columbia University, 1981), 51.

128 **"In adopting a republican form . . . "**: GM to John Dickinson, May 23, 1803, in Jared Sparks, *The Life of Gouverneur Morris* (Boston: Gray & Bowen, 1832), 3:181.

128 **"deplorable results . . . "**: Janvier, *In Old New York*, 57–61.

CHAPTER 9: GETTING SQUARE WITH RIGHT-ANGLED LIVING

129 **"The whole island has been surveyed . . . "**: Thomas Naylor Stanford, *The Citizens and Strangers Guide Through the City of New York* (New York: George Long, 1814), 3.

129 **"And young New York . . . "**: Schopfer, "The Plan of a City," 695–96.

130 **"false prophet"**: *Brooklyn Long-Island Star*, Feb 19, 1812.

130 **"Nicodemus Havens, cordwainer . . . "**: Nicodemus Havens, *Wonderful Vision of Nicodemus Havens* (Boston: Coverly Jr., 1812), *passim*.

131 **"We have now reached the point . . . "**: Stokes, *Iconography*, 1:407–08.

134 **"In 1812 & 1813 . . . "**: JR, Field Book 65.4.

136 **"After all the monuments . . . "**: JR, *Explanatory Remarks*, 15. Shortly after Randel's death, his instruments and field books were in the possession of Henry Dawson, owner-editor of the *Historical Magazine*; the field books (or many of them at least) eventually made their way to the NYHS, but the instruments have disappeared.

136 **"was done with an accuracy . . . "**: Statement by SDW, Jan 16, 1823, in Carey, *Exhibit*, 7.

136 **"men . . . who would have cut down . . . "**: [Clement Clarke Moore], *A Plain Statement, Addressed to the Proprietors of Real Estate, in the City and County of New-York* (New York: J. Eastburn and Co., 1818), 50.

137 **"Our public authorities . . . "**: Ibid., 24.

137 **"There, at least . . . "**: *The Knickerbocker* magazine, 33:2 (Feb 1849), 185.

138 **"it was thought advisable . . . "**: *Valentine's Manual* (1854), 536.

139 **"binding and conclusive"**: *Laws of the State of New York*, 1813, Chap. 136 (Apr 9, 1813).

139 **"to become a capitalist . . . "**: Moore, *Plain Statement*, 52.

139 **"spirit of divination"**: Ibid., 14.

141 **"The evils which would grow . . . "**: MCC, 10: 223 (Feb 1, 1819).

142 **"These Laws were intended . . . "**: Peter Lorillard to Daniel Webster, Jun 26, 1828, in *The Papers of Daniel Webster, Legal Papers, Vol. 2 The Boston Practice* (Hanover, NH: University Press of New England, 1983), 568–570.

CHAPTER 10: THE GRID THAT ATE MANHATTAN

145 **"The early planners succeeded . . . "**: Lewis Mumford, "The Plan of New York: II," *New Republic*, 71:916 (Jun 22, 1932), 152.

145 **"Greenwich is now . . . "**: *New York Commercial Advertiser*, Jan 18, 1825.

146 **"It has become dangerous . . . "**: *New York Evening Post*, Aug 31, 1829.

148 **"Those blocks are each . . . "**: *Documents of the Assembly of the State of New York* (Albany: E. Crosswell, 1838), No. 164 (Feb 12, 1838), 2.

149 **"Fifth Avenue is very muddy . . . "**: Catherine Elizabeth Havens, *Diary of a Little Girl in Old New York* (New York: Henry Collins Brown, 1919), 18. Havens recovered from her loss, lived to one hundred, and never married but, with her "magic" piano-playing in a Dresden hotel in 1868, aroused an emotional crisis in young imminent philosopher William James. Henry James, *A Life in Letters*, ed. Philip Horne (New York: Viking, 1999), 525.

150 **"Broadway . . . "**: Harder, "The City's Plan," 35.

150 **"In straight New York . . . "**: Schopfer, "The Plan of a City," 693, 699.

150 **"Every one of these corners . . . "**: Franz K. Winkler, "Mitigating the 'Gridiron' Street Plan," *The Architectural Record*, 29:5 (May 1911), 383, 380. Winkler was the occasional pseudonym for longtime *NYT* editorial writer Schuyler.

153 **"Could I begin life again . . . "**: Matthew Hale Smith, *Sunshine and Shadow in New York* (Hartford: J. B. Burr and Company, 1868), 117. This appears to be, two decades after Astor's death, the earliest source of the now ubiquitous and probably apocryphal quote.

153 **"in the backwoods of New York . . . "**: *The New York Sun*, Oct 2, 1906.

154 **"This I declined . . . "**: Hone, *Diary*, 1:158.

156 **"Sash-Windows, Beaufets . . . "**: *New York Post Boy*, Sep 25, 1752.

156 **"To be sold . . . "**: *New York Royal Gazette*, Oct 28, 1780.

158 **"the plan of 1811 . . . "**: Mumford, "The Plan of New York: II," 152.

158 **"Remonstrances against running . . . "**: Hone, *Diary*, 1:87, 91.

159 **"People are packed . . . "**: NYH, Oct 2, 1864.

160 "in consequence of . . . ": MCC, 13: 249 (Sep 15, 1823).

160 "that under existing circumstances . . . ": Ibid., 13: 685 (Apr 26, 1824).

160 "unadvisable at this time . . . ": Ibid., 17:108 (Apr 7, 1828).

160 "As a general rule . . . ": Ibid., 19:13 (May 3, 1830).

161 "final and conclusive": *Laws of the State of New York*, 1836, Chap. 244 (May 4, 1836).

162 "A contract made to pay . . . ": *Documents of the Board of Aldermen of the City of New York* (New York: Common Council, 1838), Doc. 82 (Apr 9, 1838), 596.

163 "civil liberty . . . ": *New York Municipal Gazette*, Mar 11, 1841.

165 "opening, regulating and paving . . . ": *Laws of the State of New York*, 1849, Chap. 187 (Apr 2, 1849).

165 "destined to work a revolution . . . ": Edward Dana Durand, *The Finances of New York City* (New York: The Macmillan Company, 1898), 68.

166 "are often made . . . ": *New York Evening Post*, Jul 19, 1839.

167 "the millions already so freely expended . . . ": James Frost, "The Art of Building," *The American Repertory of Arts, Sciences, and Manufactures*, 1:6 (Jul 1840), 412. A pioneer in the development and manufacture of British hydraulic cement, Frost was nearly sixty when he migrated with his wife and six nearly grown children to New York in 1834.

CHAPTER 11: THE CITY GRIDDED

169 "Our perpetual dead flat . . . ": *New York Sunday Dispatch*, Nov 25, 1849. The quote is from one in the series of "Letters from a Travelling Bachelor" written by Whitman under the penname Paumanok.

169 "The time will come . . . ": Frederick Law Olmsted to Board of Commissioners of the Central Park, May 31, 1858, in *Documents of the Board of Commissioners of the Central Park for the Year Ending April 30th, 1859* (New York: Evening Post, 1859), Document No. 5, 6.

169 "Have you confidence . . . ": *NYH*, Jul 8, 1849.

170 "possessors of suddenly acquired wealth . . . ": *New-York Weekly Herald*, Jul 14, 1849.

171 "I have been roaming . . . ": *Columbia* (Pennsylvania) *Spy*, May 18, 1844.

171 "I could not look . . . ": Ibid., Jun 1, 1844.

172 "The elevated and stony grounds . . . ": *New York Sunday Dispatch*, Nov 25, 1849.

172 **"the levelling system . . . ":** William Alexander Duer, *New-York As It Was, During the Latter Part of the Last Century* (New York: Stanford and Swords, 1849), 18.

172 **"How this city marches . . . ":** *The Diary of George Templeton Strong,* ed. Allan Nevins and Milton Halsey Thomas (New York: Macmillan, 1952), 2:24 (Oct 27, 1850) [hereafter Strong, *Diary*].

173 **"The plan of 1807 . . . ":** George S. Greene, memorandum, Sep. 1875, in Board of Commissioners of the New York City Department of Public Parks, *Document No. 74* (Feb 28, 1877), 20.

175 **"The time will come . . . ":** Frederick Law Olmsted to Board of Commissioners of the Central Park, May 31, 1858, in *Documents of the Board of Commissioners of the Central Park for the Year Ending April 30th, 1859* (New York: Evening Post, 1859), Document No. 5, 6.

175 **"There seems to be good authority . . . ":** "Preliminary Report of the Landscape Architect and the Civil and Topographical Engineer, upon the Laying Out of the Twenty-Third and Twenty-Fourth Wards," Nov 15, 1876, in Board of the Department of Public Parks, *Document No. 72* (Dec 20, 1876), 4–5.

175 **"The great disadvantage . . . ":** *New York Tribune,* Dec 28, 1879.

175 **"If a building site is wanted . . . ":** "Preliminary Report of the Landscape Architect and the Civil and Topographical Engineer, upon the Laying Out of the Twenty-Third and Twenty-Fourth Wards," Nov 15, 1876, in Board of the Department of Public Parks, *Document No. 72* (Dec 20, 1876), 5.

176 **"There was no place . . . ":** Clarence Cook, *A Description of the New York Central Park* (New York: F. J. Huntington, 1869), 13.

177 **"is now, and probably will ever be . . . ":** New York City Board of Aldermen, *Document No. 83,* Jan 2, 1852, reprinted in Board of Commissioners of Central Park, *First Annual Report on the Improvement of Central Park, New York* (New York, 1857), 139, 145, 146. The special committee, appointed by Mayor Ambrose Kingsland, consisted of aldermen Daniel Dodge, a Democrat representing the mercantile Second Ward, and Joseph Britton, a Republican from the wealthy residential Fifteenth. In their report and accompanying map, the name "Central Park" is used for the first time.

177 **"Central Park is too large . . . ":** Le Corbusier, *Cathedrals,* 192.

178 **"Despotic governments . . . ":** *Real Estate Record and Builders' Guide,* 2:29 (Oct 3, 1868).

178 **"a person who never looks . . . ":** James Grant Wilson, *The Life and Letters of Fitz-Greene Halleck* (New York: D. Appleton and Company, 1869), 405.

178 **"masters of the world . . . "**: Arsène Houssaye, *Les Confessions* (Paris, 1885), 4: 93–94. English translation for me by Richard Sieburth.

179 **"We have no Emperor here . . . "**: *Real Estate Record and Builders' Guide*, 2:30 (Oct 10, 1868).

179 **"brawny Alsatian"**: Robert Moses, "What Happened to Haussmann," *Architectural Forum*, 77:1 (Jul 1942), 57.

179 **"The objections at first . . . "**: "Preliminary Report of the Landscape Architect and the Civil and Topographical Engineer, upon the Laying Out of the Twenty-Third and Twenty-Fourth Wards," Nov 15, 1876, in Board of the Department of Public Parks, *Document No. 72* (Dec 20, 1876), 2.

182 **"To Fifty-ninth Street . . . "**: Strong, *Diary*, 4:155 (Oct 22, 1867).

182 **"form[ing] receptacles for . . . "**: *Report of the Council of Hygiene and Public Health of the Citizens' Association of New York Upon the Sanitary Condition of the City*, 2nd ed. (New York: D. Appleton and Company, 1866), 224.

182 **"Though expensive . . . "**: E. Porter Belden, *New-York: Past, Present, and Future* (New York: Prall Lewis & Co., 1850), 30.

183 **"at once the delight . . . "**: "Two Miles of Millionaires," *Munsey's Magazine*, 19:3 (Jun 1898), 352.

183 **"The din of wheels . . . "**: Howells, *Impressions and Experiences*, 246.

185 **"flourishing little town"**: *New York Public Advocate*, Jun 9, 1807.

186 **"ought not to be rejected . . . "**: MCC, 5:219 (Jul 25, 1808).

187 **"The general aspects of . . . "**: *Report of the Council of Hygiene*, 336.

188 **"He deserved it . . . "**: NYT, Nov 14, 1903.

189 **"Not a cent is got . . . "**: Olmsted to John Bigelow, Feb 9, 1861; Olmsted to Calvert Vaux, Mar 25, 1864, in Justin Martin, *Genius of Place: The Life of Frederick Law Olmsted* (Boston: Da Capo Press, 2011), 174.

189 **"in making a plan . . . "**: Andrew H. Green, *Communication to the Commissioners of the Central Park* (New York: Wm. C. Bryant & Co., 1866), 31–32.

190 **"the lines of property . . . "**: *Eleventh Annual Report of the Board of Commissioners of the Central Park* (New York: Wm. C. Bryant, 1868), 134–35.

190 **"If you stand in the hollow . . . "**: *Harper's New Monthly Magazine*, 61:364 (Sep 1880), 564.

192 **"impracticable, and ruinous . . . "**: *Laws of the State of New York*, 1860, Chap. 201 (Apr 7, 1860).

193 **"Instead of perpetrating . . . "**: *NYH*, Aug 27, 1860.

193 **"The surface of this territory . . . "**: Green, *Communication* (1866), 17.

194 **"first appearance in an official plan . . . "**: Herbert S. Swan, "The Minor Street," *The Journal of Land & Public Utility Economics*, 9:3 (Aug 1933), 297.

194 **"It is the only portion . . . "**: *Seventh Annual Report of the American Scenic and Historic Preservation Society* (Albany: J. B. Lyon Company, 1902), 86. Green founded the society, modeled on Britain's National Trust, in 1895. It flourished for decades before going dormant in the 1970s.

194 **"a series of lateral avenues . . . "**: George Alexander Mazaraki, "The Public Career of Andrew Haswell Green" (PhD. diss., New York University, 1966), 99.

CHAPTER 12: THE CITY UNBEAUTIFUL

195 **"The exasperating idiots . . . "**: *Real Estate Record and Builders' Guide*, 32:823 (Dec 22, 1883), 1024.

195 **"From the moment . . . "**: Edmund Wilson, *Europe Without Baedeker: Sketches Among the Ruins of Italy, Greece, & England* (Garden City, NY: Doubleday, 1947), 6.

195 **"If you suppose . . . "**: "Three Weeks in New York," *MacMillan's Magazine*, 5:30 (Apr 1862), 454. The aquatic vertebrate vision persists. Le Corbusier in 1936 saw Manhattan Island "spread out like a sole in the water of the Hudson and East rivers" and, with typically unselfconscious contradiction a hundred thoughts later, like "a kind of sole stretched out on a rock." Le Corbusier, *Cathedrals*, 87, 189.

196 **"these things are past praying for"**: *Real Estate Record and Builders' Guide*, 32:823 (Dec 22, 1883), 1025.

196 **"with its chief movements . . . "**: "Report of Samuel McElroy," *Town Survey Commission of Kings County* (Brooklyn: Rome Brothers, 1874), 6–7.

197 **"my husband was not very strict . . . "**: *Brooklyn Daily Eagle*, Jan 29, 1899.

197 **"If our remote ancestors . . . "**: "Diagonal Avenues in Cities," *Engineering News*, 26:2 (Oct 10, 1891), 334–35.

198 **"It is truly remarkable . . . "**: Harder, "The City's Plan," 34, 35, 45.

198 **"Even on the score of utility . . . "**: Janvier, *In Old New York*, 62.

199 **"It is now easy to appreciate . . . "**: Arthur Pound, *The Golden Earth: The Story of Manhattan's Landed Wealth* (New York: MacMillan, 1935), 123–127.

200 **"had probably surveyed . . . "**: *NYT*, Jun 14, 1892.

200 **"identified with all . . . "**: *NYH*, Jun 12, 1892.

202 **"severely injured and burnt . . . "**: *NYT*, Mar 31, 1852.

203 **"would be the same arrangement"**: *NYH*, Mar 14, 1867.

203 **"Now, if Mr. Serrell . . . "**: *NYH*, Mar 21, 1867.

204 **"If such a project . . . "**: *New York Sun*, Jun 21, 1879.

205 **"It can only be a few years . . . "**: Howells, *Impressions and Experiences*, 245.

205 **"At every turn . . . "**: Montgomery Schuyler, "The Small City House in New York," *The Architectural Record*, 8:4 (Apr–Jun 1899), 359.

206 **"In the original plan . . . "**: *Report of Committee on Small Parks*, 1897, quoted in Lawrence Veiller, "Parks and Playgrounds for Tenement Districts," *The Tenement House Problem*, eds. Robert W. DeForest and Lawrence Veiller, 2 vols. (New York: MacMillan Company, 1903), 2:7.

206 **"Many complaints are received . . . "**: Jacob A. Riis, "Small Parks and Public-School Play-Grounds," *Harper's Weekly*, 41:2125 (Sep 11, 1897), 903.

206 **"the failure to provide . . . "**: *Report of Committee on Small Parks*, 1897, quoted in Lawrence Veiller, "Parks and Playgrounds for Tenement Districts," *The Tenement House Problem*, eds. Robert W. DeForest and Lawrence Veiller, 2 vols. (New York: MacMillan Company, 1903), 2:7

207 **"the antagonism between a park . . . "**: "Parks and Playgrounds," *Landscape Architecture*, 1:2 (Jan 1911). The journal was (and is) the official publication of the American Society of Landscape Architects, cofounded in 1899 by Frederick Law Olmsted Jr., as devoted as his father to the purity of the park.

208 **"a truly shocking name . . . "**: *NYT*, Dec 2, 1915.

208 **"The automobilist has absorbed . . . "**: *NYT*, Jul 6, 1925.

209 **"impertinent cross-streets . . . "**: Henry James, "New York Revisited," *Harper's Monthly Magazine*, 112:672 (May 1906), 900–01.

210 **"The commissioners, after choosing . . . "**: Schopfer, "The Plan of a City," 698, 699, 700.

210 **"What a difference there would now be . . . "**: "Report of the Landscape Architect and the Civil and Topographical Engineer, Accompanying a Plan for Laying Out that Part of the Twenty-Fourth Ward Lying West of the Riverdale Road," Nov 21, 1876, in Board of the Department of Public Parks, *Document No. 72* (Dec 20, 1876), 18.

211 **"huge masses [that] rear . . . "**: *NYT*, Dec 29, 1907.

211 **"to break the bond . . . "**: Ernest Flagg, "The Plan of New York, and How to Improve it," *Scribner's Magazine*, 36:2 (Aug 1904), 253–56. Like others who have dared to challenge the grid, Flagg's subsequent life intersected with tragedy: in 1912, on East 74th Street, his dinner party–bound limousine ran over a thirteen-year-old roller skater, the son of an unemployed carpenter, who died in the bloodied laps of Flagg and his shocked wife as they raced to a nearby hospital on a futile mission.

212 **"To Destroy Central Park . . . "**: NYT, Jul 13, 1904.

212 **"was written by a man . . . "**: Robert Wheelwright, "The Attacks on Central Park," *Landscape Architecture*, 1:1 (Oct 1910), 14, 18, 19.

213 **"excellent if somewhat eccentric . . . "**: NYT, Jan 29, 1905.

213 **"break up the rectilinear enormity . . . "**: *Boston Evening Transcript*, May 5, 1905.

213 **"the most visionary scheme of all"**: NYT, Mar 31, 1918.

214 **"In the report of the earlier Commission . . . "**: *Report of the New York City Improvement Commission* (New York: Kalkhoff Company, 1907), 10.

214 **"There is not the slightest reason . . . "**: Herbert Croly, "Civic Improvements: The Case of New York," *The Architectural Record*, 21:5 (May 1907), 348, 350.

215 **"How Can New York Be Made . . . "**: NYH, Apr 29, 1900.

216 **"guarantee peace and order . . . "**: NYT, Dec 7, 1922.

216 **"handsomest man in Europe . . . "**: *Chicago Tribune*, Apr 27, 1924.

217 **"during a fit of nervous depression"**: NYT, Mar 22, 1924.

217 **"We expect of her power . . . "**: NYH, Apr 29, 1900.

218 **"Let the new cities . . . "**: Schopfer, "The Plan of a City," 700.

219 **"That more northerly and southerly . . . "**: NYT, May 29, 1910.

220 **"unless in consequence of accident . . . "**: "Hints for Breathing Places for the Metropolis," *The Gardener's Magazine*, 5:23 (Dec 1829), 687, 688.

220 **"You took my bread and butter away; now I've got you!"**: NYT, Feb 4, 1913. The *Times* used this quote when reporting Gallagher's death at a hospital for the insane. Contemporary newspaper accounts indicate a briefer Gallagher outburst, e.g., "You took my bread and butter," *Washington Post*, Aug 10, 1910.

221 **"EDISON'S DARING SCHEME . . . "**: *Raleigh* (North Carolina) *Evening Times*, Jul 28, 1906.

222 **"devoted to Art and Nature . . . "**: *Indoors and Out*, 2:6 (Sep 1906), 311.

223 **"a bit of folly . . . "**: *Brooklyn Daily Eagle*, Aug 31, 1913. Operation of the loop soon passed from the city to the Brooklyn Rapid Transit

Company as part of the "dual system" that emerged to integrate city rapid transit after 1898; the BRT eventually reorganized as the BMT (the Brooklyn-Manhattan Transit Corporation).

223 **"the serious congestion . . . ":** *NYT*, Jul 18, 1915.

224 **"Thomson is a large man . . . ":** *Brooklyn Daily Eagle*, Aug 31, 1913.

224 **"Think what a wonderful opportunity . . . ":** *NYT*, Jun 24, 1923.

225 **"I do not smoke . . . ":** *Massillon (OH) Evening Independent*, Nov 25, 1930. The same advertisement ran during the year in papers from coast to coast.

225 **"majestic structures":** *NYT*, Jun 22, 1924.

226 **"New York has been . . . ":** *NYT*, Oct 18, 1925.

226 **"Look at that traffic . . . ":** *NYT*, Apr 23, 1952.

228 **"Out of doors . . . ":** Edith Wharton, *A Backward Glance* (New York: D. Appleton-Century Company, 1934), 54–55. Wharton was born Edith Newbold Jones in 1862 in a three-story brownstone at 14 West 23rd, built by her father five years earlier, one among many similar homes going up along the street. Twenty years later her father died, the family money ran out, and she moved with her mother to a lesser address nearby; she eventually married a wealthy Bostonian. Number fourteen meanwhile was redesigned as retail space, what Wharton considered the "chocolate-coloured coating of the most hideous stone ever quarried" was replaced with cast iron, two floors and large windows throughout were added, and a fine linens store moved in. Today, the bones of Wharton's birth house hide deep within its modern cladding, with a Starbucks out front.

CHAPTER 13: BACK TO THE RECTILINEAR FUTURE

229 **"I found it the way . . . ":** Nicolas Nabokov, *Bagázh: Memoirs of a Russian Cosmopolitan* (New York: Atheneum, 1975), 187–88.

229 **"A proper city plan . . . ":** "New York City's Planning Exhibition," *The American City*, 9:6 (Dec 1913), 506.

230 **"The present almost unrestricted . . . ":** *Report of the Heights of Buildings Commission to the Committee on the Height, Size and Arrangement of Buildings of the Board of Estimate and Apportionment of the City of New York*, Dec 23, 1913, [56], 99n14, 157.

232 **"The zoning laws are the Napoleon . . . ":** *NYT*, Sep 14, 1924.

232 **"The city's illness . . . ":** *NYT*, Mar 17, 1929.

233 **"The period of the car . . . ":** Le Corbusier, *Cathedrals*, 189.

234 **"Both events have been . . . ":** "Architecture in the United States," *The American Journal of Science and Arts* 17:1 (Jan 1830), 102.

235 **"diligently kept and supply'd . . . "**: John Evelyn, *Fumifugium* (1661; Exeter: University of Exeter, 1976), 14.

235 **"Three hundred years from now . . . "**: Ernest Hemingway to Gertrude Stein and Alice B. Toklas, Oct 11, 1923, in *Ernest Hemingway Selected Letters 1917–1961*, ed. Carlos Baker (1981; New York: Scribner, 2003), 95.

235 **"I see in the distance . . . "**: Sartre, "New York, Colonial City," 133, 123.

235 **"The grid pattern is New York . . . "**: Sartre, "Individualism and Conformism in the United States," *The Aftermath of War (Situations III)*. Translated by Chris Turner (New York: Seagull Books, 2008), 93.

236 **"I looked long and fruitlessly . . . "**: Sartre, "New York, Colonial City," 124–129, 133.

236 **"As for those who have given . . . "**: *NYT*, Mar 31, 1907.

237 **"The future is but . . . "**: Vladimir Nabokov, "Lance," *The New Yorker*, Feb 2, 1952.

237 **"When we walk in New York . . . "**: Adam Gopnik, "Heaven's Gaits," *The New Yorker*, Sep 1, 2014.

237 **"The street and block system . . . "**: L[udwig] Hilberseimer, *The Nature of Cities* (Chicago: Paul Theobald, 1955), 192–93.

237 **"Manhattan distance . . . "**: Paul E. Black, "Manhattan distance." In *Dictionary of Algorithms and Data Structures*, Vreda Pieterse and Paul E. Black, eds. May 31, 2006. http://www.nist.gov/dads/HTML/manhattanDistance.html.

238 **"We define 'Manhattan Tower . . . "**: Mirela Damian, Robin Flatland, and Joseph O'Rourke, "Unfolding Manhattan Towers," *Computational Geometry*, 40:2 (Jul 2008), 102, 103. The irony of the second listed author's name cannot escape notice.

238 **"Etiolated oddities . . . "**: Martin Filler, "New York: Conspicuous Construction," *New York Review of Books*, 62:6 (Apr 2, 2015), 32, 34.

239 **"There are no right angles here . . . "**: *NYT*, Jan 21, 2015.

BIBLIOGRAPHY

THIS IS AN inclusive bibliography that presents primary and secondary materials of which I have made close use and secondary materials that have been of more background, general, or tangential interest to me and may be to others thinking and writing about the organization of cities.

UNPUBLISHED AND MANUSCRIPT MATERIALS
Alexander Hamilton Papers, LOC
DeWitt Clinton Papers, Columbia University
DeWitt Clinton Papers, NYPL
Gouverneur Morris Papers, Columbia University
Gouverneur Morris Papers, LOC
John Randel Jr. Field Books, NYHS
John Rutherfurd Papers, NYHS
Report of the Commissioners for Laying Out Streets and Roads in the City of New York, 1811, NYPL
Robert L. Alexander Papers, privately held (a comprehensive collection of materials on Joseph François Mangin, including copies of rare, obscure, and manuscript documents)
Serrell-Opdycke-Patrick Papers, NYPL
Simeon De Witt Correspondence, NYPL
Thomas Kennard Thomson scrapbook, NYPL
Stephen Wray, "The Old Village of West Farms, Now in New York City" (1942) (bound typescript), NYHS
[Surveys to be Performed on New York Island: Oaths of Office], 1811 and 1812, NYHS

THESES/DISSERTATIONS

Mazaraki, George Alexander. "The Public Career of Andrew Haswell Green" (PhD. diss., New York University, 1966).

Rose-Redwood, Reuben Skye. "Rationalizing the Landscape: Superimposing the Grid upon the Island of Manhattan" (Master's thesis, Pennsylvania State University, 2002).

Shanor, Rebecca. "New York's Paper Streets: Proposals to Relieve the 1811 Gridiron Plan" (master's thesis, Columbia University, 1981).

NEWSPAPERS

New York Times
New York Herald
New York Evening Post
Real Estate Record and Builders' Guide

PRIMARY MATERIALS

"Preliminary Report of the Landscape Architect and the Civil and Topographical Engineer, upon the Laying Out of the Twenty-Third and Twenty-Fourth Wards," Nov 15, 1876, in Board of the Department of Public Parks, *Document No. 72* (Dec 20, 1876).

"Report of Samuel McElroy," *Town Survey Commission of Kings County* (Brooklyn: Rome Brothers, 1874).

Documents of the Board of Aldermen of the City of New York (New York: Common Council, 1838), Doc. 82 (Apr 9, 1838).

Documents of the Board of Commissioners of the Central Park for the Year Ending April 30th, 1859 (New York: Evening Post, 1859).

Eleventh Annual Report of the Board of Commissioners of the Central Park (New York: Wm. C. Bryant, 1868).

Goerck, Casimir, and Joseph François Mangin, *A Plan and Regulation of the City of New York* (New York, 1803).

Green, Andrew H. *Communication to the Commissioners of the Central Park* (New York: Wm. C. Bryant & Co., 1866).

Green, A[ndrew] H[aswell]. *New York of the Future: Writings and Addresses of Andrew H. Green since December 7th, 1892* (New York, 1896).

Greene, George S. Memorandum, Sep. 1875, in Board of Commissioners of the New York City Department of Public Parks, *Document No. 74* (Feb 28, 1877).

Havens, Catherine Elizabeth. *Diary of a Little Girl in Old New York* (New York: Henry Collins Brown, 1919).

Holmes, John Bute. *Map of the Common Lands from 26th to 43rd Street* (New York, 1874).

Holmes, John Bute. *Map of the Common Lands from 42nd to 59th Street* (New York, 1874).

Holmes, John Bute. *Map of the Common Lands from 59th to 76th Street* (New York, 1874).

Holmes, John Bute. *Map of the Common Lands from 76th to 93rd Street* (New York, 1874).

Hone, Philip. *The Diary of Philip Hone 1828–1851*, Allan Nevins, ed., 2 vols. (New York: Dodd, Mead and Company, 1927).

Laws of the State of New York (various years).

Minutes of the Common Council of the City of New York, 1784–1831, 19 vols. (New York: City of New York, 1917).

Morris, Gouverneur. *The Diary and Letters of Gouverneur Morris*, 2 vols., Anne Cary Morris, ed. (New York: Charles Scribner's Sons, 1888).

New York City Board of Aldermen, *Document No. 83*, Jan 2, 1852, reprinted in Board of Commissioners of Central Park, *First Annual Report on the Improvement of Central Park, New York* (New York, 1857).

Proceedings of the Corporation of New-York, on Supplying the City with Pure and Wholesome Water, with a Memoir of Joseph Browne, M. D. on the Same Subject (New York: John Furman, 1799).

Report of the Committee of the Common Council Upon the Subject of New Streets (New York: James Cheetham, 1803).

Report of the Council of Hygiene and Public Health of the Citizens' Association of New York Upon the Sanitary Condition of the City, 2nd ed. (New York: D. Appleton and Company, 1866).

Report of the Heights of Buildings Commission to the Committee on the Height, Size and Arrangement of Buildings of the Board of Estimate and Apportionment of the City of New York, Dec 23 1913.

Report of the New York City Improvement Commission (New York: Kalkhoff Company, 1907).

Strong, George Templeton. *The Diary of George Templeton Strong*, 4 vols., Allan Nevins and Milton Halsey Thomas, eds. (New York: Macmillan, 1952).

The Private Journal of Aaron Burr During His Residence of Four Years in Europe, Matthew L. Davis, ed., (New York: Harper & Brothers, 1838).

Secondary Materials

"Architecture in the United States," *The American Journal of Science and Arts* 17:1 (Jan 1830).

"City Planning," *Seventeenth Annual Report of the American Scenic and Historic Preservation Society* (Albany: Argus Company, 1912).

"Diagonal Avenues in Cities," *Engineering News and American Railway Journal*, Oct 10, 1891.

"Hints for Breathing Places for the Metropolis," *The Gardener's Magazine*, 5:23 (Dec 1829).

"New York City's Planning Exhibition," *The American City*, 9:6 (Dec 1913).

"Two Miles of Millionaires," *Munsey's Magazine*, 19:3 (Jun 1898).

Adams, William Howard. *Gouverneur Morris: An Independent Life* (New Haven, CT: Yale University Press, 2003).

Allen, Irving Lewis. *The City in Slang: New York Life and Popular Speech* (New York: Oxford University Press, 1993).

Aristotle. *The Politics of Aristotle*. Translated by B[enjamin] Jowett (Oxford: Clarendon Press, 1885).

Augustyn, Robert T., and Paul E. Cohen. *Manhattan in Maps, 1527–1995* (New York: Rizzoli, 1997).

Auster, Paul. *City of Glass* (1985; New York: Penguin Books, 1987).

Ballon, Hilary, ed. *The Greatest Grid: The Master Plan of Manhattan 1811–2011* (New York: Museum of the City of New York and Columbia University Press, 2012).

Barthes, Roland. *A Barthes Reader* (New York: Hill and Wang, 1982).

Beck, T. Romeyn. *Eulogium on the Life and Services of Simeon De Witt* (Albany: E. W. & C. Skinner, 1835).

Belden, E. Porter. *New-York: Past, Present, and Future* (New York: Prall Lewis & Co., 1850).

Belloc, Hilaire. *The Road* (New York: Harper & Brothers, [1925]).

Black, George Ashton. *The History of Municipal Ownership of Land on Manhattan Island*, 2nd ed. (New York: Columbia University, 1897).

Blackmar, Elizabeth. *Manhattan for Rent, 1785–1850* (Ithaca, NY: Cornell University Press, 1989).

Bogart, John. *The John Bogart Letters* (New Brunswick, NJ: Rutgers College, 1914).

Brooke, Daniel. *A History of Future Cities* (New York: W. W. Norton, 2013).

Brookhiser, Richard. *Gentleman Revolutionary: Gouverneur Morris, the Rake Who Wrote the Constitution* (New York: Free Press, 2003).

Bulloch, Joseph Gaston Baillie. *A History and Genealogy of the Families of Bayard, Houstoun of Georgia, and the Descent of the Bolton Family* (Washington, D. C.: James H. Dony, 1919).

Burrows, Edwin G., and Mike Wallace. *Gotham: A History of New York City to 1898* (New York: Oxford University Press, 1999).

Cajori, Florian. *The Chequered Career of Ferdinand Rudolph Hassler* (Boston: Christopher Publishing House, 1929).

Carey, Mathew. *Exhibit of the Shocking Oppression and Injustice Suffered for Sixteen Months by John Randel, Jun., Esq., Contractor for the Eastern Section of the Chesapeake and Delaware Canal, from Judge Wright, Engineer in Chief, and the Majority of the Board of Directors* (Philadelphia, 1825).

Caro, Robert A. *The Power Broker: Robert Moses and the Fall of New York* (1974; New York: Vintage, 1975).

Collins, George R., and Christiane Crasemann Collins. *Camillo Sitte: The Birth of Modern City Planning* (1986; Mineola, N.Y.: Dover, 2006).

Croly, Herbert. "Civic Improvements: The Case of New York," *The Architectural Record*, 21:5 (May 1907).

de Certeau, Michael. *The Practice of Everyday Life* (Berkeley: University of California Press, 1984).

DeWitt, Simeon. *The Elements of Perspective* (Albany: H. C. Southwick, 1813).

Dover, Victor, and John Massengale. *Street Design: The Secret to Great Cities and Towns* (Hoboken, NJ: Wiley, 2014).

Duer, William Alexander. *New-York As It Was, During the Latter Part of the Last Century* (New York: Stanford and Swords, 1849).

Dunshee, Kenneth Holcomb. *As You Pass By* (New York: Hastings House, 1952).

Esperdy, Gabrielle. "Defying the Grid: A Retroactive Manifesto for the Culture of Decongestion," *Perspecta*, 30 (1999).

Evelyn, John. *Fumifugium; or, the Inconvenience of the Aer and Smoake of London* (1661; Exeter: University of Exeter, 1976).

Feirstein, Sanna. *Naming New York: Manhattan Places & How They Got Their Names* (New York: New York University Press, 2001).

Ferris, Hugh. *The Metropolis of Tomorrow* (1929: Mineola, NY: Dover, 2005).

Fine, Albert, ed. *Landscape into Cityscape: Frederick Law Olmsted's Plans for a Greater New York City* (1968; New York: Van Nostrand Reinhold Company, 1981).

Flagg, Ernest. "The Plan of New York, and How to Improve it," *Scribner's Magazine*, 36:2 (Aug 1904).

Fox, Dixon Ryan. *The Decline of Aristocracy in the Politics of New York, 1801–1840*, Robert V. Remini, ed. (1919; New York: Harper & Row, 1965).

Frost, James. "The Art of Building," *The American Repertory of Arts, Sciences, and Manufactures*, 1:6 (Jul 1840).

Garfield, Simon. *On the Map: A Mind-Expanding Exploration of the Way the World Looks* (New York: Gotham Books, 2013).

Garvin, Alexander. *The American City: What Works, What Doesn't*, 2nd ed. (New York: McGraw-Hill, 2002).

Gerard, J[ames] W[atson], Jr. *A Treatise on the Title of the Corporation and Others to the Streets, Wharves, Piers, Parks, Ferries, and Other Lands and Franchises in the City of New York* (New York: Poole & MacLauchlan, 1872).

Gilfoyle, Timothy J. *City of Eros: New York City, Prostitution, and the Commercialization of Sex, 1790–1920* (New York: W. W. Norton & Company, 1992).

Gill, Jonathan. *Harlem: The Four Hundred Year History from Dutch Village to Capital of Black America* (New York: Grove Press, 2011).

Greatorex, Eliza, and Matilda Pratt Despard. *Old New York from the Battery to Bloomingdale* (New York: G. P. Putnam's Sons, 1875).

Green, Andrew H. "The Scenic Beauties of Fort Washington Battlefield," *Seventh Annual Report of the American Scenic and Historic Preservation Society* (Albany: J. B. Lyon Company, 1902).

Grumet, Robert Steven. *Native American Place Names in New York City* (New York: Museum of the City of New York, 1981).

Haley, Charlie. *Spoil Island: Reading the Makeshift Archipelago* (Lanham, MD: Lexington Books, 2013).

Hamlin, Talbot. *Benjamin Henry Latrobe* (New York: Oxford University Press, 1955).

Hammond, Jabez D. *The History of Political Parties in the State of New-York*, 2 vols. (Albany: C. Van Benthuysen, 1842).

Harder, J[ulius] F. "The City's Plan," *Municipal Affairs*, 2:1 (Mar 1898).

Harris, Luther S. *Around Washington Square: An Illustrated History of Greenwich Village* (Baltimore: Johns Hopkins University Press, 2003).

Hartog, Hendrik. *Public Property and Private Power: The Corporation of the City of New York in American Law, 1730–1870* (Chapel Hill, NC: University of North Carolina Press, 1983).

Havens, Nicodemus. *Wonderful Vision of Nicodemus Havens* (Boston: Coverly Jr., 1812).

Hawes, Elizabeth. *New York, New York: How the Apartment House Transformed the Life of the City (1869–1930)* (New York: Alfred A. Knopf, 1993).

Heidt, William. *Simeon DeWitt: Founder of Ithaca* (Ithaca, NY: DeWitt Historical Society of Tompkins County, 1968).

Higgins, Hannah B. *The Grid Book* (Cambridge, MA: MIT Press, 2009).

Hilberseimer, L[udwig]. *The Nature of Cities* (Chicago: Paul Theobald, 1955).

Hilberseimer, L[udwig]. *The New City: Principles of Planning* (Chicago: Paul Theobald, 1944).

Hoffman, Murray. *Treatise upon the Estate and Rights of the Corporation of the City of New York, as Proprietors*, 2 vols. (New York: Edmund Jones & Co., 1862).

Hood, Clifton. *722 Miles: The Building of the Subways and How They Transformed New York* (NY: Simon & Schuster, 1993).

Howells, William Dean. *Impressions and Experiences* (New York: Harper and Brothers, 1896).

Hubbard, Bill, Jr. *American Boundaries: The Nation, the States, the Rectangular Survey* (Chicago: University of Chicago Press, 2009).

[Hunn, John]. *Observations on the Improvement of the City of New-York South of Grand Street* (New York: James Cheetham, 1806).

Hunter, Gregory S. *The Manhattan Company: Managing a Multi-unit Corporation in New York, 1799–1842* (New York: Garland Publishing, 1989).

Jacobs, Jane. *The Death and Life of Great American Cities* (1961; New York: Modern Library, 1993).

Jaffe, Eric. *The King's Best Highway: The Lost History of the Boston Post Road, the Route That Made America* (New York: Simon and Schuster, 2010).

James, Henry. "New York Revisited," *Harper's Monthly Magazine*, 112:669, 670, 672 (Feb, Mar, May 1906).

Janvier, Thomas A. *In Old New York* (New York: Harper and Brothers, 1894).

Johnson, Hildegard Binder. *Order Upon the Land: The U.S. Rectangular Land Survey and the Upper Mississippi Country* (New York: Oxford University Press, 1976).

Kent, James. *The Charter of the City of New York* (New York: McSpedon & Baker, 1854).

Kirkland, Stephane. *Paris Reborn: Napoleon III, Baron Haussmann, and the Quest to Build a Modern City* (New York: St. Martin's Press, 2013).

Kirschke, James J. *Gouverneur Morris: Author, Statesman, and Man of the World* (New York: St. Martin's Press, 2005).

Klein, Carole. *Gramercy Park: An American Bloomsbury* (Boston: Houghton Mifflin, 1987).

Kline, Mary-Jo, ed. *Political Correspondence and Public Papers of Aaron Burr* (Princeton: Princeton University Press, 1983).

Koeppel, Gerard. *Bond of Union: Building the Erie Canal and the American Empire* (Boston: Da Capo Press, 2009).

Koeppel, Gerard. *Water for Gotham: A History* (Princeton, NJ: Princeton University Press, 2000).

Koolhaas, Rem. *Delirious New York: A Retroactive Manifesto for Manhattan* (1978; New York: Monacelli Press, 1994).

Kostof, Spiro. *The City Shaped: Urban Patterns and Meanings Through History* (1991; Boston: Little Brown, 1999).

Kotkin, Joel. *The City: A Global History* (New York: Modern Library, 2005).

Kouwenhoven, John A. *The Beer Can by the Highway: Essays on What's American About America* (Garden City, NY: Doubleday, 1961).

Kunstler, James Howard. *The Geography of Nowhere: The Rise and Decline of America's Man-Made Landscape* (New York: Simon & Schuster, 1993).

Lawrence, Henry W. *City Trees: A Historical Geography from the Renaissance Through the Nineteenth Century* (Charlottesville, VA: University of Virginia Press, 2006).

Le Corbusier. *The Radiant City: Elements of a Doctrine of Urbanism to Be Used as the Basis of Our Machine Age Civilization* (1933; New York: Orion Press, 1967).

Le Corbusier. *When the Cathedrals Were White* (1937; New York: McGraw-Hill, 1964).

Lee, J. J., and Marion R. Casey, eds. *Making the Irish American: History and Heritage of the Irish in the United States* (New York: New York University Press, 2006).

Linklater, Andro. *Measuring America: How an Untamed Wilderness Shaped the United States and Fulfilled the Promise of Democracy* (New York: Walker & Company, 2002).

Lockwood, Charles. *Manhattan Moves Uptown: An Illustrated History* (New York, Barnes & Noble, 1976).

Lofaso, Anthony. *Origins and History of the Village of Yorkville in the City of New York* (1972; Xlibris, 2010).

Lomask, Milton. *Aaron Burr: The Conspiracy and Years of Exile, 1805–1836* (New York: Farrar Straus Giroux, 1982).

Lomask, Milton. *Aaron Burr: The Years from Princeton to Vice President, 1756–1805* (New York: Farrar Straus Giroux, 1979).

Lopate, Philip. *Waterfront: A Walk Around Manhattan* (New York: Anchor Books, 2005).

Lossing, Benson J[ohn]. *The Hudson, from the Wilderness to the Sea* (New York: Virtue & Yorston, 1866).

Maffi, Mario. *New York City: An Outsider's Inside View* (Columbus, OH: Ohio State University Press, 2004).

Mano, Jo Margaret. "History in the Mapping: Simeon DeWitt's Legacy in New York State Cartography," *Middle States Geographer*, 22 (1989).

Marcuse, Peter. "The Grid as City Plan: New York City and Laissez-faire Planning in the Nineteenth-Century," *Planning Perspectives*, 2 (1987).

Martin, Justin. *Genius of Place: The Life of Frederick Law Olmsted* (Boston: Da Capo Press, 2011).

Martin, William R. *The Growth of New York* (New York: George W. Wood, 1865).

Mason, Randall. *The Once and Future New York: Historic Preservation and the Modern City* (Minneapolis: University of Minnesota Press, 2009).

McCorquodale, Duncan, ed. *Mapping New York* (London: Black Dog, 2009).

McNeur, Catherine. *Taming Manhattan: Environmental Battles in the Antebellum City* (Cambridge, MA: Harvard University Press, 2014).

Miller, Melanie Randolph. *An Incautious Man: The Life of Gouverneur Morris* (Wilmington, DE: ISI Books, 2008).

Miller, Stephen. *Walking New York: Reflections of American Writers from Walt Whitman to Teju Cole* (New York: Fordham University Press, 2015).

Miller, Terry. *Greenwich Village and How It Got That Way* (New York: Crown, 1990).

Mintz, Max M. *Gouverneur Morris and the American Revolution* (Norman, OK: University of Oklahoma Press, 1970).

Moehring, Eugene P. *Public Works and the Patterns of Urban Real Estate Growth in Manhattan, 1835–1894* (New York: Arno Press, 1981).

[Moore, Clement Clarke]. *A Plain Statement, Addressed to the Proprietors of Real Estate, in the City and County of New-York* (New York: J. Eastburn and Co., 1818).

Moscow, Henry. *The Street Book: The Encyclopedia of Manhattan's Street Names and Their Origins* (New York: Fordham University Press, 1978).

Moses, Robert. "What Happened to Haussmann," *Architectural Forum*, 77:1 (Jul 1942).

Mott, Hopper Striker. *The New York of Yesterday: A Descriptive Narrative of Old Bloomingdale* (New York: G. P. Putnam's Sons, 1908).

Mumford, Lewis. "City Planning and the American Precedent," *The New Republic*, 39:497 (Jun 11, 1924).

Mumford, Lewis. "The Plan of New York," "The Plan of New York II," *New Republic*, 71:915, 916 (Jun 15, Jun 22, 1932).

Mumford, Lewis. *Sticks and Stones: A Study of American Architecture and Civilization* (New York: Bone and Liveright, 1924).

Mumford, Lewis. *The City in History: Its Origins, Its Transformations, and Its Prospects* (1961; New York: MJF Books, [1989]).

Mumford, Lewis. *The Culture of Cities* (New York: Harcourt Brace & Company, 1938).

Mushkat, Jerome. *Tammany: The Evolution of a Political Machine, 1789–1865* (Syracuse: Syracuse University Press, 1971).

New York City Landmarks Preservation Commission, *Upper East Side Historic District Extension Designation Report* (New York, 2010).

Page, Max. *The City's End: Two Centuries of Fantasies, Fears, and Premonitions of New York's Destruction* (New Haven, CT: Yale University Press, 2008).

Peets, Elbert. *On the Art of Designing Cities: Selected Essays of Elbert Peets* (Cambridge, MA: MIT Press, 1968).

Peterson, Jon A. *The Birth of City Planning in the United States, 1842–1917* (Baltimore: Johns Hopkins University Press, 2003).

Plunz, Richard. *A History of Housing in New York City* (New York: Columbia University Press, 1990).

Pope, Thomas. *A Treatise on Bridge Architecture: In which the Superior Advantages of the Flying Pendent Lever Bridge are Fully Proved* (New-York: Alexander Niven, 1811).

Pound, Arthur. *The Golden Earth: The Story of Manhattan's Landed Wealth* (New York: MacMillan, 1935).

Rabun, J. Stanley. *Structural Analysis of Historic Buildings: Restoration, Preservation, and Adaptive Reuse Applications for Architects and Engineers* (New York: John Wiley & Sons, 2000).

Rae, Douglas W. *City: Urbanism and Its End* (New Haven, CT: Yale University Press, 2003).

Randel, John, Jr. "City of New York, North of Canal Street, in 1808 to 1821," *Manual of the Corporation of the City of New York* (New York: Valentine, 1864).

[Randel, John, Jr.] *The Elevated Railway, and Its Appendages, for Broadway, in the City of N. York* (New York: J.M. Elliott, 1848).

Randel, John, Jr. *Explanatory Remarks and Estimates of the Cost and Income of the Elevated Railway, and Its Appendages, &C., For Broadway in the City of New-York* (New York: George F. Nesbitt, 1848).

Reps, John W. *The Making of Urban America: A History of City Planning in the United States* (Princeton, NJ: Princeton University Press, 1965).

Reps, John W. "Public Land, Urban Development Policy, and the American Planning Tradition," in Marion Clawson, ed. *Modernizing Urban Land Policy* (Baltimore: Resources for the Future, 1973).

Riis, Jacob A., "Small Parks and Public-School Play-Grounds," *Harper's Weekly*, 41:2125 (Sep 11, 1897).

Robbins, Christine Chapman. *David Hosack: Citizen of New York* (Philadelphia: American Philosophical Society, 1964).

Roosevelt, Theodore. *Gouverneur Morris* (Boston: Houghton Mifflin, 1888).

Rose-Redwood, Reuben Skye. "Re-Creating The Historical Topography Of Manhattan Island," *The Geographical Review* 93.1 (Jan 2003).

Rosenwaike, Ira. *Population History of New York City* (Syracuse: Syracuse University Press, 1972).

Rosenzweig, Roy, and Elizabeth Blackmar. *The Park and the People: A History of Central Park* (Ithaca, NY: Cornell University Press, 1992).

Rybczynski, Witold. *A Clearing in the Distance: Frederick Law Olmsted and America in the 19th Century* (New York: Simon & Schuster, 1999).

Rybczynski, Witold. *City Life: Urban Expectations in a New World* (New York: Scribner, 1995).

S[herwood], M[ary] E[lizabeth] W[ilson], "The Homes of America: Old Morrisania," *The Art Journal*, 4 (New Series) (1878).

Sanderson, Eric W. *Mannahatta: A Natural History of New York City* (New York: Harry N. Abrams, 2009).

Sartre, Jean-Paul. *The Aftermath of War (Situations III)*. Translated by Chris Turner (New York: Seagull Books, 2008).

Schopfer, Jean. "The Plan of a City," *The Architectural Record*, 12:7 (Dec 1902).

Schuyler, David. *The New Urban Landscape: The Redefinition of City Form in Nineteenth-Century America* (Baltimore: Johns Hopkins University Press, 1986).

Schuyler, Montgomery. "The Art of City-Making," *The Architectural Record*, 12:1 (May 1902).

Schuyler, Montgomery. "The Small City House in New York," *The Architectural Record*, 8:4 (Apr–Jun 1899).

Schuyler, Montgomery. *American Architecture and Other Writings*, 2 vols. (Cambridge, MA: Belknap Press of Harvard University Press, 1961).

Schwartz, Seymour I., and Ralph E. Ehrenberg. *The Mapping of America* (1980; Edison, NJ: Wellfleet Press, 2001).

Scobey, David M. *Empire City: The Making and Meaning of the New York City Landscape* (Philadelphia: Temple University Press, 2002).

Sennett, Richard. *The Conscience of the Eye: The Design and Social Life of Cities* (New York: W. W. Norton, 1990).

Serrell, James E. *Plan and Description Proposing to Re-model the City of New York and Its Vicinity* (New York: Bergen & Tripp, 1869).

Serrell, James E. *Memorial . . . Asking the Action of Congress on the Proposed Change of the Eastern Boundary of the City of New York by the Construction of A New East River, and the Filling up of Hell-Gate* (New York, 1867).

Shanor, Rebecca Read. *The City That Never Was: Two Hundred Years of Fantastic and Fascinating Plans That Might Have Changed the Face of New York City* (New York: Viking, 1988).

Shvidkovsky, Dmitry. *Russian Architecture and the West* (New Haven, CT: Yale University Press, 2007).

Smith, James Reuel. *Springs and Wells of Manhattan and the Bronx at the End of the Nineteenth Century* (New York: New-York Historical Society, 1938).

Smith, Matthew Hale. *Sunshine and Shadow in New York* (Hartford, CT: J. B. Burr and Company, 1868).

Spann, Edward K. "The Greatest Grid: The New York Plan of 1811," in *Two Centuries of American Planning*, ed. Daniel Scheffer (Baltimore: Johns Hopkins University Press, 1988).

Spann, Edward K. *The New Metropolis: New York City, 1840–1857* (New York: Columbia University Press, 1981).

Sparks, Jared. *The Life of Gouverneur Morris*, 3 vols. (Boston: Gray & Bowen, 1832).

Stanford, Thomas Naylor. *The Citizens and Strangers Guide Through the City of New York* (New York: George Long, 1814).

Stein, Mark. *How the States Got Their Shapes* (New York: Harper, 2008).

Steinberg, Ted. *Gotham Unbound: The Ecological History of Greater New York* (New York: Simon & Schuster, 2014).

Stern, A. M., Thomas Mellins, and David Fishman. *New York 1880: Architecture and Urbanism in the Gilded Age* (New York: Monacelli Press, 1999).

Stevenson, David. *Sketch of the Civil Engineering of North America* (London: John Weale, 1838).

Stilgoe, John R. *Common Landscape of America, 1580 to 1845* (New Haven, CT: Yale University Press, 1982).

Stillman, Damie. "New York City Hall: Competition and Execution," *Journal of the Society of Architectural Historians*, 23:3 (Oct 1964).

Stokes, I. N. Phelps. *The Iconography of Manhattan Island, 1498–1909*, 6 vols. (1915–28; New York: Arno Press, 1967).

Swales, Francis S. "New York and Its Plans, 1," "New York and Its Plans, 2," *Pencil Points*, 15:6, 7 (Jun, Jul 1934).

Swan, Herbert S. "The Minor Street," *The Journal of Land & Public Utility Economics*, 9:3 (Aug 1933).

Swiggett, Howard. *The Extraordinary Mr. Morris* (Garden City, NY: Doubleday, 1952).

Tauranac, John. *Manhattan Block by Block: A Street Atlas* (Santa Barbara, CA: Tauranac Maps, 2000).

The Encyclopedia of New York City, 2nd ed., Kenneth T. Jackson, ed. (New Haven, CT: Yale University Press, 2010).

The Encyclopedia of New York State, Peter Eisenstadt, ed. (Syracuse, NY: Syracuse University Press, 2005).

Tillson, Geo[rge] W[illiam]. *Street Pavements and Paving Materials: A Manual of City Pavements: The Methods and Materials of Their Construction* (New York: J. Wiley & Sons, 1903).

Trachtenberg, Alan. "The Rainbow and the Grid," *American Quarterly*, 16:1 (Spring 1964).

Traub, James. *The Devil's Playground: A Century of Pleasure and Profit in Times Square* (New York: Random House, 2004).

Valentine, David Thomas, ed. *Manual of the Corporation of the City of New York* (New York) (annual volumes 1842–1870).

Vance, James E., Jr. *This Scene of Man: The Role and Structure of the City in the Geography of Western Civilization* (New York: Harper & Row, 1977).

Viele, Robert L. *The Transval of the City of New York* (New York: Johnson & Company, 1880).

Wharton, Edith. *A Backward Glance* (New York: D. Appleton-Century Company, 1934).

Wheelwright, Robert. "The Attacks on Central Park," *Landscape Architecture*, 1:1 (Oct 1910).

White, Norval, Elliot Willensky, and Fran Leadon. *AIA Guide to New York City*, 5th ed. (New York: Oxford University Press, 2010).

Williams, Edwin. *The New York Annual Register 1836* (New York: Edwin Williams, 1836).

Wilson, James Grant. *The Life and Letters of Fitz-Greene Halleck* (New York: D. Appleton and Company, 1869).

Wilson, Rufus Rockwell. *New York: Old & New*, 2 vols. (Philadelphia: J. B. Lippincott, 1902).

Winkler, Franz K. [aka Montgomery Schuyler]. "Mitigating the 'Gridiron' Street Plan," *The Architectural Record*, 29:5 (May 1911).

Wood, Elizabeth A. *Science from Your Airplane Window* (1968; New York: Dover, 1975).

ACKNOWLEDGMENTS

W HAT I HAVE learned about the grid for this book has come with the help of many people—in casual conversation to considerable assistance—including Diana Agrest, Betsy Aidem, Harriett Alexander, Albert Appleton, Bob Augustyn, Jason Barr, Carla Bauer, Mary Beard, Eugenia Bone, Kevin Bone, Kevin Brown, Marta Cabrera, Dorothy Carpenter, Meredith Cherven-Holland, Ken Cobb, Paul Cohen, Tuck Edelstein, Elizabeth England, Frank Griggs, Joan Geismar, David Goldman, Christopher Gray, Bill Green, Nick Hardy, Elizabeth Harris, Kristina Harvey, Elizabeth Hazan, Steve Hicks, Marguerite Holloway, Eric Holzman, Bill Hubbard (whom I wore out with surveying questions), Stephane Kirkland, Charles Lauster, Chuck Levey, Peter Marcuse, Tom Mellins, Melanie Miller (whom I wore out with questions about Gouverneur Morris, whose papers she is preparing for publication), Alex Neil, Kathy Ogawa, Dennis Powell, Kazimira Rachfal, Andrea Renner, Jack Repcheck, John Reps, Richard Sieburth (and Gilles Depardon, Cecile Droz, Francoise Gramet, and Amadou Ly, for French translations), Carolyn Swartz, (John Rutherfurd descendant) Lupo Talamo, John Vennema, and (John Randel descendant) Ann Weeks.

I plumbed the resources of many institutions, including the Museum of the City of New York, the New-York Historical Society, the New York Public Library (especially Thomas Lannon in the Manuscripts and Archives Division), the New York City Municipal Archives (especially intrepid director Ken Cobb), the New York City

Department of Records (especially its online photo gallery), the New York City Department of Parks and Recreation (in particular its historical reports posted online), and the Library of Congress (especially its American Memory Collection and other online resources).

A word or more about online resources. Google Books is, of course, invaluable to the modern researcher but it is a troubling resource. Google Books is to a library as a toddler's playthings are to a toy store: the goods have shifted from ordered shelves to a maltreated jumble of often sloppily digitized volumes. Fortunately there are options, especially Internet Archive (archive.org), where books' digitizing sponsor most often is an academic library or other responsible institution that produces a cover-to-cover, high-quality, searchable reproduction.

Acknowledgment is also due to Wikipedia. My children's teachers are wary, but, if you filter out the junk, Wiki is the best starting place on any number of subjects, especially the many entries with good footnotes and source references.

Special acknowledgment also to the cornucopia of websites and blogs related to urban planning and New York City history. The website Urban Planning, 1794–1918: An International Anthology of Articles, Conference Papers, and Reports (urbanplanning.library .cornell.edu/DOCS/homepage.htm), assembled by Cornell's venerable John Reps, is no longer updated but remains highly useful. Gothamist (gothamist.com) is an excellent Internet "daily" with good historical material and links. More specialized sites include ephemeralnewyork.wordpress.com, forgotten-ny.com, manhattan past.com, manhattanunlocked.blogspot.com, daytoninmanhattan .blogspot.com, newyorkinplainsight.com, nyc-grid.com, oldstreets.com, untappedcities.com/newyork, thegreatamericangrid.com, and discoveringurbanism.blogspot.com. One could (and I did) get lost for hours (or days or more) in the vast landscape of material posted online by professional, scholarly, and amateur fans of New York and urban history and planning. New sites are born, and others go dormant or die, as surely as restaurants and storefronts open and close in New York.

I also made regular use of historic maps posted online in a variety of places, but especially the incomparable David Rumsey Map Collection (davidrumsey.com), which is as intelligent and rigorous as any traditional library map collection.

The Greatest Grid: The Master Plan of Manhattan 1811–2011 is cited in the bibliography, but it and its editor, Hilary Ballon, deserve special mention. If you're reading my book, you should read hers too. The companion volume to her Museum of the City of New York exhibit of the same name, it is a virtual encyclopedia of Manhattan's grid and was an essential guide for my research. And the highlights are now online: thegreatestgrid.mcny.org.

My books don't get published without the approval of Russ Galen, my agent. If Russ can't sell it, I don't write it. I threw him a succession of different pitches for this book before he liked my stuff.

At Da Capo, erudite editor Rober Pigeon shaped the manuscript with his seasoned touch, always praising and suggesting, never criticizing or demanding; this is our second of what I hope are (many) more books together. If you're reading this, it's probably because publicity director Lissa Warren did something that brought this book to your attention. Thanks also to project editors Carolyn Sobczak and Cisca Schreefel, Sean Maher, Justin Lovell, and everyone else at Da Capo who had a hand in the book.

As always, my wife, Diane, eased me through the process, reading and commenting and, in the late going, bringing dinner over to my office. I was born on Manhattan (in a hospital long replaced by a high-rise condo), grew up on the suburban mainland, returned to the island as soon as I could, and made sure to raise our three now mostly grown children, Jackson, Harry, and Kate, here. I think they love the place as much as I do.

INDEX

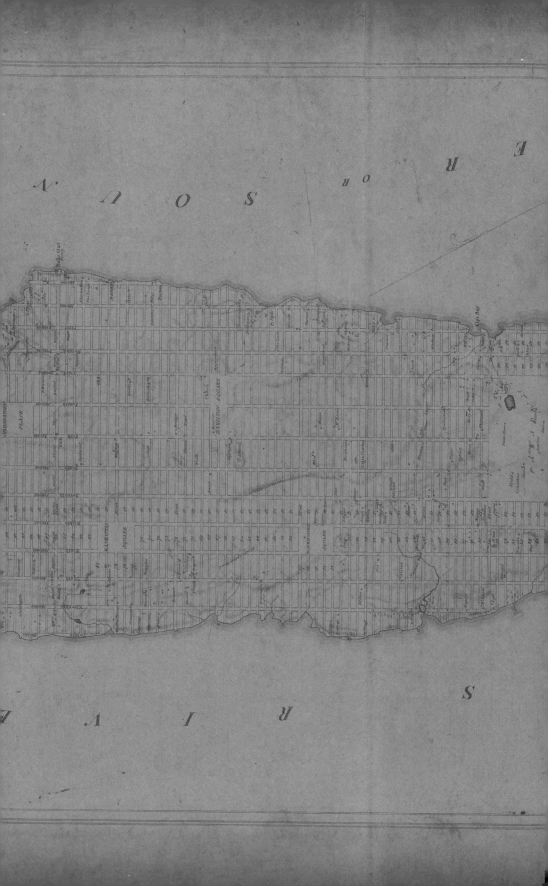